Creating the Ideal School

Where Teachers Want to Teach and Students Want to Learn

Albert Mamary

Rowman & Littlefield Education
Lanham, Maryland • Toronto • Plymouth, UK
2007

Published in the United States of America
by Rowman & Littlefield Education
A Division of Rowman & Littlefield Publishers, Inc.
A wholly owned subsidiary of The Rowman & Littlefield Publishing Group, Inc.
4501 Forbes Boulevard, Suite 200, Lanham, Maryland 20706
www.rowmaneducation.com

Estover Road
Plymouth PL6 7PY
United Kingdom

British Library Cataloguing in Publication Information Available

Library of Congress Cataloging-in-Publication Data

Mamary, Albert.
Creating the ideal school : where teachers want to teach and students want to learn / Albert Mamary. p. cm.
ISBN-13: 978-1-57886-577-2 (hardcover : alk. paper)
ISBN-13: 978-1-57886-619-9 (pbk. : alk. paper)
ISBN-10: 1-57886-577-8 (hardcover : alk. paper)
ISBN-10: 1-57886-619-7 (pbk. : alk. paper)
1. School improvement programs—United States. 2. School management and organization—United States. 3. School improvement programs—United States—case studies. 4. Educational change—United States. I. Title.
LB2822.82.M357 2007
371.200973—dc22 2007017386

∞™ The paper used in this publication meets the minimum requirements of American National Standard for Information Sciences—Permanence of Paper for Printed Library Materials, ANSI/NISO Z39.48-1992.
Manufactured in the United States of America.

To all educators who have a positive influence on the lives of their students

Contents

Foreword

For more than 20 years I have known Dr. Albert Mamary and have observed firsthand his work in the Johnson City schools. In my book *The Quality School*, I wrote, "The Johnson City schools are probably the best model in the United States of what could be called quality schools." Under Dr. Mamary's leadership, the Johnson City schools achieved the distinction of being the only education program validated and revalidated by the United States Office of Education.

For years I have encouraged him to describe in some detail the process used to gain such dramatic results in student achievement in a school district not expected to produce them. In this book, *Creating the Ideal School: Where Teachers Want to Teach and Students Want to Learn*, Al Mamary presents a program that will allow you to create your own ideal school in a clear, commonsense language that all involved, or who wish to be involved, in the education of our children will understand.

Dr. Mamary explains that the only way to achieve long-lasting results is to take a comprehensive systemic approach and examine every aspect of ideal schools and classrooms. He points out that the "fix of the day" solutions will not produce long-term results, but in fact may have a negative effect on the morale of staff and students.

As a practitioner, Dr. Mamary examines many different issues facing teachers, including getting all students to achieve at highly competent levels. In my book *Every Student Can Succeed*, I state, "With the exception of the Johnson City, New York school district under the leadership of Superintendent Albert Mamary as it operated in the years between 1976 to 1993, no other school district I know of has ever seriously suggested eliminating low grades and making competence (B grade) the minimal standard for credit. During these years, Johnson City schools were lauded nationwide."

Not only does Dr. Mamary examine the classroom practice of grading, he also explains how to manage time when giving retests to achieve competence. Other classroom practices that have a profound influence on student learning such as testing, homework, and discipline are also examined.

There are times when the traditional system of teacher assessment is confrontational and doesn't work as intended. A new system of self- and co-assessment is explained and a detailed perceptual check is provided. Dr. Mamary explains how staff performance will improve in a noncoercive environment.

Finally, Dr. Mamary shows that for schools to become ideal schools, they must have well-structured continuing professional education for all staff. He provides a guide for funding a program that gives all staff time to learn and plan while being away from children.

Anyone interested in improving student achievement and preparing our students to compete in the world market will find this book rewarding and a must read. *Creating the Ideal School* will be useful in the training of new teachers and administrators as well as those who have been in the profession a long time.

Dr. Mamary knows that, in the long run, getting teachers and administrators to create their own ideal schools is the only meaningful way to create substantive change, and he provides the structure and framework to do so. By doing this, Dr. Mamary's book makes a major contribution to the field of education.

William Glasser, MD

Acknowledgments

It would not have been possible to write this book without the help and influence of many others, both within and outside the teaching profession. Many deserve my thanks.

Mary, my wife, had the most influence. She encouraged me to put my educational knowledge and experience into a book about schooling. She also encouraged me to make the book as accessible as possible to all readers. Her advice and love kept me going and on target.

My daughter, Anne Mamary, a professor of philosophy, advised me to include my personal stories. She reminded me that people always responded wonderfully to these stories during workshops and presentations, and that they would serve to make the book more interesting and human.

I want to acknowledge and thank the entire staff of the Johnson City schools during my tenure. It was a pleasure and a joy to be associated with these true professionals. They were willing to read the educational literature, have meaningful discussions, and then take the necessary action to get better. Visiting educators were always impressed by the commitment and enthusiasm of the Johnson City staff.

Ideas, knowledge, and solutions to complex educational problems often came from the staff. I listened, participated, and learned from them. While many influenced my thinking, Dr. Frank Alessi must be cited for the key role he played. Through many conversations, discussions, and brainstorming sessions, Dr. Alessi was at the forefront of the Johnson City school district's effort to improve what we were doing. He deserves a special thanks.

Many read the manuscript while it was still a work-in-progress, each from a different perspective. I want to thank Drs. Patricia and Henry Binzer. They made detailed suggestions about the content, the order of the chapters, and the wording. Pat and Hank were gentle, and sometimes not so gentle, when making a point. We had some heated discussions, which only ended when I agreed with them. Well, I usually did.

A very special thanks goes to Joan Davis, a retired high-school English teacher and department chairperson at Owego Academy, New York. She read every word with the sharp eye of an outstanding English teacher. I am sure she knew how to use a red pencil but she chose to use an ample supply of post-it notes instead. Joan is a master of grammar, punctuation, and sentence structure. She commented in detail, as any good high-school English teacher would, and I can't recall a time when I didn't agree with her suggestions. I am grateful for Joan's generosity of knowledge and spirit.

My good friends Ross and Carole Peduto read all the chapters and had especially helpful comments about the early ones. Ross is a remarkable business leader who offered many incredibly useful suggestions. He wanted the book to reach a wide range of readers and posed this penetrating question: Why would a reader want to read the next chapter? He advised me to be sure that each chapter was as provocative as the next one. Carole kept Ross and me focused, and ensured the book was readable.

Dr. Floyd McDowell, PhD, PhD (he has two of them), read the manuscript for professional accuracy. His suggestions were always appropriate, professional, and accurate. Floyd is one of those educators who always wants to do what was best for children and to add quality to their lives. He played a role in getting the law passed that provides an appropriate education for children with disabilities. Dr. McDowell is a true scholar and gentleman, and children are better off thanks to his efforts. I thank him for that.

Dr. Fannie Linder is a good friend and a practicing psychotherapist. Her varied suggestions and advice came from a unique perspective. She read the manuscript as a parent, teacher, counselor, and humanitarian. This encouraged me to write at an appropriate level throughout the book.

I appreciate all the comments made by Patricia Dovi, a school superintendent. Pat used the concepts presented in this book in her school district. The positive comments received from her teachers and principals reinforced the importance of this work.

I have known Dr. Robert Carpenter, interim dean at Binghamton University, for many years, and was pleased when he accepted the invitation to read my manuscript and share his personal and professional thoughts. His comments were poignant and well received. Bob has been my colleague, and has made many contributions to our local schools with his expertise and personality. Our education community is better off because of him.

I want to thank Cecelia Cancellaro, my agent and founder of Idea Architects, for her valuable assistance in editing this book and in finding a publisher for it. Her editing was the work of a true professional. Whenever I encountered a problem or had a question, I would contact Cecelia and get a professional answer immediately. Her advice was impeccable.

I also want to thank Paul Cacciato, assistant managing editor at Rowman & Littlefield Education, for keeping me on track, moving the publication forward, and seeking my thoughts during the entire process. Paul is, in every sense of the word, a true professional in the publishing business.

Finally, I owe a special thank-you to Dr. William Glasser, MD, a world-renowned educator. Not only did he write the foreword but his ideas and teachings helped shape my psychological perspective as I led the Johnson City school district and as I wrote this book. I also appreciate his many kind comments about my work as superintendent of the Johnson City schools. It is good to have a friend's support and encouragement. Many years ago, Bill prompted me to write this book but I didn't have the time. Over the years, the thought of a book kept resurfacing and when I did sit down to write it, my ideas and experience were more focused than ever. Thanks to Bill for planting the seed those many years ago.

Introduction

When I arrived as the assistant superintendent for instruction in 1972, Johnson City, New York, was a village of modest homes, primarily low- to middle-income families, and a school system with mediocre test scores and expectations. Six years later the demographics remained the same but the test scores had improved dramatically. Later, the school district earned the distinction of having the nation's only validated and revalidated comprehensive effectiveness program. The Joint Effectiveness Panel of the United States Department of Education conducted the review, validation, and revalidation process.

The teachers and administrators of the Johnson City public schools didn't start with a comprehensive plan and process to create an ideal school. There was none to be had. Rather, a small number of teachers and administrators volunteered and made the commitment to read the educational literature about implementing programs that would enable all students to be successful learners. This seemingly simple decision transformed the Johnson City school district from one with mediocre achievement to one with outstanding achievement.

Just talking about getting all students to learn was a major breakthrough for educators at that time. Not many really believed it was possible. I am not sure I did. Even though I attended the University of Minnesota, Stanford University, and Columbia University, where I studied and received my graduate degrees, nothing in my education taught me that it is possible for all students to learn well.

My own ideas about learning and teaching began to change when, by chance, I read University of Chicago professor Benjamin Bloom's article

"Learning for Mastery" and his book *Human Characteristics and School Learning* (1983). Bloom explained that under the right conditions most students could learn what was once reserved for a few. I didn't believe what I was reading. How could all students learn the mathematics I was teaching? How could everyone learn algebra, geometry, and calculus? After years of assuming student learning would fall on the bell curve, I doubted Bloom's assertions.

But I read and reread his article and book and became convinced that his ideas were sound. Exploring his research and compelling assertions, we started the transformation of the Johnson City schools. While the process was not always easy and was certainly not without mistakes or frustrations, it began with discussion and implementation of the following assertions that Bloom and others made:

1. One of the most destructive practices in American schools is the sorting and labeling of children and the expectations that accompany that sorting and labeling.
2. A student's learning aptitude is not his or her capacity to learn but the amount of time needed to learn. Furthermore, teachers should abolish the use of the IQ test to make any decisions about students.
3. Not only do students learn at different rates, they learn in a variety of ways.
4. When instruction and assessment are carefully aligned to the desired outcomes, student achievement increases dramatically.
5. Earned success in learning is one of the greatest motivators in student learning. Teachers agree that making mistakes is necessary to learning, but that mistakes should not be viewed as failures.
6. Teachers' expectations have a profound influence on student learning.

These compelling observations challenged all teachers and administrators to question their beliefs and practices. After discussion, we agreed upon the following beliefs:

- Cooperation in the classroom will replace competition in the classroom.
- All students will be included in every activity where possible.
- Each student's talent will be recognized and developed.
- All teachers will develop an atmosphere of trust and encouragement in the classroom.

- An optimistic "I can do" attitude will be encouraged for all students.
- Assessment will be used for the purpose of helping students learn. After they demonstrate they have learned well, they will receive a good grade.

In approximately six years, most teachers (K–12) were involved. They were committed to inclusion—to refusing to separate students physically or mentally from regular classrooms and activities. They intentionally aligned instruction and assessment to learning outcomes rather than including some problems on tests that only a few might be able to do, some not everyone could do, and some every student could do. Teachers made an important distinction between viewing aptitude as the capacity to learn and the rate of learning. Teachers, while still providing some lecture, were now allowing students time to explore, investigate, interact, share knowledge, explain, discuss, and learn in a variety of ways. They made it plain to students that all could earn good grades given enough time to learn material well. While most teachers embraced the changes, some did not. In response, we showed those teachers nothing but respect, and we kept providing them opportunities for involvement.

Although we were doing our best with what we knew, we made mistakes. We tried to learn from them, to correct our errors, and to do a better job. Many times, educators revert to what they have always done when they encounter difficulties. This was never in our thinking.

A classic mistake was made when we accepted and interpreted the phrase "Given enough time, most students will learn what was once reserved for a few." Time was mismanaged. Students took advantage of teachers by taking more time than needed. They became intellectually lazy, and we were the enablers. There were few deadlines, and our classes became fragmented. Teachers couldn't manage it.

After lengthy discussions and modifications, teachers adopted the phrase "Given enough time today, most students will learn well." Teachers learned to manage time and their class. Approximate time limits were placed on each unit of study. All students were responsible for learning at least at the competent level, while the faster learners were able to carry on investigations. Extra time was provided for those students who did not achieve at the minimum level of competency.

Although the superintendent and I, as the assistant superintendent, were involved with the teachers from the very beginning of the school's climate and cultural transformation, we were both new to the district. We knew that it was common practice for administrators to want teachers to make a commitment to making changes but rarely make commitments of their own to teachers. We had to earn their trust over time with consistently supportive behavior and setting the right conditions for change. Teachers were working hard to make profound changes, and they wanted to know if they would get the support they needed. Some of the commitments we made to our teachers included the following:

1. We will never ask you to do something you are not trained to do. We will provide the time and training.
2. We are colearners, coworkers, and codoers. We, along with the principals, will not use our positions to gain power. Everyone has the power to influence and develop the process.
3. We will have most of the staff training during the school day or during the summer.
4. It is OK to make mistakes, for if we don't make mistakes we can't learn. Don't bury mistakes. Identify them, so we can solve them and learn.
5. We will provide summer employment.

Together we made an agreement to abolish all "killer phrases." After a brainstorming session, teachers, principals, and some students published all the phrases they could think of and then placed them on the walls of the classrooms, offices, and lounges. These included "Here we go again," "It won't work here," "Our students are not like their students," "We won't be supported," "We already tried and it didn't work," and "It's not in our budget." Everyone agreed to be held accountable not to use them. Students even held their teachers and principals accountable. One class conducted a funeral service for these killer phrases and buried them in the schoolyard, vowing never to use them again.

Parents, students, teachers, principals, and the entire support staff functioned as a team in which everyone's ideas were valued and given a fair hearing. Dr. William Glasser's ideas on basic human needs and choice theory helped explain why what we were doing was so successful. We now had a model to create a psychologically safe and nurturing environment systematically. Everyone had ownership, the key to successful change.

We gained many positive results from our use of knowledge to refine our beliefs, classroom practices, culture, management, and instruction. Student achievement as measured by state and national tests exceeded everyone's expectations. This was not supposed to happen in this community of low- to middle-income families. Everyone told us that, including other superintendents. As a matter of record, they conducted an investigation of our achievements. When they found out they were wrong, they might have apologized and even emulated us, but they didn't. But, for us, the best rewards came from our students. At the end of eighth grade, with no students exempt, students were achieving three years above grade level in reading and three and a half years in math. Title I students were reading and computing at least two years above grade level.

The other surprise happened at the end of fourth grade. National scores tend to level off or even decline at this point; our scores showed the greatest increases. The longer students were within our schools, the better they achieved. But even students who came to the district for only a year or two did well. Although Johnson City's low-cost rental properties contributed to families' moving in and out of town, and there was often more than a 35% change in student body each year, the national and state scores remained high.

Furthermore, in New York State, at that time, approximately 35% to 40% of a high school graduating class received the coveted Board of Regents diploma. The Johnson City High School granted more than 70% of its graduating class this diploma. To earn it, students had to take strong academic courses and achieve well on state examinations.

Because of these achievements, the *New York Times* published an article about the district, followed by a feature story "The School Where Everyone Gets As" in *Family Circle* magazine. Thousands of educators visited our schools, where they were able to observe what teachers and principals were doing to get such good results.

We were encouraged to apply for National Validation from the United States Office of Education. To write a proposal, we had to determine all the components that contributed to our success. This led us to write a comprehensive systems process.

Had we not decided to apply for validation, we might not have discovered a total systems process. We might have been satisfied with a series of related ideas. We did apply, and we were validated. We were now able to explain to others our Total Comprehensive Process—the total picture.

While test scores were remarkable, there were many other achievements. During a Middle States accreditation critique, the chair of the visiting committee made the following comments:

> Where are the real kids and where is the real building? Did you import the kids and do you use this building only for evaluation? All these students seem to be happy. When we asked students, selected at random, how many good teachers they had, they seemed impatient with the question. Many responded with, "Why do you ask?" But then they would say all of our teachers are good while the usual response rate at other schools was 4 or 5.

The committee reported that most students were involved in their learning and proud of their school. They also noted that graffiti was almost nonexistent. Students were not only taking responsibility for their learning, they were taking responsibility for the cleanliness of their school.

Community enthusiasm for the schools was overwhelming. Every two years the district administered a survey to parents during the parents' open house. To ensure anonymity, surveys were deposited in boxes placed in the halls. These are some of the survey questions and responses:

1. Do you have an understanding of how teachers are working with your children? Answer: 98.1% of the parents said they did.
2. Do you feel that you need more explanation of any aspect of the educational program? Answer: 98.8% of the parents said they didn't.
3. Were you welcomed to visit your school last year or this year? Answer: 96.1% of the parents said yes.
4. From what you have observed, heard, or read, do you feel that this school district is moving in the proper direction in its efforts to ensure that your children are learning well? Answer: 92.7% of the parents said yes.

Parents, teachers, and administrators were asked to present their points of view concerning this comprehensive systems process. A selection of comments from parents, principals, and teachers follows.

A PARENT'S VIEW

This comprehensive process with the major emphasis on all students learning well sometimes seems overwhelming. Teachers, principals, other administrators, and parents talk on a regular basis about how they can better educate our children. I have two children. One happens to be a self-directed learner, who does not need much help. My other child really needs to be pushed, but I see firsthand how this process is working for both of my children.

The one child who is self-directed assumes much responsibility for her own education. Not only does she achieve what is expected but is encouraged to go well beyond. She is not held back by slower learners and studies given topics in depth. She works either independently or with other students to carry on a full investigation. All students are taught how to investigate a topic, so when they have time they are given the freedom to explore additional topics related to the unit of study. Now, my other child is also being helped but in a different way. She gets the special attention she needs, but she knows that unless she applies herself on each unit of work, she will not get credit or a grade for that unit. She knows she must learn at least at a highly competent level. Both children are learners, know what they are supposed to learn, know that they are expected to learn well, and that teachers will guide them through the necessary experiences to be successful. Yet one goes well beyond the standard curriculum while the other learns at least the standard curriculum.

One point that is really interesting about the comprehensive process is that when all children leave high school, they are not only going to have a good education, they will also be able to deal with life. As a parent, that is almost the most important education I want my children to have. Sure, I'd love to have them be National Honor Society students, to be chair of the board, or bank president, but that is not the reality of life. The reality of life is that they have to learn to deal with life wherever it takes them, experiencing both the ups and downs.

By going through this process they are learning to be responsible for themselves from kindergarten. By the time they reach high school and graduate, they know that they have to take responsibility for themselves and go on from there. It is very comforting to parents to know that for approximately

180 days a year, our children are in classrooms where teachers and administrators are trying to show them this process day in and day out. Most parents want the process and support the school in its efforts.

A PRINCIPAL'S VIEW

A principal's role in the comprehensive system used in Johnson City had many special challenges as well as many rewards. The principal's major activities include intense daily involvement in all aspects of curriculum and instruction. Being a principal in Johnson City requires a strong adherence to the school's vision, beliefs, culture, and, above all, making decisions using the most compelling research-based information available. A principal could not operate from the power of the position and expect good things to happen. Working together with teachers and other administrators, sharing ideas and planning, produced great results.

Great attention was paid to establishing and maintaining an effective communication process so everyone was involved in all major planning and decisions. In a given week, the principal would not only meet formally with each team in the school but would also informally communicate with each member of the staff. Much was accomplished by "managing by walking around" and by being where the action and problems were. Visiting with each member of the noninstructional staff was also very important.

If one were to follow a principal during his or her everyday management duties, one would have observed the principal as a learner, listener, teacher, team worker, and a person who fully understood that his or her influence made an essential difference between a good school and an ideal school.

You will also see a principal who created the conditions for teachers to get the time and training they needed. You would see a principal basking in the glow of the achievements of teachers and students and being their biggest cheerleader.

A TEACHER'S VIEW

After I became involved in Johnson City's comprehensive instructional process, many of the frustrations I had vanished. The more involved and sophisticated I became in the process, the more students learned and the happier we became about our success.

When I was first introduced to the research, beliefs, and some practices, my initial reaction was "I do all those things. What is so different?" The difference was that I was sporadic rather than systematic in my approach. My teaching was far from an intentional/thought-out process that would enable most students to learn and learn well.

As I analyzed the process and compared it to my existing practices, I found many differences:

1. I knew there were certain skills students needed to know to be successful in the unit, but I never bothered to assess, remediate, or review what students needed to know to be successful each day. Some students, therefore, didn't understand my lesson.
2. I never told students at the beginning of the lesson what they were to learn that day or summarize what they should have learned at the end of the lesson.
3. I never altered the learning time from one student to another.
4. I never consciously decided on the best modes of initial instruction or about the specific learning outcomes expected.
5. I did not create active student participation. I was not active while they were in the guided practice. I did not form needs groups for those having difficulty.
6. I continuously assessed student performance, not to help them learn but for giving a grade.
7. I did not align my tests with what I taught. Many times I wanted students to go to higher levels of thinking, when, in fact, I had never taught them to do this.
8. I did not certify students for learning but for time spent against other students.
9. I did not provide reteaching, correcting, and retesting for those who needed it but rather taught the next unit to everyone.
10. I assigned student grades even though they had not learned well. I did not give retests or adjust grades to reflect new learning.

I do not look back with regret. I was doing the best I could with the knowledge I had. With my present knowledge of instruction, learning rates and modes, expectations, psychological needs, and classroom practices, I look at the present and to the future with much enthusiasm.

CONCLUSION

I chose the title *Creating the Ideal School: Where Teachers Want to Teach and Students Want to Learn* after much deliberation. Because some Chinese educators remarked that Johnson City was a "very good school" (their highest compliment), I considered this as a title. Understanding that in the United States, however, "very good" is not good enough, I also realized that we must strive to make all our schools ideal ones. Why would anyone not want to create the ideal school?

No one can give schools a program to replicate. Each school or district must take on the task of developing its own framework for creating the ideal school. I have shared what worked for us. Feel free to use what you want, but whatever you decide to do, make sure it represents the most comprehensive picture possible. Don't be satisfied with the process presented in this book. Be critical and determine which of the components need to be changed, modified, and even removed. Add components as faculty wishes. Only our best thinking can be provided, and this is what I attempt to do in the following pages.

Chapter One

Here We Go Again

All children have a wonderful brain and mind, and if you think they don't, just pretend they do.

Focus Questions

1. Make a list of some of the many innovations in education that have come and gone. Why do you think some innovations have survived in part or whole? Why do you think most have been abolished?
2. Based on your professional experience, name some programs that have been mandated that have made a difference in student learning. Make a list of political slogans concerning education.
3. What are some alternatives or modifications you would implement to the state standards and high-stakes testing?

Every child has special gifts and talents waiting to be discovered and nurtured. Our job as teachers is to find and develop these gifts and talents, to see more in children than they see in themselves, and to encourage—certainly never discourage—every single child with whom we come in contact during our lives.

Teachers do make a difference in the lives of children—a profound one. Other adults do as well, but it is the teacher who influences thousands of children during his or her career.

My teachers did. Entering first grade four months after my fifth birthday and totally unready to learn, I was nurtured and encouraged by my teacher Miss Monahan. It would have been so easy for her to give up on me, but she didn't. I learned to read and to love first grade and Miss Monahan.

Since my elementary school was in the poorer section of the city, there was no library in the school or in my neighborhood. Students were not allowed to take home any of the books that were available. My parents were first-generation immigrants and were never told to have books in the home or to encourage their children to read. They simply didn't know, and even if they had known they couldn't afford books anyway. My mother left school during her sixth grade to help take care of her six brothers and sisters after their mother died. My father finished ninth grade and worked in a local factory. Love, food, used clothing, and chores were given in abundance in my family. After finishing my usual Saturday morning house cleaning one day, I decided to explore outside my immediate neighborhood. I was ten years old. I found the YMCA and went in. The kind gentleman at the desk showed me around. He gave me some used gym clothing and sneakers and I was in business for my usual Saturday afternoon jaunt. The wonderful man never mentioned money; he must have known I couldn't afford to pay.

One afternoon after leaving the Y, I took a different route home through the wealthier part of town. I saw a sign for "The Osterhout Library." I was never in a library before then. I entered not knowing whether I was welcome or not, and to my surprise the rooms were filled with books. No one said I couldn't stay even though I was expecting to be escorted to the nearest exit at any minute. I found a book and after an hour I carefully put the book back in its vacated spot. No one told me I could check out books. But they were nice to me and even smiled occasionally. This routine continued for eleven months until I went to junior–senior high school, which included a wonderful library with a lot of books.

My life continued to be influenced by my teachers and other adults. It took only one positive comment by my seventh-grade mathematics teacher to inform me that I had some math talent. Miss Rizik, my ninth-grade Latin teacher, helped me develop my language talents. She gave me encouragement and private time to develop my writing skills. Then there was my high-school math teacher Mr. Chalis, who told my mother that he thought I should go to college. But going to college was out of the question at that time. In those days, college was reserved for the affluent.

After graduating from high school, I worked for three years to help support my family. This allowed me to save enough money to attend a state college, Mansfield University, for one semester. When that semester was over I was going to return home. Dean Long, the dean of students at Mansfield, heard about my plight and found a dishwashing job to pay my expenses.

My story is not unique. Every day, every minute, some teacher and some adult somewhere are having life-changing influences on the life of a child. These stories go unreported most of the time; nevertheless, they are incredibly influential.

Activity: Influence of a Teacher

Virtually everyone I've ever asked has a story about how a teacher or adult influenced his or her life. Has a teacher had a profound influence on your life? What did she or he say or do? Be as specific as possible. Is your life better for that influence? Why or why not?

During an interview with Maya Angelou, a reporter asked, "Are you a role model for others?" Maya's response went something like this: Each of us famous or infamous is a role model for someone else and even if we think we are not, we should behave as though we are, for you can be sure someone is watching and taking diligent notes.

As educators we are role models for students whether we like it or not and we can be sure they are watching us and diligently taking notes, mostly mental. Our influence is profound. We must always ask ourselves, "What kind of message do we want to send?" When students know we care and we provide a first-rate education, they will have a greater chance at becoming academically competent with a positive attitude. They will have a better chance of living a fulfilling productive life. Everyone is entitled to learn well and if they don't, the consequences to them and society are severe.

This book will help you develop your own ideal school where every child will have a well-rounded education and learn well. This won't happen by hoping or by applying the latest innovation. The only way you can get all students to learn well is to implement a comprehensive process known to influence student learning, while celebrating the life, goodness, and potential of each child.

THE MAJOR PROBLEM: QUICK FIXES, INSIDIOUS ILLUSIONS

Virtually everyone agrees it is imperative that we have a highly educated society. Our workforce demands it. The process of education starts at the time of birth and continues more formally when a child enters school. We know that some students turn off to learning early in their school career and this problem continues to grow. Schools then search for solutions, frequently looking to the next innovation that offers the hope that more students will want to learn and learn well. Schools have tried them all. Remember open education and flexible scheduling? Remember modern mathematics, management by objectives, transformational outcomes, zero-based budgeting, individualization of instruction, block scheduling, and now standards-based education? Not one of these practices is bad. As a matter of fact, many are good. Many are promising. However, not one of them alone will change our schools significantly enough to get more students to learn better. It is imperative that we reject the tinkering approach and instead employ a systematic plan to solve the complex problem of getting all students to learn well, of getting all teachers and administrators to feel job satisfaction, and of getting parents to feel satisfied with the performance of their children's schools. When we fail to plan systematically, we systematically plan to fail.

The consequences are severe to those students who are not learning well. More and more jobs now require a highly skilled workforce and a highly sophisticated learner and worker. Manufacturing jobs are rapidly disappearing and many are being shipped abroad. Corporations are downsizing, with automation replacing many low-level unskilled jobs. Computer-driven robots are replacing workers, and consequently the remaining workers must have knowledge and technical skills and be able to function well as a member of a team to keep their jobs. Basic communication skills including reading, writing, speaking, and listening are essential to today's job world. Facility with technology is rapidly becoming a necessary basic skill as well.

Getting and keeping a good job that pays well with good benefits, a job that brings workers to at least middle-class status and financial stability is still the dream of most people. Without good knowledge and skills, workers may be subject to a life of low-paying jobs, periods of unemployment, or, even worse, long-term welfare. The future is often bleak for those without a good education and demonstrated skills. Knowledge, both formal and that obtained through on-the-job training, is a key resource today; it can be transferred from job to job. Having good knowledge and skills won't guarantee a good job but without them, getting and keeping a good job is almost impossible.

More than a decade ago the Secretary's Commission on Achieving Necessary Skills, of the U.S. Department of Labor, examined the demands on the workplace and concluded that more than half of our students leave school without adequate knowledge to get and keep a good job (U.S. Department of Labor, 1992). The only way to fix this problem is to design schools so that each one develops the capacity to manage itself, ensures that all teachers and administrators are performing well, and all students, not just some, are learning well. As a friend once said, "What part of 'all' don't we understand?"

RENEWED HOPE, STATIC RESULTS

We begin each school year with a renewed hope that this year is going to be a good one—a year where all students will choose to learn well and do what is required to achieve and, in fact, choose to learn at high levels. We also begin each year with the hope that schools will get the supplies and equipment they need and that their buildings and grounds will be clean, neat, and in good repair.

Parents also have high hopes that their children will love school, attend with enthusiasm, and learn well. They hope that all students will read easily and write fluently, that they will understand math and science, will be informed citizens, will be competent in world affairs, and will understand geography and home and financial management. They also hope that the arts and music will receive proper attention.

The beginning of every school year is exciting for parents, teachers, and students. It brings a renewing of friendship, a fresh start for learning and teaching, a new optimism, and a positive hope for achievement.

There is some encouraging news concerning student achievement, and publicly stated standards have contributed to this. However, the truth is that results remain virtually unchanged. Approximately one third of students achieve quite well. Another one third achieve well but not at high levels, and yet another one third are not learning well at all. By their own admission, these students come to school primarily to socialize and are just putting in their time. While these results vary from class to class and school to school, and while the level of achievement in suburban schools seems to be higher than in inner-city schools, these results represent the range of achievement found in most classrooms.

Many students who are not learning well often feel negatively about their teachers, their school, and the necessity of education. They often refuse to do their work and turn to disruptive, antisocial behavior. They indulge in vandalism, graffiti, and, in extreme cases, violence. Teachers do their best to motivate, counsel, remediate, and encourage, but often in vain.

Schools are facing more and more challenges, including cuts in state and federal funding and increasingly diverse students, who come to school struggling to learn English as a second language. And although some students enter school ready to learn with a foundation of stimulating home experiences, many others have had very few educational experiences at home, few or no books at home, and no one reading to them.

These problems, however, are not excuses. Schools do their best to compensate for and cope with them even as they have a profound impact on the educational experience. It is not that teachers and administrators don't care or don't work hard; most do. Their jobs are very difficult. They put in long hours, work extra time with students who need help, often have poor working conditions, and are criticized by the public and by politicians, who always seem to have their pet slogan for how to fix schools—all of this at a time when they are in the process of furthering their own formal education. Most teachers and administrators want all students to want to come to school, to work hard, and to achieve. They want their students to love learning, they want them to learn, and to do what is expected. However, when they don't see this happening, they themselves often lose hope, get discouraged, and in some cases give up. Sometimes they just put in time or commit what I call job suicide. Some, if not many, leave the profession that once offered them hope and the promise of a fulfilling career.

It is tough enough managing a school or classroom where students want to learn, but it is nearly impossible when they don't. Teachers often think students don't want to learn and students often think teachers don't care. Both are generally wrong. Most students do want to learn and most teachers do care. Not wanting to learn was learned and not showing caring was the result. This cycle must be broken. But doing what we have always done won't break the cycle.

PARENTS' DEMANDS AND LEGISLATIVE MANDATES

When parents see their children "giving up," not wanting to learn, and not learning well, they often retreat from this unsuccessful experience by divorcing themselves from the school. They might demand that their schools do better and apply pressure for real choice either within the school system, in other public schools, or through private schools.

Parents know that their children's future is bleak if they do not have at least a high-school diploma and the necessary skills to get and keep a job. Not only are parents demanding that schools do what it takes to get their children to learn well, but they are also seeking greater involvement in the education of their children. In some instances, school councils have been formed to give parents a greater voice in the dealings of their schools. When managed well, and without special-interest groups trying to control the council, this can be welcome news for educators, for they know that they can't do the job alone.

Upon seeing dismal results on state and national tests, and hearing parents complain, legislators become anxious to demonstrate that they are doing something to solve the perceived problem. What often follow are knee-jerk, quick-fix legislation and mandates. These rarely solve the problems at hand and, at times, even contribute to them. Each year new mandates appear with catchy titles offering much hope but producing little positive change. Who can disagree with phrases like "leave no child behind" or "back to basics"? They sound great, but do they really make meaningful changes? Probably not. What does a school or teacher do with the phrase "you will leave no child behind"? What changes must they make? To many, the phrase "back to basics" means having children memorize lots of facts and recall lots of information. Those students, however, simply don't retain isolated facts. This is just one of many examples of mandates that have little positive impact, and often cause harm.

Yet legislators continue to get involved in trying to improve education. Just listen to virtually every politician who is running for office; you will hear the slogan improve education, improve education, improve education. They all say it, but they have little to offer after being elected. At the beginning of the twenty-first century, legislatures and the state departments of education took direct aim at improving education through more regulations, legislation, and required state-sponsored exams. More than at any other time in the history of education, students are required to pass an abundance of state examinations with the hope that they will have the knowledge and skills needed to further their education, or to be able to get and keep a good job. Some progress is reported. Students appear to be writing, reading, and computing better than before. To be sure, dropout rates have declined somewhat; however, achievement in this area is modest at best. There is still a high dropout rate in urban schools. Many students are still not learning well, not required to do much thinking in schools or to do much schoolwork, not taking more difficult subjects, and not paying full attention when teachers are teaching.

Many students think school is boring; they believe that no one cares about them or that they make a difference in the vitality of their schools. These same students often get the feeling that teachers would be happy if they didn't show up. Legislative mandates, public criticism, and an abundance of state tests do not make a difference. Teachers and school administrators, if given the opportunity and the support, make the difference.

While there are many outstanding teachers, principals, and schools, and there are pockets of very good schools and practices, many students continue to be denied the education to which they're entitled. There is no such thing as a good or bad learner. Rather, there are faster and slower learners and even different kinds of learners. Perhaps we don't give students the time they need to learn or teach them the way to learn. Students also report that most of their classes are neither high quality nor have expectations of high quality. All of the tests that are now mandated may even stifle any quality and creativity that had been present.

The practice of setting expectations sometimes begins when students enter school. They are too often given a test, sorted into groups, and then labeled. This practice may be damaging, for it often sets an expectation, leading to the self-fulfilling prophecy that some students will not learn. But even when we don't give a test, we often label children in our minds. Students then behave according to our perceptions of whether they have the aptitude to learn what we are teaching.

It doesn't take long for a child to realize what the teacher expects and, by fourth grade, or even earlier, some students give up. Throughout their years in school, these same students often continue to be denied equity in learning opportunities.

TOTAL SCHOOL IMPROVEMENT: A COMPREHENSIVE APPROACH

While many hope that the next innovation will be the medicine that will make education well, we know from past experiences that there is no simple solution to a very complex problem. If schools are going to get significantly better, that is, get to the place where students learn well, then school personnel must change their thinking and examine more realistic, sophisticated solutions. Rather than examining just one or two aspects of a school, school personnel must look at the total school structure. They must identify all school components, examine each of them intentionally and intently as to their effectiveness, and then take the actions necessary for improvement. While total school improvement may seem overwhelming, it is not. Total school improvement means having a systematic process to intentionally examine every aspect of the school operations that are known to influence student achievement, such as teacher performance, administrative leadership, and policy support. Without the inclusion and management of every vital component along with a process to make meaningful decisions, total school improvement will not be effective. To address the real issues, school personnel must have a comprehensive and systematic process of examining and improving every aspect of school operations. Doing so will result in higher achievement for all students.

CONCLUSION

This book is dedicated to examining the components that contribute to making a school an ideal school, to making every learner a very good learner, and to making every teacher and administrator a very good professional. Consider the focus questions at the beginning of each chapter. You may also wish to determine a comprehensive set of components on your own or with colleagues that would make every school an ideal school.

You may wish to answer the focus questions at the beginning of each chapter before reading the chapter. Record your discussion and conclusions. It is not necessary to read all the chapters in the order presented, but it is recommended that you begin with the first three chapters. After reading a chapter you may wish to return to the focus questions to see if your initial reactions were confirmed or changed. "Learningful" and meaningful discussions are encouraged.

Chapter Two

Characteristics of an Ideal School

Children will choose to learn when what they are asked to learn is useful, relevant, interesting, and personally meaningful.

Focus Questions

1. What are some characteristics or attributes of all highly successful ideal schools?
2. What are parents, business leaders, and educators now demanding that all students *know* and be able to *do* when leaving school?
3. If you could create an ideal school without restrictions, what would be your design? What would be your plan? (Assume everyone will cooperate and support your design and that a reasonable amount of money will be available.) What would you see? What would you never see?

As you read this chapter, think about your school. What do you really want for your students and your staff? The choice for any school improvement must be yours. Positive change is possible. You can make your school better. You can even make your school an ideal school.

Thirteen characteristics of an ideal school are presented in the following pages. Each characteristic is explained briefly and a more detailed explanation, with concrete examples, is provided in later chapters. The "can you imagine" introduction to each characteristic is meant to highlight practices that are utilized in many schools. A description of how things would be in an ideal school follows. You should feel free to add new characteristics or delete those that don't apply to your school. This process must be adapted to fit the needs of your particular situation.

After reading chapters 4 through 14 (which can be read in any order), it might be useful to return to the characteristics outlined in this chapter. This will promote meaningful ideas and discussions. As you work through this book, record all agreements, disagreements, and suggestions, whether they are your own or those of your colleagues.

Remember, no one can mandate excellence for you. No one can make you do much of anything. Real meaningful changes come from within. Be patient with yourself and others as you examine current and desired practices.

CHARACTERISTIC 1: DEVELOP THE UNIQUE TALENTS OF EACH STUDENT

Can you imagine a school where many students come to school and don't want to learn, come to school only because attendance is mandatory, come to school only to socialize, and do just enough to get by?

Can you imagine a school that believes only a few students have the talent to perform and learn well, where the talents of many students are being submerged and never developed, and where most students start school excited about learning but eventually end up believing they are talentless, dumb, and not capable of learning well?

Wouldn't you rather imagine an ideal school in which students want to learn, are learning well, and their unique talents are nurtured, developed, and unleashed? In an ideal school:

- Destructive practices such as sorting, labeling, passive learning, and an overabundance of work sheets and busy work have been abandoned.
- Teachers and parents identify the unique talents of each student and devise a plan to develop, nurture, and expand them.
- Teachers view the aptitude of a student to learn not as the capacity to learn but as the amount of time the student needs to learn. This means all students can learn but some need more time and some less. Given enough time and good teaching, most students will learn well.
- Teachers identify students who are not doing what is expected and then provide additional time and vary the teaching modes to the way students learn.

- Each day teachers review or reteach the necessary skills for students to be successful that day and assure each student that he or she can succeed. Success is for everyone—not a few.

CHARACTERISTIC 2: EXPECT ALL STUDENTS TO LEARN WELL

Can you imagine a school where students do not work hard and do not achieve? A school where some students are not expected to learn and some teachers believe some students can learn and some can't?

Can you imagine a school where students go through the motions of learning, and where just getting by is the norm?

Can you imagine a school where students spend most of their time studying just to pass a standards test, where creativity and exploration of ideas are all but lost, and where memorization without understanding is the mode?

Wouldn't you rather imagine an ideal school in which students work hard and are expected to learn and achieve, while feeling that what they are being asked to learn is relevant, interesting, and personally meaningful? In an ideal school:

- Teachers and administrators believe one's ability cannot be measured by a single test, which therefore should not be used to create an expectation of a student's performance.
- All students are expected to learn and achieve and these expectations are genuinely communicated through practices and positive action.
- Students are encouraged to explore, question, discover, investigate, and be creative with their use of knowledge without fear of failure. The result is that more students will find their education to be relevant, interesting, and personally meaningful.

CHARACTERISTIC 3: HAVE HIGH AND CLEAR EXPECTATIONS

Can you imagine students having to guess what teachers want them to learn, and guess what is expected of them even after the teacher taught the lesson?

Can you imagine students having to guess what will be on a test knowing if they guess right they will do well and, if not, they won't?

Can you imagine a teacher who tells the class after they do poorly on a test, "Don't worry, I will mark on the curve?" Does that mean students learned what was expected?

Can you imagine teachers grading on the curve, comparing students in assigning grades, rather than grading against predetermined stated expectations? Is it possible for all students to get high grades?

Wouldn't you rather imagine an ideal school in which teachers are very clear about what is expected of their students, students understand what is expected of them, and both strive to meet expectations? In an ideal school:

- Teachers have determined and agreed on what all students should know and be able to do.
- These expectations are explained to students, and they understand and strive to meet them.
- The expectations include the requirements for state and/or national exams but go way beyond that.
- It is possible for all students to do well and even get As.
- Students know the bell curve of grading will never be used.

CHARACTERISTIC 4: CREATE A NO-EXCUSE SCHOOL

Can you imagine a school where teachers go through the motions of teaching and ignore what the educational literature is saying about good teaching?

Can you imagine a school where teachers do not care what students learn and expect them to learn just a little?

Can you imagine a school where everyone makes excuses why some students don't learn, why some teachers don't teach well, and where students and teachers blame each other?

Wouldn't you rather imagine an ideal school in which teachers are demanding and teach well, but don't make excuses when students don't learn, and don't accept excuses either? In an ideal school:

- Teachers plan and teach well. They fully understand that teaching is both a science and an art. They understand that when using acceptable teaching practices the results will be better. They know, for example, that when they teach using a single mode of learning, many students will not learn. They know they must use a variety of teaching–learning modes.
- Teachers know students learn at different rates, so they give students appropriate amounts of time to learn while still managing time effectively.
- You never hear excuses but you do see teachers continuing to search for ways to include more students in the learning process. Excuses neither make learning nor school better. Excuses bring everyone down and must never be used, not even in the faculty lounge. Excuses serve as "killers" of all initiatives.
- Teachers and administrators find reasons why and never reasons why not.

CHARACTERISTIC 5: BE CARING AND COMPASSIONATE AS WELL AS DEMANDING

Can you imagine a school where students are afraid to take risks and where they hide behind the students in front of them to avoid being embarrassed?

Can you imagine a teacher who is not compassionate and who routinely embarrasses students by using "put down" comments rather than encouragement?

Can you imagine a teacher who merely puts a grade on papers without letting students know what they have to do to improve their learning?

Can you imagine a teacher who does not let students correct learning errors to improve their grade?

Wouldn't you rather imagine an ideal school in which teachers are caring and compassionate, encourage students to take risks, and correct learning errors until students learn well and succeed? In an ideal school:

- Teachers are compassionate and never embarrass a student either in private or in front of other students.
- Teachers encourage students to take risks, to try to integrate their knowledge and skills, and to demonstrate their new understandings.

- Teachers know that students will never try to be creative or to learn beyond what is required if they are not encouraged to take risks without fear of being penalized.
- Teachers can be demanding as long as students know the teacher cares.
- Teachers give students the help they need, correct learning errors, and assign grades only after students learn well.
- Teachers set standards, hold students accountable to standards, and help each student achieve them. Students are never compared to each other.

CHARACTERISTIC 6: INVITE ALL STUDENTS TO BE CREATIVE THINKERS

Can you imagine a school where teachers are interested only in students' passing a state or national test and where little thinking or creativity is encouraged or expected?

Can you imagine a school that takes away from students what they possess naturally? Most students enter school with profound thinking processes in place, asking their parents the kind of provocative questions that don't have simple answers. But because of mandated pressures on schools to prepare students for state and national exams, students frequently are discouraged from thinking, being creative, or even learning.

Can you imagine a school whose only slogan is "Let's get them ready for The Tests"? (This slogan is often implied rather than stated.)

Wouldn't you rather imagine an ideal school in which teachers invite and encourage thinking, and students are thinking and demonstrating this all the time? In an ideal school:

- Teachers prepare students for The Tests, but they also encourage students to think. Getting students ready for a test and encouraging them to think are not mutually exclusive events. Excellent teachers know that when students are not turned off to thinking they ask unusual questions, and when they challenge basic assumptions, they do even better on The Tests.

- Grades don't get in the way of thinking. When students are free to try out new ideas and don't have to worry about grades, increased learning will take place. Remember that when students are making an honest effort to learn, teachers should assign grades only after they learn well.
- Children enter school thinking and wanting to learn. Our job is to encourage this.

CHARACTERISTIC 7: BE EXCITED ABOUT TEACHING AND ABOUT THE SUBJECTS YOU TEACH

Can you imagine a teacher trying to teach a subject he or she doesn't know very well? A student might ask a teacher who is teaching mathematics, and who does not have a good understanding of math, why when finding the area of a triangle you multiply half the base times the height (i.e., why is $A = \frac{1}{2} bh$)? Without an understanding of basic geometry and algebra, the teacher cannot explain why. Is it any mystery why students don't understand when the teacher doesn't?

Can you imagine a teacher who is not excited about his or her subject or teaching and is just waiting to retire or get another job? How can you teach what you don't know or understand? Why would students get excited about learning if the teacher is not excited about teaching?

Wouldn't you rather imagine an ideal school in which teachers know their subject well and are excited about teaching it, and students respond positively to this enthusiasm? In an ideal school:

- Teachers understand what they are teaching, can explain it well, and help all students understand what they are learning. When students understand what they are learning, they remember their initial learning longer. They may even gain a greater appreciation for different subjects.
- Teachers are excited about what they are teaching and students get caught up in the excitement. Students' learning potential is increased.

CHARACTERISTIC 8: CREATE A PSYCHOLOGICALLY SAFE AND NURTURING SCHOOL

Can you imagine a school where only some students and some teachers are accepted unconditionally, and feel valued or worthwhile?

Can you imagine a school where some students are expected to learn and some are not? For example, a beginning teacher in a school was told by parents during a parent–teacher conference that their five-year-old daughter was slow (meaning she moved slowly, did her work slowly, and even ate slowly), and the teacher soon wanted to have the girl tested and classified. Words influence perceptions, perceptions influence expectations, and both influence actions.

Can you imagine a school where a family's history, a student's looks, and placement tests influence a school's perceptions and expectations about who will be accepted, valued, respected, and thought worthwhile, and in which teachers think only certain students have talent?

Wouldn't you rather imagine an ideal school in which everyone is accepted unconditionally, all are valued and included, and teachers create a psychologically safe and nurturing environment? In an ideal school:

- Every child and adult is accepted without any conditions. Each knows he or she is valued and worthwhile.
- Teachers understand that every child has a talent just waiting to be discovered and nurtured.
- Students know they make a difference and that school would not be the same if they weren't there.
- Teachers also know that they would be missed if they weren't there. Think about people who go to work, put in time, and continually look at the clock knowing they are just "another employee."
- Everyone is in a psychologically safe environment.

CHARACTERISTIC 9: REMOVE ALL SARCASM, HUMILIATION, AND BLAME

Can you imagine a school where people simply don't care for each other, where everyone looks out only for himself or herself?

Can you imagine a school where teachers' good ideas about getting all students to learn are killed by uncaring teachers? You will hear expressions like:

- It won't work here.
- We don't have students who will learn.
- This too shall pass.
- They won't support us.
- Here we go again.

Can you imagine a school or classroom that is filled with sarcasm, blame, and humiliation?

Can you imagine a school or classroom where validation and affirmation are rarely used?

Wouldn't you rather imagine an ideal school in which everyone cares for one another; there is no sarcasm, humiliation, or blame; and all are validated for honest effort? In an ideal school:

- Staff genuinely care for each other, not just in a time of crisis but on a daily basis.
- Staff are interested in each other and their families, ideas, and welfare.
- Staff never use sarcasm, blame, or humiliation in the classroom or in any part of the school, including the faculty lounge. They know how destructive these practices are, personally and educationally. They also know that humor at the expense of someone else is destructive and therefore never tolerated.
- Staff validate each other and students for honest effort and achievement. They know that their job is to help everyone be successful and achieve.
- Staff listen to one another as well as to their students' ideas, draw them out, encourage them, and help put good ideas into operation. They know that a spark of an idea may eventually have a major impact on student achievement.

CHARACTERISTIC 10: FIND PLEASURE AND JOY IN TEACHING AND LEARNING

Can you imagine a school where there is little joy or laughter, where learning and teaching are viewed as unexciting, boring chores?

Can you imagine a school where some teachers find little pleasure in teaching, don't want to come to school, and can't wait until they retire? Can you imagine being a student in those classrooms?

Can you imagine a school where students only find joy and pleasure in extracurricular activities instead of in mandated classes?

Wouldn't you rather imagine an ideal school in which everyone finds time to laugh, teaching and learning are satisfying and enjoyable, and pleasure and fun occur on and off the job? In an ideal school:

- Teachers and students laugh with each other but never at the expense of each other.
- Students and teachers have a voice in what happens. Together they establish the expectations of the classroom and school and live by them.
- Joy and pleasure are derived from the everyday classroom experience.

CHARACTERISTIC 11: HAVE A FEW POSITIVE RULES, INCLUDING RESPECT AND RESPONSIBILITY

Can you imagine a school filled with rules that are usually expressed in negative terms? Rules like "don't run," "don't use bad language," "don't do this," "don't do that," all with listed consequences.

Can you imagine a school where teachers and students don't even know the rules or consequences?

Can you imagine a school where the rules were created by a person or group that did not have to live by them?

Wouldn't you rather imagine an ideal school in which there are very few rules and the ones that do exist were created cooperatively by students, teachers, and principals and where respect and responsibility foster peace and harmony? In an ideal school:

- There are few rules, and those rules have been developed jointly by students, teachers, and principals.
- Rules and consequences are published and reviewed with students regularly.

- Teachers and principals never put students in conflict with themselves, but rather in conflict with the mutually developed rules.
- You might find a teacher pointing to a rule and asking, "Is what you are doing consistent with a published rule?" "We agreed on the rules, so what are you, the student, going to do about it?"
- A few positive rules usually suffice. Good examples are "We will respect each other and our school" and "We will be responsible for our own behavior."
- Discussions of what is meant by the rules must take place on a regular basis, especially in the beginning.
- When a student forgets or violates a rule, he or she can be reminded in a very positive, caring way. With few exceptions, a gentle reminder is usually all that is needed. There are exceptions, but generally a gentle reminder works.
- Teachers model good behavior. When a teacher and principal show respect and responsibility, students often do as well.
- Peace and harmony are the rule, with few exceptions.

CHARACTERISTIC 12: DEVELOP A WELL-DEFINED, CLEAR VISION

Can you imagine a school where teachers, parents, or principals are not clear what direction their school is taking?

Can you imagine a school where there is no well-defined, articulated, clear, and measurable vision? A school where the direction is confusing?

Can you imagine a school where parents, teachers, and administration are not involved in setting the direction or vision for their school?

Can you imagine a school that lives by slogans that have little influence on decision making or in improving student learning?

Can you imagine a school that has a vision or written direction that cannot be verbalized without notes?

Can you imagine a school where there is no dream of what can be, where individual teachers might have a dream or vision, but there is no collectively articulated one?

Can you imagine a school where the only vision is to have all students do well on some state tests?

Wouldn't you rather imagine an ideal school in which everyone creates, understands, and is committed to the vision of the school? In an ideal school:

- Teachers, administrators, parents, and students have developed a collective vision of what they want their school to accomplish. They have all agreed there is much more to accomplish than test preparation.
- Parents are asked what they would like their children's teachers and school to accomplish by the end of the school year.
- A collective vision is the driving force behind all planning, decision making, and school thinking.

CHARACTERISTIC 13: STRIVE TO MAKE YOUR IDEAL SCHOOL BETTER

Can you imagine a school where staff is not given the time to learn continually and be engaged in meaningful and thought-provoking discussions and planning, and where staff is expected to be actively involved in school improvement after teaching all day and having to go home to take care of their families?

Can you imagine a school where a few staff members are always called on to make meaningful decisions and many are either ignored or if they have ideas, their ideas are ignored?

Can you imagine a school with little pride and no plan to make school better?

Can you imagine a school where only some students have pride in their school and many talk with less-than-glowing comments?

Can you imagine a school where some children feel they don't belong and that school is for the "in group" and not for them?

Can you imagine a school where students who do well academically are picked on by other students?

Can you imagine a school that is slowly being destroyed by some students?

Can you imagine a school that has no plan to continually assess how well they are doing either with students or with improving the climate and culture of the school?

Can you imagine a school where the improvement plan is based on opinion rather than objective and acquired data?

Wouldn't you rather imagine an ideal school in which everyone contributes to making the school an ideal school, all feel a sense of pride and responsibility, and everyone strives to make the school even better? In an ideal school:

- Everyone—students, parents, teachers, administrators, and the community—talk glowingly about their school. Their school is busting with pride.
- Students, staff, and administrators feel their school is the place to work and learn.
- The school is clean and well kept and everyone makes sure it stays that way. Students pick up after themselves and don't tolerate anyone who doesn't contribute to keeping their school safe and clean. Staff would not want to work anywhere else. They are treated fairly by those in charge. They are given the supplies and support they need to do a good job.
- Staff is provided time both during the school year and when school is not in session to plan, learn, and have meaningful thought-provoking discussion.
- Everyone feels that the least among us is as good as everyone else.
- Everyone feels that it is his/her responsibility to make the school even better.

These characteristics of an ideal school should stimulate your thinking, assist you with planning new directions, and enable you to determine how well you are doing. Use them as a guide as you implement positive change and strive to make your school better.

Chapter Three

It's All in the Perception

All children have a genius, intelligence, and a creativity inside that is ready to be discovered, nurtured, and developed.

Focus Questions

1. Does your school perceive, believe, and expect all students to learn well? How do you know? Support your answer.
2. How do teachers' perceptions influence student learning?
3. How do teachers' expectations influence student learning? How do we communicate our expectations? How do students feel when teachers expect them to learn and when they don't expect them to learn?
4. How do teachers treat and teach those students who are expected to learn? Who are not expected to learn? Consider how teachers teach differently, plan differently, grade differently, and test differently when they expect some students to learn and some not to learn.
5. Does your school expect quality learning for all students? How do you know? What is your evidence?
6. What will the future hold for those students not expected to learn well?

STORY 1: A NEW TEACHER'S PERCEPTION

When a young teacher, new to the profession, received her fifth-grade class list, she thought the numbers next to each name were the children's IQ. The numbers ranged from 114 to 138. During her teacher preparation, this teacher was told that IQ, Intelligence Quotient, is a measure of a child's ability that is fixed and won't change much. She believed that and she was delighted about what the numbers on the class list would mean for her classroom experience during the year ahead. Who wouldn't be, when the entire class had IQs well above normal?

The school year was a great one. The teacher constructed thought-provoking learning outcomes and designed activities that challenged everyone. The students, working cooperatively, encouraged each other to work hard and achieve. The teacher was patient with all students, encouraging them as a group and individually. She was positive in her approach, never embarrassing anyone, smiling frequently, providing friendly reinforcement, and exhibiting warmth and care to every student. All the students were her favorites and they knew this.

The teacher used many and varied teaching–learning modes. She convinced each student that they were capable of learning even the most complicated concepts and showed each of them that learning can be fun. When anyone needed more time to learn, she provided it. When someone didn't learn, she taught the same lesson using a different mode of instruction.

As for discipline problems, there were very few and these were handled easily and without humiliation. All problems were solved in a positive, constructive way, with students learning how to be responsible for their own behavior and how to solve their own problems.

Students came to expect more of themselves; they raised their hands frequently, spoke out, and volunteered answers. They became self-confident as learners and initiated interactions and learning situations with other students and with their teacher.

As a result of the actions of the teacher and her students, test scores and grades were high. Students knew what was expected, what they had to learn and what was to be tested. Predetermined published learning outcomes were aligned with assessments, and assessments were always aligned with the learning outcomes.

Because of earned high grades, few problems, inspired teaching, much student involvement, and great learning, students went home each day and told their parents what a wonderful day they had at school. They understood that learning was demanding but it was also satisfying and fun. Parents naturally were ecstatic, and why wouldn't they be?

Later in the school year during a conversation with a colleague, the teacher was talking about her very special class with so many high IQs.

The experienced teacher was surprised and asked how she knew. She told him the IQ scores came with the class list and were next to each student's name. The experienced teacher, with a smirk on his face, told her that the numbers on the class list were the students' locker numbers.

The school year ended with fine results, not the least of which was a new teacher who learned a great deal about perceptions, expectations, beliefs, and teacher behavior.

Activity

1. Describe how the new teacher perceived her class and how these perceptions influenced her attitude, beliefs, and expectations of her students. How do you think she might have communicated these to her students? Describe both verbal and nonverbal clues.
2. How do you think this new teacher would perceive her class if the numbers on the class list ranged from 87 to 112? How do you think she might communicate her perception to students? Describe both verbal and nonverbal clues. Do you think she would treat students differently? Do you think she would teach differently? How?

STORY 2: A PERSONAL STORY

When I was a brand-new teacher, I encountered my first disturbing class. At least I thought they were. There were five math teachers in the job the year before and according to the administration, the kids just "ran them out." Naturally, this made me perceive the kids as the "enemy." How can they be good, I thought, if five certified teachers couldn't last the year? Sure enough I was brewing for a fight. After all, I thought, I had to establish myself and my turf with those kids.

My perception was that the kids were bad, unwilling to learn, uncaring, and irresponsible, and that it was my job to tell them how to behave, how to think, what to believe, and what was right and wrong. My perception was exactly right. They misbehaved, didn't do their work, didn't care, and were irresponsible. I tried moralizing, preaching, and even yelling, but matters just got worse. I didn't dare smile for they might perceive me as "easy." I was even given the advice that no first-year teacher should ever smile until Christmas. Someone even suggested that first-year teachers should postpone that smile until the last day of the first year. Needless to say, I didn't smile. I was going to be strict. Homework on the desk when you arrive in my class, copy the homework assignment off the board for tomorrow, and if you talk, there will be a short quiz. My quizzes were for control only. I went over all the homework each day, and even though no one asked a question, I had little time for teaching after that homework routine. Then I assigned new homework. If they didn't behave, I gave them double the number of exercises. I was really into control. The problem was that the more I tried to control, the more I lost it. I would call on kids to respond to my questions even though they didn't raise their hands. I never heard that embarrassing a child was one of the worst things that a teacher could do. I was hoping to last until Thanksgiving, which, in September, seemed very far away.

Without knowing why, I figured out that what I was doing was not working. I realized that I couldn't change the students but I could change my approach and my strategies. I knew that these students were driving me crazy, but if I decided to have faith that underneath it all they were talented, smart people with great potential, then I could treat them in this manner and have half a chance at steering the classroom dynamics and learning environment in a new and better direction.

I now know it is quite common to perceive a bunch of out-of-bounds kids as, well, out of bounds. The conclusions I was drawing from these perceptions are most important. If I concluded that a class, like this, was beyond help, then there was no hope for changing the classroom dynamics.

I knew I had to think differently about the students. I knew that if I kept doing what I was doing, it would not get me the desired results. Like most teachers, I really wanted to be a good teacher. I really wanted my students to learn well, and like most students, my students wanted to learn well in spite of their behavior. Most students don't come to school with the intent to do poorly. That is an acquired habit. I really wanted my students to have the same love of mathematics that I had. I really wanted my students to see the beauty in an elegant proof, a neat solution to a problem, and the challenge that exciting problems pose. I wanted them to see the power of mathematics and to understand that modern medicine, modern transportation, and modern architecture all require the use of mathematics. I also wanted them to have pride in themselves, to study, to do their work, to ask good questions, to ask when they didn't know, and to share my enthusiasm for learning.

I knew what I wanted, but I didn't get it until I began to realize that my own thinking and perceptions were getting in the way. I certainly didn't perceive the students as capable and I definitely perceived them as actively trying to force me out of their classroom in order to add another notch to their belt—the sixth one.

I forced myself to begin to think about the good in each student. I remember asking myself, "How would I want a teacher to behave if one of those kids were my son or daughter?" "Are all these kids bad or is that just my perception?" I began to perceive all students as capable and willing. I had nothing to lose and much to gain from trying out this new perception. The change that resulted was remarkable. When I changed myself and my approach, I opened a door that allowed the students to change themselves as well. I began to see them as wanting to learn and most began to learn. I began to see them as responsible and many became more responsible. I began to see them as good learners and many became good learners.

As my perceptions changed, my beliefs, expectations, and actions changed. I began to smile and have fun. I didn't wait until Christmas to smile. I still checked their homework only to be sure it was done. I even said that if for some good reason, a student couldn't get his or her homework done, he or she should let me know. I allowed students to choose not to do all the assigned problems if they could demonstrate performance. I decided and vowed never to embarrass a child again.

I realized that if I wanted the students to respect me, I had to respect them. I had to show them that I was genuinely interested in them, and that I wanted to get to know each one of them personally. I demonstrated that I was a caring person. Relationships make a difference.

When I asked for the secrets of more experienced and well-respected teachers who seemed to have few problems in the classroom, I found stories quite similar to my own. These teachers knew each student well and each student knew that. They called each student by name and always reinforced good behavior before bad behavior occurred. They complimented students when they caught them doing something worthwhile. One of them even shared the phrase "Catch them doing something good."

Another important fact was, and still is, that these teachers were well respected for their subject competence as well as their teaching competence. Students respect teachers who know their subject well, who can teach well, and who are caring. Students respect competence and respond in kind.

That year I gathered information about each of my 130 students. I learned their names and the activities they were involved in, both in and out of school. I learned, when possible, about their hobbies, 4-H clubs, sports activities, music activities, what they were especially good at, and many of their academic and nonacademic achievements. Whenever possible, I attended school activities. I saw some plays, concerts, school choirs, and sports events, to name a few. My students saw me attending these events.

I also began to engage each student in conversations relevant to their lives. I remember talking to one of the football players in my class about our favorite professional baseball team. I recall saying "Did you hear about Robin Roberts and the game he pitched last night?" This student's entire demeanor changed after we started having these conversations. I also remember a student, Steve, who did not participate in school activities but who loved motorcycles. I knew little about Harleys but I engaged Steve in a conversation about them. He told me more than I wanted to know but I listened and asked questions. He no longer acted out in class after this relationship was forged. I remember telling a student that I liked her proof on a geometry problem. She acted surprised and said that no teacher had ever complimented her before.

It took a few months of agony and doing all the wrong things before I realized that establishing personal relationships with each student would go a long way in preventing and reducing problems. I began to regularly "Catch them doing something good."

I also started to understand that students really want to learn—a fact that no one had ever shared with me during my teacher training. I started a math club where we solved nonroutine math problems that were not found in texts. Since there were no tests and the club was a volunteer one, both the students and I were getting along well. In fact, I was doing so well with the students that I was assigned lunch duty for an hour and a half each day so I could spend more time with them! Teaching had become what I hoped it could be and what most teachers enter the profession hoping for.

Activity

1. How did I perceive the students and how did these perceptions influence my attitude, beliefs, and expectations? How did I communicate these to my students? Describe both verbal and nonverbal clues.
2. I was a first-year teacher coming into a position that had worn out five teachers the year before. I had no idea how to act or what to do. What advice would you have given me before I entered the class that September? How should I have perceived that class? What should I have believed, expected?
3. List some specific practices that would have helped me achieve all, or most, of what I wanted or deserved that year.

LESSONS TO BE LEARNED

If you perceive you can or perceive you can't, you are correct. If you believe you can or believe you can't, you are also correct. If you expect all students to learn well or you don't, you are correct.

If your attitude and behavior toward students who are expected to learn is different from your attitude and behavior toward those not expected to learn, those expected to learn will, and those expected not to learn won't.

When we know what we want for our students and we perceive them as being capable, then we can get what we want. If we don't perceive all students as being responsible, caring, and eager and enthusiastic to learn, then it is almost impossible for us to achieve the desired results. Perceptions and expectations alone won't get us what we want, however. We still must have a driving set of beliefs, and a plan of appropriate action.

EIGHT ACTIONS TO INCREASE STUDENT ACHIEVEMENT

1. Give all students time to think before expecting an answer or participation in a discussion. Silence is for thinking.

2. Be persistent, warm, supportive, and friendly, and expect good performance from all, not just some, students.
3. Be sensitive to all students when teaching, testing, correcting specific errors, assigning homework or projects, and assigning grades.
4. Expect positive participation and quality responses from every student.
5. Provide equal opportunities, time, and materials and accept all students.
6. Provide equal attention to all students, acknowledging successes of specific achievements.
7. Perceive, believe, and expect all students to produce high-quality work.
8. Give informative feedback and complimentary comments to specific responses instead of global ones.

Chapter Four

The School

Children will choose to learn when they know someone in the school cares, makes an effort to get to know them, and when very good teaching is provided.

As explained in chapter 1, there are no simplistic solutions to the very complex problem of getting all students to learn well. Teaching is difficult even when students come prepared and want to learn. Mindless mandates don't make teaching any easier or learning any better. What is needed is for school personnel to intentionally examine every component that can contribute to making their school an ideal school and all learners very good learners.

To illustrate this point, think of putting a picture puzzle together. What is the first thing you do after emptying the box and before you start trying to get the pieces to fit? Some will say, turn all the pieces over. Some will say find the corners or locate the edges. But, in fact, we all look at the picture of the completed puzzle first.

Herein lies the problem in education. The complete picture of what would make every school a very good one is rarely available to all school personnel. Most of them simply have not been shown the whole picture. It is no mystery why teachers get upset when the next so-called innovation or practice comes along. It is no wonder that comments like "Here we go again" or "This too shall pass" are heard in the faculty lounges of schools throughout America.

What is the complete comprehensive picture? What does it look like? To help you develop your own educational picture, read through the following exercise about choosing a doctor. The subject might be different but the goals and approach are transferable and quite useful.

CHOOSING A FAMILY DOCTOR

Imagine that you and your family have to choose a medical doctor or practice to take care of all your medical and health wellness needs. You call a meeting of everyone in your family—parents, children, grandparents, and extended family members—to make this important, even life-saving, decision.

Part of this process would involve listing all of the characteristics and criteria you want the doctor or medical practice to possess. You would also likely make a list of questions that you want answered when interviewing doctors. Then you would be ready to meet with doctors to conduct interviews. To help you and your family with this decision, consider these five important areas:

1. The vision and mission of the doctor and practice
2. The knowledge and continuing knowledge of the doctor and practice
3. The philosophy and beliefs behind the doctor's decisions
4. The psychology and relationships the doctor and practice will employ and maintain with your family
5. The actions and practices the doctor and practice will use to ensure maximum wellness of everyone in your family

VISION AND MISSION

What if you walked into a doctor's office and saw a sign or received treatment that conveyed this message: Some of our patients will get well.

Contrast this with a sign or attitude that conveyed the following messages: We will do everything in our power to ensure that all of our patients receive optimum medical care and achieve wellness. We will help each patient design a personal wellness program, both nutritionally and physically, to prevent illness. We will treat each patient with dignity and concern independent of financial or social status. We will seek other medical advice when we encounter a problem outside of our area of specialty.

Which of these visions do you want your doctor and medical practice to possess and to practice? Now think about the statements above in relation to a school. Which statements do you want the administration, staff, and faculty of your school to promote and practice?

KNOWLEDGE

When interviewing doctors, you'd probably ask about their medical training and whether or not they stay abreast of changes in the medical field, no matter how busy they are. It would likely impress you if you learned that they regularly read professional journals, attended medical seminars, and had educational conversations with their peers.

You might also ask what this doctor does if he or she is unsure about a diagnosis or if a patient has concerns that are outside the doctor's area of medical specialty. If the doctor was willing to provide referrals to other medical specialists who would be better able to handle certain situations, you would probably feel more confident about trusting this doctor with your health and medical issues. After all, in many instances, the knowledge to seek out the advice and expertise of others is a strength, not a weakness.

Now imagine that you were posing these questions to a principal or a teacher. What kind of responses would make you feel confident and secure? What kind of responses would make you feel you could trust these educational professionals with your child's academic, social, and emotional well-being?

PHILOSOPHY AND BELIEFS

When interviewing a prospective doctor, many of your questions would address this person's beliefs and philosophies. The following questions, or similar ones, would likely be on your list of interview questions:

- Do you perceive, believe, and expect all of your patients to have a good quality of life no matter how ill they are?

- Will you include and treat every member of our family equally when making medical decisions regardless of his or her age or sex?
- Do you believe that we all deserve quality medical services without consideration of costs?
- Will you acknowledge our beliefs when you make important life decisions even if this belief is not the one you hold?

Now imagine yourself asking these questions to educational professionals and instead of asking about their beliefs and philosophies regarding patients and medical services, you were asking them to tell you their beliefs and philosophies regarding students and their educational practices.

PSYCHOLOGY AND RELATIONSHIPS

A doctor's bedside manner is a very important component of a patient's comprehensive medical experience. Yes, we all want a doctor who comes highly recommended and is impressively trained, but if that doctor does not know how to talk or listen to patients, then it is likely that we'd find ourselves looking for a replacement pretty quickly.

When thinking about the kind of relationship you'd like to have with your health care professional, it is likely that you'd want that person to possess the following characteristics and qualities:

- The ability to listen attentively while treating and analyzing health problems
- The ability to make each patient feel as though they are receiving careful, fully focused attention, even if there is a full waiting room on the other side of the door
- The ability to respect each patient's ideas and intelligence
- The ability to take the necessary time with patients and speak to them clearly and compassionately
- The ability to put patients at ease, even during difficult conversations
- The ability to provide choices and alternative treatments when necessary

Wouldn't you want the same kind of relationship with the teachers and principals you meet during your child's educational journey? And perhaps more important, don't you want your children to have teachers and administrators who exhibit the qualities and characteristics listed above?

ACTIONS AND PRACTICES

Finally, but quite important, you would want to know and agree with the way your doctor practices medicine. You'd be interested in learning how the doctor treats and responds to a variety of medical conditions and concerns. Your interview might include some of the following questions:

- Once we have agreed on a wellness or treatment program, will you and your staff assume a mutual responsibility to monitor our progress?
- Will you continue to search for additional or new treatments if the initial or prescribed treatments are ineffective?
- Will you persevere and never give up on any of us?

As was the case with each of the points discussed above, you can replace the word *doctor* with the word *teacher*, you can replace *medical practice* with *school*, and you can replace the word *patient* with *student*. You would want the same kind of professionalism, care, treatment, and belief system whether you were choosing a medical doctor or an educational professional.

CONCLUSION

Putting together a comprehensive picture that will serve as a guide as you create a very good, even an ideal, school must include paying careful attention to the five major components outlined above. There are no shortcuts when building a process in which all children learn well. However, when your comprehensive picture is complete and when your total process has been established, you will experience long-term benefits, and you'll also have a strong planning model, decision-making scheme, and problem-solving strategy to call upon whenever new situations or challenges arise.

There are many benefits in developing your own comprehensive systems-driven process, including:

1. You have determined your own future. You will be able to state your beliefs and your vision as well as your strategies for achieving them. By being an active participant in creating a total systems process, you will help avoid externally mandated solutions.
2. The process will unite virtually everyone involved and this will lead to a focused and effective effort. Everyone is valued, valuable, and involved in developing the process and they know it. Everyone is accountable to the process and will have agreed to live by it until it is changed. The thinking of your school will be connected and aligned.
3. The process creates a totally inclusive system. Students know exactly what school personnel expect and believe, and they have seen and experienced the human side of the process. Parents understand the beliefs and values of the school, and feel involved in creating the school vision and influencing decisions. All teachers and administrators are involved in every part of the process, which combines personal and collective vision and beliefs. While no one will get all of what he or she wants and believes, a compromise will be reached that feels fair to all. Academic freedom and personal style and activities are not in question as long as they are in concert with the agreed-upon key areas:

    - Vision and mission
    - Knowledge
    - Philosophy and beliefs
    - Psychology and relationships
    - Actions and practices

4. You will develop the skills to self-assess, make necessary adjustments, and continually get better.
5. Your staff development program will be aligned to the entire process. Teachers will have a voice in determining their staff development needs and how they will be met. This will be done in concert with administration and based on self-inspection and process.
6. Finally, a real sense of pride and professionalism will emerge. Professional communications, planning, and decision making are hallmarks of the entire comprehensive process.

Chapter Five

Vision and Mission

Learning that matters is the only learning that matters.

Focus Questions

1. If a vision is a picture of a desired future, what is your school's vision for its students?
2. What do you want students to know and be able to do when the school year is over?
3. What is your clear, measurable, and short mission statement? Can it be easily remembered and repeated by everyone in the school? How does a mission statement differ from a slogan?
4. Were your mission and vision created and endorsed by all?

The vision and mission component introduced in chapter 4 is the focus of this chapter. Although we have chosen to begin with this component, you should feel free to examine and implement the components in whichever order works best for you.

As a teacher, your vision is a personal and professional ideal that expresses a desired picture of what you and your colleagues really want for all of your students while they are a part of your school. This vision will be realized for each and every student by the time they leave your classroom or school. While every future holds uncertainty, we must still determine, to the best of our ability and knowledge, what students need to *know* and *do* to increase their chances of having a productive and successful future.

A vision is never static. It is always a work in progress. New insights and new knowledge are always evolving, and so is your vision. A common vision that has been developed mutually has many wonderful characteristics and benefits:

1. It is compelling, gives clear direction, unifies staff and community, and is attractive and measurable.
2. It gives you and your school a clear picture of what everyone is trying to accomplish and achieve.
3. It will allow you and your colleagues to implement your hopes and desires and to realize your personal and professional ideals.
4. It will align all of your thinking and actions. The entire staff will be working cooperatively and intentionally.
5. It will give you and your colleagues the power to determine your own future. To create a unified and effective effort, you must create and promote your agreed-upon vision, and be willing to verbalize and defend it. If you are proactive, rather than reactive, others will be less likely to head off in other, less focused, directions.
6. It gives you long-term goals and direction as well as short and intermediate ones.

Create your vision by involving teachers, administrators, school committees, parents, students, business leaders, and members of your community. Let everyone know that the purpose of visioning is to arrive at a comprehensive picture of what you all want for the students in your school. It probably won't come as a surprise when you learn that almost everyone involved wants the same things for the students and the school, even though he or she hasn't shared his or her desires before. Creating a collective vision for the children of your community is a necessary first step in making your school an ideal school.

When was the last time anyone asked you to determine and visualize what you want your students to know and be able to do in order to have a productive and successful future? This is precisely the question that must be posed to everyone who plays a part in your school community—teachers, administrators, staff, parents, local business leaders, and community members.

Everyone must be involved in creating your school's vision. Committees can be formed, but it is essential that each individual feels as though he or she has had the opportunity to express his or her desires and ideas.

Teachers will play a major role in this process. Even those who seem somewhat negative must be included. Every school has some teachers who don't want to change or even examine the possibilities. However, it is important to continue on the path to change while trying to involve these teachers along the way. Chapter 13 provides some effective strategies for managing change.

Parents play an important role as well. When parents attend an open house or visit their children's teachers, be sure they have a chance to share their views. Ask them what they would like their child's teacher to accomplish this year. Make a composite list of responses. Parents generally want their children to love learning, feel good about themselves as learners, have good academic preparation, understand what they are learning, be responsible for themselves and their learning, and be creative thinkers and independent learners. Parents also want to be sure their children have a good grasp of the basics, and this includes effective communication skills. More recently, parents increasingly express the desire for their children and their peers to show concern for one another. In short, parents want their children to be prepared for the future.

Ask everyone involved in the process the following question: If you could go back to school, what would you study more intentionally? What would you do differently? Almost every time this question is asked, the responses are similar:

I would learn to be a better reader.
I would spend more time honing my public speaking skills.
I would develop better writing skills.
I would become more technologically literate.

When asked what characteristics and qualities students will need to succeed in today's work world, the responses sound familiar:

Having good communication skills, both verbal and written
Willing to be a good and effective team player with solid interpersonal skills

Being responsible, flexible, and adaptable
Having a strong work ethic
Showing concern and honesty
Possessing good basic skills and knowledge
Nurturing a desire to be a lifelong continuous learner
Being accountable and detail oriented
Being able to think analytically and problem-solve
Being an effective decision maker
Being self-directed, motivated, and not afraid to take initiatives
Possessing strong technical skills

The world's markets and job opportunities are changing rapidly, making it essential that students leave our schools with the knowledge and skills they need to succeed in today's economy. The characteristics listed above are important to consider while creating your vision.

As you read the vision for our schools presented in the next section, please be sure to think about it in terms of your specific school or educational environment. Use it as a guide as you create a vision that fits your particular needs.

CREATING YOUR OWN VISION

The following plan can be used to build a comprehensive school vision that encompasses what all students and educational professionals should know and do in order to be successful. This general discussion can be used with the more detailed curriculum-planning process in chapter 11.

Know

The knowledge part of a Vision Statement consists of three parts:

1. Concepts and understandings
2. Information and facts
3. Skills and procedures

Always begin your planning with the simple yet profound questions: What does it mean to understand what I am teaching? What do students have to demonstrate to show they understand what I am teaching? Does it mean students should memorize facts? Gather information? Does it mean students should discover concepts? Be creative thinkers? Have good subject matter procedures and skills? Understand the tools and structures of the subject they are studying?

The answer to all of the above questions is yes.

Do

The *do* part of the Vision Statement is divided into five skill parts:

1. Connecting skills
2. Communication skills
3. Learning skills
4. Life skills
5. Social skills

Connecting skills allow students to think critically about what they are learning and doing. In addition to learning and understanding course information, concepts, procedures, and facts, students must also learn, for example, to compare ideas, determine how one piece of information is different from another, and to find reasons why. They must also be able to analyze, discover, create, and look for trends and patterns. Some connecting skills are:

construct	create	develop
explain	synthesize	apply
analyze	evaluate	justify
find examples	find similarities	
find differences	find patterns	

Communication skills help students share ideas in many different forms. All students should be able to read, write, and speak clearly and coherently about a concept and theory in every discipline they are studying. By doing this, students will develop a better understanding of that concept and theory. Students should also know how to listen for understanding, view materials critically, and be able to express their thoughts coherently.

What good is having knowledge if one cannot communicate effectively? Communication skills are the foundation of all learning and should be included in every discipline and not just in language arts. When students perfect communication skills in one area, all of their communication skills will improve. For example, when students learn to write well, their reading skills will show great improvement. Some communication skills are:

read	write
speak	listen
illustrate	view

Learning skills are those skills designed to help students become lifelong learners. All students should be self-directed learners who do not have to rely on others to direct their learning. To be self-directed, students must understand the tools and concepts of the discipline, conduct creative investigations, and be able to make meaningful connections. These very important skills must be intentionally and systematically taught.

How can we tell when students possess these skills and are self-directed learners? We can only judge student competency by knowing the corresponding indicators. Some learning skills are:

be a self-directed learner	employ the tools of the discipline
carry out investigations	make meaningful learning connections
use the structure of the discipline	learn how to study and understand each discipline

Life skills allow students to develop the personal skills necessary for a productive and rewarding life. Virtually every employer wants every employee to be a team player. They want their employees to be independent, to explore and develop new ideas, and to be productive and personally responsible. They want them to be able to share ideas, build a composite from their collective creativity, and to possess a strong work ethic.

It is also important and necessary to have updated technology skills. Not only will good technology skills help on the job, they are necessary skills in the pursuit of knowledge. Technology has changed the nature of inquiry, investigations, and learning. Constructing models, having discussions, creating new ideas, testing hypotheses, searching for information, communicating ideas, and observing patterns, just to name a few skills, have been greatly enhanced by modern technology. Some life skills are:

be technology savvy	able to self-motivate
create and test hypotheses	willing to take initiative
use problem-solving skills	pay attention to detail
build team skills	possess honesty and integrity
behave responsibly	able to make decisions

Social skills are designed to help students develop a concern for themselves, others, and the environment. What good is having all we have if we don't show concern and caring? When children are taught what it means to show concern and this is discussed and modeled in the home and classroom, not only will their grades get better, they will become better learners. When students do not have to worry or fret about criticism in their classroom, they will have more energy to learn.

To teach students about concern and caring, ask them to describe a situation in which a person is showing concern for someone else. What would this person be saying and doing? Ask them to describe what the person wouldn't be doing and saying as well. Ask them how expressing concern would look in a classroom. Brainstorm with them and classify their ideas.

Following are some comments made by students when they were asked how teachers might show concern:

- They will never laugh at you.
- They will never put a student down or bully.
- They will always encourage and never embarrass students.
- They will never make fun of students or the answers they give and they will try to understand each student's intent.
- They will invite everyone to participate and no one will ever be excluded.
- They will expect everyone to learn and not just a few.
- Teachers will allow time for students to think, take risks, and make mistakes without fear of failure.
- Teachers will keep the classroom calm and, even in stressful times, never yell and never embarrass anyone.

These are just a few of the attributes students will state when asked this question. Once your students have come up with a list, make it public. List the positive attributes—the ones you should see in the classroom. Also, list the negative ones—the ones you shouldn't see. You may want to involve parents in this activity and hold them accountable as well.

Social skills and concern can be discussed in every classroom. Using the attributes developed by you and your students, you can critique history, literature, novels, stories, music, art, and science. You can also critique student activities, leaders, and school decisions using these attributes. Discuss whether the school rules in your school show concern. No value judgment should be made by teachers during this exercise. Allow students to judge for themselves. Some social skills are:

ability to show compassion
attentiveness when listening
ability to understand other points of view
maintaining a positive and encouraging outlook
cooperative attitude
sensitivity to the needs of others
willingness to share ideas

CONCLUSION

A vision is what and who you are. It is compelling, purposeful, and drives all of your actions. When creating your vision, the following list of key words will be useful:

Visualize
Compelling
Attractive
Connects
Desired future
Wants
Unites
Measurable
Aligns
Growth
Knowledge-driven

Without a vision there will be:

- Vague responses
- Vague results
- Vague efforts
- Vague focus
- Vague direction

With a clear vision there will be:

- Clear response
- Clear results
- Clear effort
- Clear focus
- Clear direction

A vision leads to a mission, which describes for whom your vision has been developed and how it will be implemented. In light of the ideas that have been presented in this chapter, a possible mission statement might read: Given enough time, high-quality instruction and planning, and involvement of parents, community, students, and the entire staff, all students will learn well and be prepared for a bright future.

Chapter Six

Best Knowledge, Research Literature, and Data

Children will learn when they are developmentally and emotionally ready to learn.

Focus Questions

1. Are planning and decision making in your school based on opinions or on the best knowledge and research literature available?
2. What best knowledge and research literature have you used to get more students to learn well?
3. It has been said that knowledge is what makes education and teaching a profession. Do you agree? Do you disagree? Support your conclusions.
4. How does your own data about student learning influence your decisions?

KNOWLEDGE

It has been said many times that knowledge is power. But in reality knowledge has the potential to give you power.

I asked a group of educators when and how they and their school were using educational research, articles, and compelling observations to make decisions; design curriculum, instruction, and programs; solve problems; create a vision; determine beliefs; and plan an effective staff development program. I waited and waited but got no response. They readily admitted that they almost never refer to educational literature.

I don't believe their answer was unusual. Most schools do not use professional literature on a regular basis. Rather, they make decisions according to past practices or according to their recently adopted, ever-changing "program of the year." Herein lies the problem. School and student achievement can never get significantly better until the body of professional literature on educational research is used on a regular basis.

When I asked teachers what they hear around school and in the faculty lounge when the question of professional research came up, their responses came quickly and to the point:

We can find research to support any position and since there is no common or agreed-upon acceptable research, we will ignore it.
Research has little to do with how we are teaching.
We are practitioners and we know how it is done.
I have been a teacher and principal all my life and it's experience that really counts. What do they know?
I have all I can do to handle discipline problems teachers send me, and I don't have time for much else.
We have so much to cover at a faculty meeting there is no time to talk about educational literature.
We are too busy to spend time reading and discussing the literature.

In summary, they were politely saying don't bother me with all that research nonsense when I am too busy with teaching and administration. I don't have time to use it, and it won't make any difference anyhow.

Unfortunately, this sounds all too familiar. Yet how can we lay claim to our professional status if, in fact, we don't use our own professional literature? After all, we wouldn't go to a doctor who wasn't up to date with the professional literature in the medical field. Most of us wouldn't go to any professionals who didn't know what the latest advancements were in their respective fields. But schools generally operate in a mode that Rip van Winkle would identify with were he to wake up today. Virtually little has changed, and yet we want the public to respect us more and to consider us professionals. If we want that title, we must act professionally and make it our business to stay familiar with the professional literature in our field.

It is impossible for any school or district to maintain high quality or to improve significantly if professional literature is ignored. If we continue implementing current detached practices, we will continue to get less than one half of our students learning well or ready to get and keep a job. Discipline problems, attendance problems, dropouts, and repeated failure will continue to be the norm.

But if we really want to have ideal schools where most students learn well, discipline problems decline, dropout rates approach zero, and academic achievement skyrockets, then studying the professional literature is essential. If you want your students to be responsible, self-motivated, self-directed, lifelong learners who are prepared for a knowledge-based society, then you must begin to examine the abundance of research about learning, motivation, organizational development, and classroom instructional practices that is available.

While there is no perfect research with the ability to get all students learning well, attending school regularly, being responsible for their behavior, and getting ready for a bright future, there is much good knowledge; quantitative, qualitative, and action research; proven professional practices; and good common sense that will get more students to achieve at higher levels. When you find yourself faced with divergent research, which you undoubtedly will, place it on the table, discuss it, and then make your best decision. If you always wait around for the definitive answer, your educational and learning environment will never improve.

Perhaps the problem is not whether to use the professional literature but what professional literature should be used. Only you and your colleagues can make this determination once you engage the research and assess whether or not it has the potential to change your particular situation in a positive manner. Read, discuss, and act. Then observe the results and determine what must be changed or discarded.

You can also use the compelling observations that I've included below. These are knowledge-driven observations that come directly from the educational literature in our field. I purposely call them observations because one may argue that they are not universal truths and that there may be exceptions to each of them. I concur. Nonetheless, each statement is powerful and can influence your classroom and school in a positive way.

BENEFITS OF USING KNOWLEDGE-DRIVEN OBSERVATIONS

- Using knowledge is the hallmark of being a professional in any field but especially in education. It's what we do.
- Knowledge determines your vision, beliefs, and the psychology employed in your school.
- Since knowledge is always evolving, teachers and administrators continue to change and renew. It also empowers and encourages creative thinking.
- Knowledge influences all we do, eliminates baseless opinions, and is the basis for planning, problem solving, decision making, and meaningful change.

COMPELLING OBSERVATIONS

Students

1. One of the most destructive practices in schools is the sorting and labeling of children. This practice may influence our perceptions, attitudes, beliefs, and expectations of students (Bloom, 1983).
2. Children who know their parents and family value education perform better in school than other children.
3. A student's aptitude for learning is the rate at which that student learns and not the capacity to learn as measured by a standardized test. A student's aptitude or rate of learning is dependent on the skills or concepts to be learned. A student's aptitude to learn a skill or concept is influenced or affected by previous learning.
4. Most students can learn what we want them to learn if given the appropriate amount of time to learn and if they have high-quality instruction.
5. Students will invest time, effort, and energy in learning, if they value what is to be learned.
6. Students remember a great deal if they use their learning immediately.
7. Students rarely say they have quality experiences in their classrooms. They do say they experience quality in activities like athletics, music, clubs, and driver training.

8. When students know what they are to learn, why they are to learn, how they can go about learning, and how they will be assessed, they will learn better.
9. Not only do students learn at different rates, they learn in many, varied, and different ways.

Teachers

1. When teaching is carefully aligned to the course, unit, and daily lesson learning goals and when assessment is also carefully aligned to these goals, students who learn more slowly (rate of learning) can learn as well as learners who learn more quickly (Cohen, 1987).
2. When teachers prepare students each day for success rather than waiting to provide correctives or remediation, students will not only learn well but learning time will decrease, and students will feel successful as learners.
3. Teachers along with students' families control the conditions for success even when students bring many problems with them.
4. Most teachers will be committed to making their school much better when they are invited, involved, and given a genuine voice in the planning and decision making.
5. When teachers teach concepts for understanding rather than bits and pieces and rote learning, students will retain learning better.

Psychology

1. Students will choose to reject learning and others if they have been humiliated, fear failure, or fear rejection or if they believe the teacher does not care (Glasser, 1999; Kohn, 1999).
2. Frequent use of rewards and punishments may produce short-term gains but in the long term may actually have the opposite effect of what is intended. There may be a decrease in student motivation, responsibility, and achievement.
3. Earned success in learning and a record of that success are some of the greatest motivators. They may even cause students to learn better, feel better as learners, and enjoy learning.
4. Gold stars, smiley faces, and other extrinsic incentives are not only ineffective in the long term in motivating students to learn and behave

but may have a negative effect and produce the opposite of what is intended.

5. A school or classroom that operates with fear or coercion can never get students to learn well or be responsible for their own behavior.
6. Criticism and humiliation are two of the greatest destroyers of confidence and self-esteem as a person and a learner.

Beliefs/Philosophy

1. When students believe that their teacher believes in and expects them to learn, they will learn better than when they don't believe it.
2. Students may reject learning when there is unhealthy and unfair competition in the classroom and will learn better when they cooperate in learning.
3. When students trust their teachers to help them learn, they will learn better.
4. When students sense their teachers are excited and optimistic about teaching and student learning, they will learn better.
5. When students are led to believe that their teachers want to develop their talent and the teacher expects excellence from them, they will learn better.
6. Failure in the primary school often leads to dropping out, antisocial behavior, and other social problems.

Vision

1. Perhaps 90% of all jobs in the future will be highly skilled ones; less than 50% of our students are learning the necessary skills to perform at highly competent levels (U.S. Department of Labor, 1992).
2. All students will need to possess key understandings, information, and facts to be successful in the future.
3. Life, social, communication, and connecting skills are necessary for students to be successful in the future.

Classroom Practices

1. Students should be certified only when they can demonstrate learning in a meaningful way.

2. Student learning will improve when assessment and correctives are continuous, not just at the end of a unit, chapter, or course.
3. Student learning will improve and students will take greater risks when they view assessment as a tool to help them learn.
4. Student learning will improve when grades are assigned only after students have learned well.
5. Students often reject homework when they view it as mindless. They will want to do homework when they view it as a tool to help them learn well.

Principal

1. Student learning will improve when the principal establishes a learning culture in the building.
2. When the principal helps each staff member self-assess and establish a personal growth plan, teaching and learning will improve.
3. The principal is the chief climate and cultural leader in the school. This influences everyone and has a direct impact on student learning as well as staff morale.

Continuous Assessment, Renewal, and Accountability

1. Self-inspecting, self-assessment, and self-reflection are the ways to improve performance for students and staff.
2. When all assessment and renewal are done in a cooperative way, students and staff will improve their performance.
3. The typical teacher assessment does not contribute to more effective teaching or improve student achievement. It does just the opposite of what is intended.

Continuous Staff Development

1. In most schools, staff development is conducted poorly and has little effect on instruction or student achievement.
2. Staff development during after-school hours is rarely effective.
3. In most schools, teachers rarely have a meaningful voice in deciding the direction of their staff development.
4. In most schools, staff development lacks long-term direction and consistency.

SIX STEPS FOR IMPLEMENTING KNOWLEDGE-DRIVEN AND COMPELLING OBSERVATIONS

1. Know what the educational literature is saying. Gather it from a variety of sources such as research reviews and summaries, books, articles, and journals.
2. Agree to a set of knowledge-driven observations, discuss each, and determine how they might be implemented.
3. Modify or eliminate any existing practices that are in conflict with the observations.
4. Design an action plan to implement observations with your current information.
5. Decide what knowledge you still need for those observations that can't be currently implemented.
6. Involve everyone in the implementation, including parents and students.

Ask these four key knowledge questions when planning or making decisions:

1. What compelling evidence do we have about ________?
2. What do we need to know about ________?
3. What do we want to know about________?
4. What data do we have about ________?

When thinking about knowledge-driven and compelling observations, consider the following:

defines professionalism	enhances wisdom
is always evolving	eliminates opinions
is data-driven	drives actions
determines vision	influences beliefs
develops psychology	creates mission

Activity: Revisiting Focus Questions

Use the compelling observation statements included in this chapter and return to the questions asked in chapter 1 to assess your current thinking and planning. This can be done individually or in small groups.

Chapter Seven

Beliefs, Values, and Dominant Philosophy

There is no such thing as a universally bad learner. There are faster learners, slower learners, and different learners.

Focus Questions

In schools there are often competing beliefs and philosophies.

1. What would a school be like if the dominant belief and philosophy was that all students will learn well and succeed? Cite examples of the kind of teacher behavior and school practices that would support this belief.
2. What would a school be like if the dominant belief and philosophy was that only some students will learn well and succeed? Cite examples of the kind of teacher behavior and school practices that would support this belief.
3. What would teachers do if they believe all students can learn well? Cite examples.
4. What would teachers stop doing if they believe that only some students can learn well? Cite examples.

Our beliefs influence our thinking and actions. When we believe we can, we will. When students believe they can, and when they know we believe in them, they will perform well and learn better.

To create an ideal school, it is important and absolutely necessary to have a set of shared beliefs. Your vision cannot be achieved if your beliefs are not compatible with your vision. For example, many students will choose not to learn well if they don't trust their teachers or if they experience too much failure. But when students trust their teacher to help them learn and when earned success replaces failure, students' behavior and learning get enormously better. Similarly, teachers will not be empowered, make meaningful decisions, or design effective programs if a set of shared beliefs is not developed.

"You Gotta Believe." Tug McGraw, a famous baseball relief pitcher for the New York Mets, and then the Philadelphia Phillies, popularized the phrase "You Gotta Believe" in 1973 (Popik, 2005). He repeated this phrase many times in the clubhouse and on the field. The Mets came from behind that year to win their division, and then the National League pennant. His enthusiasm became contagious and it rubbed off on his teammates and the fans. Tug used this phrase when he was a Phillie too. With Tug on the mound, in 1980, the Phillies won the World Series. Naturally, both teams had talent, but one has to wonder if the outcomes would have been the same without the positive thinking that Tug instigated. Tug was a winner and he wanted his teammates to believe they could be winners too. If the players didn't believe in themselves, it seems unlikely that they could have achieved such success.

"Whether You Believe You Can or Can't, You're Right." Henry Ford had a vision that he could mass-produce cars that would be affordable to most people. During an insecure moment, Ford was encouraged by his good friend Thomas A. Edison to proceed. With Edison's help, Ford believed in and realized his dream. Subsequently, Ford's vision and beliefs changed the world.

"One Person with a Belief is Equal to a Force of 99 Who Only Have Interests." In most schools, you will find many people who say they want to make their school better. According to J. S. Mill, one person who believes can influence many others and lead the way to substantive change. It only takes one person, whether it's a teacher or a principal, to believe that this possibility can become a reality. How can you design a program of inclusion, for example, if the belief in inclusion is not stated and practiced?

In most schools, unstated beliefs dominate thinking. Some teachers may believe, for example, that competition for grades will motivate all students. They feel that if competition is good for business then it must be good for schools. Schools and some teachers act on this belief by grading "on the curve." There are other teachers who believe that having students cooperate in the classroom and compete only against themselves for grades will motivate all students. These teachers believe that all students are capable of achieving good grades but they must earn them by being measured against predetermined published standards. They believe competition against standards and not others is healthy competition.

Competing beliefs are usually not extremes. However, it is often the case that one belief is more dominant than another in any given school culture. For example, inclusion and exclusion are competing beliefs. This does not mean, however, that they are extremes even though they might appear to be. One may believe in inclusion but still might have to exclude some students from their classroom. The belief of inclusion might be dominant, but for many reasons some students are excluded. For example, there may be some students who have educational needs that cannot be met by an individual teacher. A teacher may require extra training and further knowledge to teach students with special needs. If additional support services are not available for this particular teacher and student, the student might be taken out of the class. (The criteria for inclusion will be discussed in chapter 9.)

Some teachers believe that classified students will not benefit from being in an inclusive classroom. They believe that the needs of these students are better met in a segregated classroom. They might even believe that these students can be included in certain activities, but certainly not all. Perhaps with knowledge, training, and proven examples of inclusion, these teachers would modify their exclusion belief. However, one belief, in this case exclusion, usually dominates in a school setting, even if some exceptions are made.

Success and failure are competing beliefs. This does not mean that a class will be made so easy that students will succeed just by being present. This also does not mean that a class will be made so tough that many students will fail. Students must make mistakes if they are to learn, but this certainly doesn't indicate failure.

Some teachers believe that the greatest motivator is success but that students must study, prepare, and earn success. These same teachers believe that prolonged periods of being unsuccessful results in students' giving up. Other teachers feel that when fear of failure is present, students will work harder. Some of these same teachers want to have the reputation of being "tough" and therefore the fear of failure dominates their classrooms. Most teachers have high expectations and standards for everyone in their classroom, want all students to succeed, and hold themselves responsible for ensuring that this happens.

There are many competing beliefs. It is tremendously useful to think about your beliefs and the beliefs of those around you. The following activity will help you determine your beliefs and consider their consequences.

Activity: Competing Beliefs and Developing Beliefs

Competing Beliefs

Think of teachers you know as you read the following sets of competing beliefs. List behaviors that you might observe in each of their classrooms.

1. What might you see in a classroom if the dominant belief is *competitive learning*? What might you see in a classroom if the competing belief is *cooperative learning*?
2. What might you see in a classroom if the dominant belief is *exclusion*? What might you see in a classroom if the competing belief is *inclusion*?
3. What might you see in a classroom if the dominant belief is *some students have talent to be developed*? What might you see in a classroom if the competing belief is *all students have talent to be developed*?
4. What might you see in a classroom if the dominant belief is *high expectations for a few*? What might you see in a classroom if the competing belief is *high expectations for everyone*?
5. What might you see in a classroom if the dominant belief is *misalignment of learning outcomes, testing, and teaching*? (This is when teachers expect students to learn certain outcomes, but they teach and test other outcomes.) What might you see in a classroom if the competing belief is *alignment of learning outcomes, testing, and teaching*? (This is when teachers expect students to learn certain outcomes, and they teach and test what is expected.)
6. What might you see in a classroom if the dominant belief is *remedial instruction*? What might you see in a classroom if the competing belief is *prevention instruction*?
7. What might you see in a classroom if the dominant belief is *fear*? What might you see in a classroom if the competing belief is *trust*?
8. What might you see in a classroom if the dominant belief is *failure-driven instruction*? What might you see in a classroom if the competing belief is *success-driven instruction*?

9. What might you see in a classroom if the dominant belief promoted *pessimism*? What might you see in a classroom if the competing belief promoted *optimism*?

Developing Beliefs

Choose a belief that you want to develop and get consensus from the staff in your school. Then, as a group, analyze that belief as well as its competing belief. For example, if you choose the belief of earned success, complete the following sentence as it relates to students and their learning: I believe earned success in the classroom will ____________________. For example, I believe earned success in the classroom will be an important motivator.

Brainstorm everyone's completed sentence. List and display all the sentences. Remove duplicates and compromise on language. Draw conclusions and get consensus. Make your agreements public.

Next, complete the following sentence for the competing belief as it relates to students and their learning: I believe continued failure in the classroom will ____________________. For example, I believe continued failure in the classroom will result in many students' giving up.

Brainstorm everyone's completed sentences. List and display all the sentences. Remove duplicates and compromise on language. Draw conclusions and get consensus. Make your agreements public.

BELIEFS TO CONSIDER

The following set of beliefs was formulated in the Johnson City, New York, schools when I was superintendent. Some have been modified to reflect current thinking.

1. We believe most learning should be *cooperative* rather than competitive and we should create the conditions where all students benefit by cooperating while learning. We do not believe that students should have to compete for learning or for grades.
2. We believe that we should search continuously for ways to *include* all students. We do not believe students should be excluded from the classroom for long periods of time.
3. We believe that *all students have talent*, which should be developed and nurtured. We do not believe that only some students have talent.

4. We believe *trust* is the glue that holds the entire learning community of students, teachers, parents, administrators, and school committees together. We do not believe fear has any place in our schools.
5. We believe *success* is possible and should be the norm for all students. We do not believe failure should be encouraged or accepted. While students and staff must take risks in order to grow, setbacks must not be considered failures but instead should be viewed as normal and as opportunities for growth.
6. We believe that student learning errors can and should be *prevented*. Teachers will provide review, reteaching, or teaching of the necessary prerequisites for student success before teaching a new lesson, so the need for correctives can be reduced. Place the emphasis on prevention and reduce remediation.
7. We believe *high expectations* are for everyone. We also believe that all students can achieve these expectations if we provide and create the right conditions. We do not believe high expectations are for a few.
8. We believe students should know what they are expected to learn, how they are to learn, why they are to learn, and what will be tested. We also believe in the *alignment* of learning outcomes, testing, and teaching. We do not believe that students should have to guess what to study, what methods the teacher will use, or what will be tested. We also believe schools should not have to guess what the states are testing. We do not believe guessing enhances teaching or learning.
9. We believe that if everyone has an optimistic, "can do" attitude, students will be influenced positively. Teachers', administrators' as well as parents' attitudes affect student learning. We do not believe that pessimism of staff produces any good effects in learning.

BELIEFS, VALUES, AND CONVICTIONS

Beliefs in schools must be a collaborative as well as a personal choice. These beliefs should be stated clearly and persuasively. However, if these beliefs are not bolstered by actions, they have little meaning. When beliefs are acted on, they become values. These values have transformative power.

Many of us believe something, and although we know we should act on it, choose not to. Still others are willing to act on their beliefs, but are unwilling to defend them. When you defend your values, you have convictions.

In schools it is important for the entire staff to be involved in the formation of the school's beliefs. A committee can do much of the brainstorming and initial work but the entire staff must be involved in final decisions. Staff must claim ownership if the stated beliefs will become values and convictions. In addition, parents and the community will provide even more support when they are involved and understand the final set of beliefs.

When thinking of beliefs, values, and dominant philosophy, consider the following:

Beliefs, values, and dominant philosophy:

act like a rudder	are compelling
unite staff	are the basis for action
enable staff	provide stability
drive action	are knowledge-driven

Activity: Evidence of Your Beliefs

Review the beliefs presented in this chapter and answer the following questions. Feel free to delete or add to this list as you see necessary.

1. What is your current set of beliefs?
2. What evidence do you have that your beliefs are being achieved?
3. What evidence do you have that your beliefs are not being achieved?
4. Are the current beliefs getting you what you want?
5. What will you do or change so that your actions are aligned with your beliefs?

CONCLUSION

What comes first, the beliefs or the action? Many teachers have told me that they really wanted to believe that all students have talent, that all should be included, that all have the ability to be successful learners, but that they weren't completely sure that this was true. My response, always, is that you must act as though you do believe. Align your practices with your vision, beliefs, prevailing knowledge, and your positive psychology, and see what happens. Most of the time, if you believe in something and act accordingly, that belief will become a reality.

Remember, results often get worse before they get better. This is true when learning any new skill. Don't give up. Keep acting as though you believe. If, after some time, the belief becomes a reality, the belief is a value. With more time and with more results, you will begin to defend your belief with vigor. Now you have convictions.

Beliefs should be driven by knowledge and by your compelling observations. Beliefs will guide all your actions, help you make decisions, and will be the rudder in the design of your programs. Beliefs must be consistent with and help you achieve your vision.

Activity: Revisiting Focus Questions

After studying and formulating your beliefs, return to the questions in chapter 1 and see how your thinking and ideas may have progressed and/or changed. This can be done individually or in a small group.

Chapter Eight

Relationships, Culture, and Dominant Psychology

All children want to learn, and they enter school with a desire to do so.

Focus Questions

1. What would a school be like if the dominant psychology was a controlling one? That is, do what I want you to do and I'll reward you; don't do what I want you to do and I will embarrass you. Cite examples of this psychology at work. Does or doesn't it work?
2. What would a school be like if the dominant psychology was one of helping all students be responsible for their own behavior and personal motivation? Cite examples of this psychology at work. When does it work? When doesn't it work?
3. How can we help students be more responsible for their own behavior?
4. What motivates you in the short term? In the long term?
5. Can you force students to learn? Give examples. Can you force students to behave? Give examples.

PSYCHOLOGY AND RELATIONSHIPS

When schools prioritize isolated goals like raising test scores, reducing dropout rates, increasing student attendance, or decreasing vandalism, all of which are important, it is highly unlikely that these goals will be achieved in any significant way. There may be short-term increases, but probably not long-term gains.

When schools realize that educating all students is their most important goal, long-lasting achievement will result. An understanding of and commitment to this most important goal will create an environment in which all the other goals, mentioned above, will be readily achieved.

What motivates students? What motivates us? Why do we choose to do what we do? What lowers our motivation? Why do we sometimes say no even when we agree? Why do students work hard and achieve for some teachers and not others? What do good teachers do that results in higher test scores, reduces dropout rates, increases student achievement, and reduces or eliminates disruption or distraction in their classrooms?

The answer is a simple one. Successful teachers establish a wonderful relationship with each student. These teachers know that any attempt at coercion or any type of external force or motivation rarely works and, if it does, the results are shortlived.

These teachers help students become internally motivated. They know that all people, students included, can't be forced to do anything they don't want to do for long periods of time. Instead they establish a relationship with each student by creating a classroom in which all students feel and are included, have positive learning experiences, feel in control of their own lives, and have freedom to explore new ideas.

External Motivation

Attempts to motivate students using external pressures or rewards have been used in most schools for as long as most of us can remember. Teachers using this psychology offer rewards, including gold stars or smiley faces, to some students and not to others. They praise some students and threaten others. They bribe some students and humiliate others.

All attempts at external motivation are designed to get students to behave and to learn. Teachers who use this approach believe that children who don't get the gold stars or smiley faces will be motivated to work harder and learn better so they can earn these "rewards." There are words and phrases associated with external motivation that guides teachers' behavior:

blame	praise	control
motivate	humiliate	manage

supervise	reward	sarcasm
assess	coerce	comply

This language can be heard in schools in which external motivation is the dominant psychology. It is difficult to believe that giving frequent rewards for performance is not a good motivator. Yet there is a great deal of research that convincingly illustrates that offering rewards for performance will not have a lasting effect on student motivation (Glasser, 1999; Kohn, 1999). Following is a summary of some of this compelling research as well as observations of educational situations in which rewards are used to motivate students.

1. Children who always get rewards for learning will work for the reward and probably learn less.
2. The more prominent the reward, the more performance and learning is undermined.
3. Watching other students get rewards reduces motivation for students who are not getting them. It also reduces motivation for the students who get them in the long term.
4. Students who expect to be rewarded for doing something creative become less creative than those not receiving rewards.
5. Over time, performance declines for students who always get rewarded for achievement. They:
   - develop a negative view of learning
   - work to get rewarded and not to learn
   - are less self-motivated
   - take fewer risks
   - work quickly to get the reward, and their work may be inaccurate as a result
   - lose a sense of self-control

If this type of external motivation psychology worked, our schools would have few problems and all of our students would learn well. But it is clear that attempts at external motivation do not solve our problems or have long-lasting effects. The major question then is what will have lasting positive effects on student motivation? What will motivate students to be responsible and want to learn? How can we establish a relationship with each student so we can achieve our vision for them?

Internal Motivation

Getting students to choose to be responsible for their own behavior, to do their schoolwork on time and well, to attend school regularly and with enthusiasm, to pay attention in class, to want to learn, to be self-directed as learners, and to show concern for self, building and others may be the most important desires teachers and administrators have for their students. While these desires may appear difficult to fulfill, they are absolutely achievable and within the reach of virtually all students. When the conditions are created in which each student has his or her basic psychological needs satisfied effectively, then we will be successful in fulfilling all of the desires listed above. When students and staff see their school as a good, needs-satisfying place, then all they want and desire will be achieved. While we can't place these needs-satisfying behaviors in the minds of students, we can provide the conditions in which they can develop.

To create needs-satisfying conditions, we must understand the psychology created by William Glasser, MD, a noted psychiatrist and educator. The work of Dr. Glasser and his colleagues has provided our schools with the knowledge and practices to help all students become internally motivated—the only motivation that works over the long haul (Glasser, 1999).

Many schools have applied his ideas successfully and his psychological ideas are included throughout the pages of this book. Following is a summary of some of Dr. Glasser's ideas:

Choice theory (what Glasser previously referred to as control theory) helps us understand that what we do in our lives (our choices and our behavior) is our best attempt to control the world and environment that surrounds us. Choice theory is all about how we control ourselves, the only ones we can control, and not about controlling others. All decisions are choices.

Choice theory contends that all behavior we choose is our best attempt to satisfy one or more of our basic psychological needs, even when the chosen behavior is ineffective or socially unacceptable. When students choose an irresponsible behavior or action, they are doing so to satisfy one or more of their psychological needs. Even though their action may be irresponsible and ineffective, it is still their best attempt at satisfying their basic needs.

The job of a teacher is to help students make more responsible choices regardless of their situation, and help them take effective and socially acceptable control of their lives.

FOUR BASIC PSYCHOLOGICAL NEEDS

According to choice theory, each of us is born with five basic needs: one physiological need and four psychological needs. The physiological need is to survive—to get food, water, air, and to reproduce so that the species survives.

The four psychological needs are the needs that we are always attempting to satisfy—sometimes effectively and sometimes not, sometimes in a socially accepted manner and sometimes not. These needs, which are listed below, are the needs that students are attempting to satisfy both inside and outside of school.

1. Belonging, Connecting, and Fitting In

Each of us is born with the need to belong, connect, fit in, and relate positively with others. Each of us needs to be involved with others, to have friends, both in and out of school, and to have human beings in our life. Each of us has the need to care for and be cared for and to give and have love in our lives.

The opposite of belonging, connecting, and fitting in is isolation, loneliness, and despair. Yet many students, and sometimes teachers and administrators, come to school and feel that no one cares for them or loves them. They feel that they don't belong or connect with others. These students feel there are those who are accepted and those who are not. They feel there is an "in group" and that they are not part of it. They feel they don't fit in. For some students, the only connection and belonging they have is with other students who don't belong or fit in. These students often learn this early in their schooling and usually by fourth or fifth grade.

Students must connect and belong somehow. They will seek out and fit in with other students like them. They must do this for survival. Many times this creates an unhealthy, ineffective, and socially unacceptable group. We as educators must search for ways to include all students so everyone belongs and fits in.

Sometimes a school's practices are the cause for students disconnecting. In some schools, IQ or other tests are used to sort and label students, to reduce expectations, and to fix and often destroy children's educational lives. "Winners" and "losers" are the results.

Special education often does exactly the same thing with its practice of sorting, labeling, and disconnecting students from their peers. This separation is not normal and if there is a separation from peers it should be for short periods of time. Kids of all aptitudes and abilities should be taught to connect in a natural setting—the classroom.

There are some exceptions, however, which are discussed in chapter 9.

Activity: Addressing the Basic Need and Revisiting Focus Questions

1. What can we do in our schools to establish conditions and practices that will allow all students to satisfy this basic need?
2. What can we do in our schools to establish conditions and practices that will allow all staff to satisfy this basic need?
3. What should we stop doing in our schools because it interferes with students' and staff's satisfying this need?

Now revisit the focus questions at the beginning of this chapter and see how your thinking has evolved. This can be done individually or in a small group.

2. Sense of Power, Self-Control, and Worthiness

Each of us is born with the need to be in control of our own life, to feel worthwhile, to have a sense of accomplishment, to feel important, to have and maintain our dignity, to feel that we make a difference, and to be valued.

When we learn, gain knowledge, and accomplish, we gain a sense of power and feel in control. Notice how good you feel when hard work and focus allows you to acquire an understanding of new concepts and use them. You always feel in control when you are directing your own learning and assessment.

We all need to be in control of our own lives. But perhaps one of the greatest paradoxes, both in and outside of school, is that we have people all around us trying to control our lives. Principals do it; school committees do it; teachers do it, both to each other and to students; and students do it, both to teachers and to each other.

In the long run it is important for everyone to feel a sense of control over their own lives. Being in control does not mean being free to do whatever one pleases. Schools are a society and like any society, mutual rules must be established and all must live within that consensus.

Real power is chosen, shared, and necessary so everyone is productive. Real power is respecting oneself and understanding that each of us is special and unique. Real power comes from understanding that it is OK to be different and that each person has talents just waiting to be nurtured and developed. Real power is understanding that brilliant thoughts and ideas can come from anyone and that they often come from the least expected sources.

We must establish the conditions in our schools so that everyone can satisfy this basic need.

Refer to the section earlier in this chapter entitled "Activity: Addressing the Basic Need and Revisiting Focus Questions." Now revisit the focus questions at the beginning of this chapter and see how your thinking has evolved. This can be done individually or in a small group.

3. Freedom and Choice

Each of us is born with the basic need to have freedom and choice in our lives. Throughout history people have fought and died for freedom.

Some schools and classrooms provide little choice, or freedom, to manage, teach, and learn. As long as mindless mandates continue to flow from above, freedom will be absent from schools and classrooms. As stated earlier, not only do these mandates have little positive influence on our classrooms, they often have a negative effect. They result in a loss of freedom for everyone involved and they reap no long-term rewards. It is no mystery why so many principals, teachers, and students are unhappy and are basically just going through the motions of teaching and learning.

When principals, teachers, and students have the freedom to be involved in the policy and operations of their school and classroom, administrators will perform well, teachers will teach well, and students will learn well.

To be clear, academic freedom does not mean that teachers can do whatever they want because they have an academic degree. Academic freedom to administrate and teach must be exercised within mutually established parameters, which are often dictated by law. Each administrator or teacher can exercise freedom, providing his or her action contributes to achieving the school vision, is consistent with the agreed-upon beliefs, is based on the most compelling knowledge available, and contributes to positive psychological relationships.

We all need the freedom to take risks and to question without fear of humiliation, embarrassment, or being "cut down." We all need the freedom to create, influence, be involved, and develop alternatives and options. We all need the freedom to think, to create, and to try new ideas.

Students need the freedom to take risks in the classroom, to present new ideas from their readings and discussions, and to do all of this without the fear of receiving negative grades. If you want your students to be free to learn, free to create, and free to be self-directed, then rethink your classroom practices of assessment and grading. These ideas will be discussed in detail in chapter 11.

We all have the need to be free, to make reasonable informed choices, and to make these choices without the fear of being manipulated or coerced. We must establish conditions in our schools that allow everyone to satisfy this basic need.

Refer to the section earlier in this chapter entitled "Activity: Addressing the Basic Need and Revisiting Focus Questions." Now revisit the focus questions at the beginning of this chapter and see how your thinking has evolved. This can be done individually or in a small group.

4. Fun and Contentment

Each of us is born with the basic need to have fun, contentment, enjoyment, and happiness in our lives. Learning can be fun; recognition can be fun; being included and invited to participate can be fun; earning good grades without fear of failure can be fun; and the freedom to choose alternative ways of learning and assessment can be fun.

It is no fun for principals, teachers, or students to always be told what to do, what to teach and learn, and even how to teach and study. It is no fun to get students ready for ill-prepared high-stakes tests. It is no fun for teachers to be criticized continually by politicians who know little about education and learning and who make these criticisms for their own reelection purposes. It is no fun for principals and teachers to be at the receiving end of ideological maltreatment. It is no fun for principals and teachers to be at the receiving end of caustic statements because a few in the profession violate their unwritten or unstated oath of what it means to be an educator.

Administrators, teachers, and students can find learning fun, feel a sense of pride, feel worthwhile, and feel that they are in control of their lives and make a difference in the lives of others.

Teachers will find teaching fun when they feel their community cares about them, values what they are doing, and supports them. Teachers will find teaching fun when they have freedom to question openly without reprisals, and when disagreements are resolved amicably. Teachers will find teaching fun when everyone is intentionally trying to achieve the stated vision and mission, make decisions based on best compelling evidence and knowledge, and live by the agreed-upon beliefs and values in a psychologically safe, nurturing, and needs-satisfying environment.

Students will find learning fun when their teachers create a psychologically safe and nurturing classroom. Students will find learning fun when they are learning well and succeeding. This will not happen with a coercive teacher and classroom.

We must establish the conditions in our schools so that everyone can satisfy this basic need.

Refer to the section earlier in this chapter entitled "Activity: Addressing the Basic Need and Revisiting Focus Questions." Now revisit the focus questions at the beginning of this chapter and see how your thinking has evolved. This can be done individually or in a small group.

CONCLUSION

The discussions in this chapter lead to the five most important kinds of questions that can be asked as you plan, make decisions, solve problems, and live your personal and professional life.

Vision and Mission Questions

- What do we really want?
- For whom do we want it?

Knowledge Questions

- What do we know?
- What do we need to know?
- What does our data tell us?

Beliefs and Values Questions

- What do we believe?
- What should we believe?
- Are our beliefs consistent with our vision and mission?

Psychology and Relationship Questions

- Is what we are doing or going to do psychologically safe?
- Is it nurturing?
- Does it satisfy everyone's basic needs?

Action Questions

- Does what we are doing or going to do get us what we really want (vision)?
- Are our actions consistent with our beliefs?
- Are our actions based on knowledge?
- Are our actions needs-satisfying?

Activity: Using the Five Kinds of Questions and Revisiting the Focus Questions

1. Choose a problem you face in your school or personal life and try to solve it using the above questions.
2. Revisit the focus questions in this chapter and see how your thinking has evolved. This can be done individually or in a small group.

Chapter Nine

Children as Students

All children can learn, learn well, and at very deep levels.

Focus Questions

1. It has been said that one of the greatest problems in American education is the sorting and labeling of children, and the perception, expectations, and attitudes of the teacher that accompany these practices. What evidence is there in your school to either support or refute this statement?
2. What are some barriers to students' learning? What are some reasons that some students do not (or choose not to) learn well? What interferes with student learning?
3. Why is it that most children enter kindergarten wanting to learn well, but many turn away or turn off to learning by the fourth or fifth grade?
4. How can we get more students to learn well? What should we start doing to make this happen? What should we stop doing to make this happen?
5. Follow a student's schedule for a day. Decide whether learning is:
   - active or passive
   - meaningful or rote
   - relevant or mindless
   - appealing or boring
   - understandable or confusing
   - for everyone or a few
   - encouraging or discouraging
   - inviting or fearful
   - success-driven or failure-driven

A GREAT BIG FISH STORY

My good friend Rob, a principal in Australia, told me a wonderful great big fish story. He claims it is true; I believe him. Rob said that behavioral researchers placed a great big fish, a three- to five-pound walleye, into a large fish tank along with an abundance of minnows. The large fish roamed freely in the tank eating as many of the minnows as it desired. More minnows were added as needed and the walleye never went hungry. Its food supply was always there; it never had to compete with any other fish. All the walleye had to do was swim and eat as many minnows as possible. This was natural for this great fish and also for its survival.

One day a large glass wall was placed in the middle of the tank with the minnows on one side and the walleye on the other. The walleye tried to do what it always did. It tried to eat minnows, but each time, the walleye hit its head on the glass wall. It tried again and again but each time it was repelled by the glass wall. The walleye tried repeatedly to get the minnows, but as time went on it tried with less enthusiasm. It finally gave up and quit trying. The glass wall won.

The glass wall was then removed and the minnows roamed freely around the tank. They even came close to the walleye. To everyone's surprise, the walleye made no attempt to eat any of the minnows even though it was quite hungry. The researchers tried to get this large fish to eat, but their remedial efforts were unsuccessful. The walleye grew weaker and weaker and still wouldn't eat. The walleye gave up and died. The glass wall really won.

How can we use that story to examine classroom behavior? A child entered school for the first time and was excited. The parents were excited and optimistic as well. The child even had some clean clothes, perhaps new, but not always. At first the child learned a great deal without even knowing it. There were no tests, worksheets, or endless drills, just a caring teacher. The children were actually learning but in a very natural way. They were socializing and having fun, recognizing letters, having play time, exploring and discovering ideas, learning number sequences, identifying patterns, learning letter sounds, and having many stories read to them. They were encouraged to talk about the story line, characters, and create new story endings. They were encouraged to use their imaginations and be creative. The children learned and were free to let their minds roam freely like the walleye before the glass wall. The children found school fun and enjoyable and were learning much without knowing it.

The teacher also got to know each child, to make each one feel special, and to laugh with them. She was kind and respectful to each child and made it a point to speak in a calm and reassuring voice. Her classroom was welcoming to everyone. She modeled caring behaviors and the children liked it. They liked their teacher and she liked them too.

During art time children did not have to draw between the lines and were even allowed the freedom to create using many colors and shades. Roses did not have to be red. At all times, the children were free to express themselves, try new ideas, explore, discover, create, and to be the children they were. There were no glass walls.

As time went on and a different teacher entered the picture, school became much more serious. Now children had to get ready for "The Tests." There was an abundance of worksheets, much seat time, stickers and smiley faces only for those doing good work, many quizzes, and lots of red ink for the wrong answers. Rules were now made by those in charge and most rules were the *don't* ones:

- Don't misbehave.
- Don't hit.
- Don't yell.
- Don't, Don't, Don't!

Furthermore, after an endless battery of tests, some children were labeled. Then they were sorted and often sent away from their classroom to be "fixed." Perceptions, expectations, and attitudes changed for labeled children.

For some children, some of them labeled and some not, difficulties began to occur and it didn't take long before the glass wall came down. While most of these children had originally come to school excited to learn and to do what was natural for them, they gave up and didn't try anymore, like the walleye. Some quit and refused to eat from the learning table. These children were leaving the classroom with less—not more—than when they entered.

Activity: Glass Walls

When glass walls begin to form, some children will give up. Although they may graduate, these children won't have enough skills to lead a productive and satisfying life.

1. What are the glass walls that some teachers, perhaps unknowingly, place in front of children? Think of all grade levels.
2. What might teachers say that children will perceive as a glass wall?
3. Think of a teacher you know who turned children off to learning. What did he or she do?
4. Think of all the glass walls teachers face while trying to do their job. What are they? What can we do to eliminate them?
5. What glass walls do principals and parents face? How can we eliminate them?

With pressures to get students ready for mandated tests and uncertainty about what will be tested, some teachers forget the human side of teaching and learning and focus their concentration completely on the tests. Learning can become tedious when test preparation is the only goal. There is no time to think, explore, make connections, investigate, or be self-directed—all valuable and necessary skills. There is no time for joy.

STATEMENTS AND ANALYSIS ABOUT FEELING UNSUCCESSFUL IN SCHOOL

Following are several descriptions of children's feelings about being unsuccessful in school. If we use the compelling observations, psychology, and beliefs discussed in chapters 4 to 8 of this book, we can see and understand these feelings in a whole new light.

I guess it was the whole sticker thing. Just once, one time to go home and say, "Look what the teacher gave me." It never happened. Compelling observation: Gold stars, smiley faces, and other extrinsic incentives are not only ineffective in the long term in motivating students to learn and behave, but may have a negative effect and produce the opposite of what is intended.

I wasn't shy. Teachers like shy, quiet kids. I heard so many "not nows" and "sit downs" that I thought they were compound words. Compelling observation: Students will choose to reject learning and other students if they have been humiliated, fear failure or rejection, or if they believe the teacher does not care. The basic need of feeling in control, of feeling worthwhile and maintaining dignity is violated. How many times can one hear "not now" and "sit down" before one says not here and doesn't hear?

It was all the times teachers stood in the doorways talking to other teachers. Why did they think we couldn't hear? We knew what slow, impossible, and bottom group meant. Later we even knew what "his elevator doesn't go all the way to the top," "nobody's home and nobody's moving in," and "not playing with a full deck" meant. Were they talking about me? Compelling observation: Criticism and humiliation are two of the greatest destroyers of confidence and self-esteem.

It was when I never got to help teachers. I really wanted to, but I couldn't because I couldn't cut, or keep quiet, or do my work, or stand tall, or walk in a straight line. I learned that I couldn't do a lot of things. Compelling observations: (1) The basic need to feel worthwhile, have self-control, and be empowered is violated in this statement. Rather than the child knowing what he or she can do, he or she learned what couldn't be done. Teachers must concentrate on what a child can do and keep the child actively engaged. (2) In chapter 3 we learned that a teacher's attitude influences student performance. (3) When students are led to believe that their teachers want to develop their talent and the teacher expects excellence, they will learn better.

I never got to be the leader. You know, the kid who gets to be first. The kid who tells the other kids how long they can stay at the water fountain. I wanted to be the leader one time. It never happened. Compelling observation: The basic need to have some power, to feel worthwhile, and to have self-control is violated. All children have these needs and sometimes they just want to be recognized and put in charge. It is also no fun to always be the follower.

I started out wanting to be good. I really did. But so many worksheets! I tried. I wanted the teacher to like me, to smile at me, to hang up my work. Sometimes she would give me extra help. She gave up. So did I. Compelling observations: (1) Earlier we learned how a teacher's perception, attitude, and expectation influence a student's actions. If the teacher gives up, why shouldn't the student? When students think their teacher believes and expects them to learn, they will learn better than when they don't believe it. (2) When basic needs are violated, the child does not feel he or she belongs or fits in and has no freedom or choice. They also feel powerless and not worthwhile.

Even when we eliminate all glass walls, getting students to be responsible for their own behavior and learning, to do their schoolwork on time and well, to attend school regularly and with enthusiasm, to pay attention in class and to want to learn, to be self-directed as learners, and to show concern for self and others are still the important goals and vision that teachers and administrators have for their students.

While these goals may appear difficult to achieve, we must do all we can to attain them. The job gets somewhat easier, however, when you identify all the glass walls and strive to eliminate them. By reviewing the compelling observations, beliefs, values, psychology, and relationships in chapters 4 to 8, you will learn how to identify and avoid glass wall behavior.

We won't get what we want by blaming previous teachers, parents, or society. We won't get what we want by making excuses about ethnic background, divorced parents, or low socioeconomic conditions. We won't get what we want if we make excuses or put down good ideas or each other. These are all glass walls.

I recall a story about a high-school teacher who placed many glass walls in front of students and himself. John was not a good teacher; he was misguided and wasn't getting much of what he wanted. He was one of those teachers who forgot or never understood the vision of the school, gave minimal attention to the agreed-upon beliefs, and described himself as being from the "old school." He didn't realize this was just an excuse to do what he had always done. He still tried external motivation and force to get students to behave and learn; he had little to show for it.

John always complained when he had the ear of the superintendent. Since my office was in the high school, I frequently passed him in the hall and he would tell me how hard it was to teach, forgetting that I had taught high-school mathematics for twelve years along with teaching graduate school mathematics at a university. I often wondered whether anything was positive in his life. I knew it wasn't positive in school. One day after John talked and I listened for what seemed like an eternity, I asked him a key question that had to do with his vision and mission: "John, what do you want for your students?" He responded quickly by saying, "I want them to behave, to do their homework, to come prepared to learn, and pay attention when I try to teach them." This meant John talks and students listen.

I said every teacher wants that. But I also said, "John, if you had the ideal class, what would you want for your students?" Without hesitation John said, "I would want all of them to be responsible for their behavior and learning. I really want them to want to learn without my being on their back all the time. I really want them to love what I am teaching and to show concern for each other."

I asked him if what he was doing in the classroom was getting him what he really wanted. He responded immediately with a no. When I asked if he'd be willing to talk more so he could get closer to achieving his goals, he replied that he would. He also agreed to let other teachers, who seemed pleased with their classroom experience and their students' behavior and learning, to join the conversation.

Many meaningful discussions followed and John's teaching skills improved. As was the case with John, the simple question "Is what I am doing now getting me the results I desire?" can serve as the catalyst for much-needed change.

While John verbalized his desires for his students, we need to recall the vision presented in chapter 5. We want all students to have knowledge and to be able to do something with this knowledge. We want all students to exit our schools with knowledge and with important skills, including the ability to be self-directed learners and responsible and caring people. We often verbalize these wants, but pay little attention to their meaning.

THE SELF-DIRECTED LEARNER

If a student were a self-directed learner, what would we see that student doing? A student who becomes a self-directed learner has some of the following attributes and characteristics:

1. They are able to use technology to gain information, do research, and to create and test certain hypotheses.

2. They are able to make connections, analyze information, find and create examples and nonexamples, find similarities and differences, observe patterns, and synthesize ideas and concepts.
3. They are able to communicate their findings in many and various ways.
4. They take the initiative, pay attention to detail, and assume responsibility for their behavior.

By using all the skills represented in the *do* section of the stated vision, students will be on their way to becoming self-directed.

Activity

1. Brainstorm attributes and characteristics of a self-directed learner.
2. Group them into categories and label each category. Remove duplicates.
3. Try to get an agreement.
4. How close did these match the five skill parts of the *do* section of the vision presented in chapter 5?

THE RESPONSIBLE LEARNER

It is important to go through the same process to determine what it means for a student to be responsible. If students were responsible people what would we see them doing? Students who become responsible people and learners have some of the following attributes and characteristics:

1. They participate in all discussions and activities, and they, in turn, include all other students. Everyone fits in.
2. They choose wisely and allow themselves and others the freedom to choose without criticism. They take risks and encourage others to do the same.
3. They feel that what they are doing is worthwhile. They also recognize and value everyone's views as worthwhile. They are open to changing their views when new information is presented.
4. They find joy in doing their job well and never at the expense of others.

Children become responsible students and people when their basic psychological needs are satisfied effectively and are socially acceptable. Students become irresponsible when their basic psychological needs are satisfied in an ineffective or socially unacceptable way.

All behavior is chosen to satisfy one or more of the basic psychological needs. Sometimes students know, and sometimes they don't, that they are behaving to belong or fit in, to have some choice and freedom, to feel worthwhile and in control, and to find joy and satisfaction in what they are doing. Sometimes students will join cliques or groups in school to satisfy these needs. But this is often ineffective and unacceptable. Their needs must be satisfied effectively as a result of the climate and culture presented in the classroom and school. When teachers and administrators (and other school personnel) provide the conditions that allow students to satisfy their basic needs effectively, they are more apt to be responsible.

One of those conditions is determining how everyone will live together in harmony and contentment. This implies that the responsibility to make this happen must be determined by the students and teachers.

One of the activities used in the Johnson City schools was to involve students in creating the ideal living and learning conditions for their classroom and to determine mutual responsibilities. While the phrase "my job/your job" was used, I prefer to look at "student responsibility" and "teacher responsibility."

Activity

1. Brainstorm attributes and characteristics of a responsible student.
2. Group these into categories and label each category.
3. Try to get an agreement.
4. How close did these match the basic psychological needs as discussed in chapter 8?

The following activity can be used at any grade level. Karen, a sixth-grade teacher, shared some student responses with me. She asked her students within a few days of the start of the school year what their responsibility would be to make this classroom a really good one. She also asked what her responsibility would be. Some of their responses and agreements included:

1. It is our responsibility (students) to:
   - Be responsible for ourselves.
   - Come prepared to learn each day.
   - Be on time.
   - Ask questions.
   - Participate in discussions.
   - Be cooperative with everyone.
   - Give our best effort.
   - Take good care of our school.
   - Be respectful of everyone.
   - Be a good listener.
2. It is your responsibility (teacher) to:
   - Be prepared.
   - Plan well.
   - Be organized.
   - Help everyone to learn.
   - Respect everyone.
   - Answer questions.
   - Make learning interesting and fun.
   - Prepare us for tests.
   - Be nice.
   - Listen to everyone.

Note that none of the student or teacher responsibilities are expressed in negative terms.

It is equally important to determine actions that are not the responsibility of students as well as those not the responsibility of teachers. Some of these are stated below:

1. It is *not* our responsibility as students to:
   - Tell on others unless it is a dangerous situation.
   - Disrupt the class or disturb others.
   - Be disrespectful.

- Destroy property.
- Hurt our class or school.
- Invade others' space.
- Put others down.

2. It is *not* your responsibility as a teacher to:
   - Give surprise quizzes.
   - Be disrespectful of anyone.
   - Talk about kids behind their back.
   - Let us fail.
   - Chat with other teachers or use a cell phone during class time.
   - Criticize us.
   - Yell at or humiliate us.
   - Put us down.
   - Make us feel stupid.
   - Give us busy work.

The teacher and students agreed to these ideas. Using large print and in four different colors, the teacher put these on the walls for everyone to see and to live by. The teacher reviewed these statements many times over the first few weeks and periodically during the year. When someone was not being responsible the teacher gently reminded the student of their agreements. Generally all the teacher had to say, for example, was "Green 3." This meant don't be disrespectful.

This process goes both ways. I was in a New York City elementary school when a third-grade student raised her hand and said "Red 6." When the teacher looked at the printed statements, she reminded herself that it was not her responsibility to yell at students. The teacher really wasn't yelling, I observed, but she did raise her voice.

Activity: Student and Teacher Responsibility

1. Do the activity described above with your class.
2. You may also want to do this with parents.
3. Be sure you get agreement and publish results.

A CONCERNED, CARING LEARNER

As you look at the responsibility agreements above, you can see that many of these can be summarized by the words "respect" and "concern." It is more important than ever to help students show respect and concern for themselves and others. Following is an activity you can use with your students to determine the attributes and characteristics of concern.

Activity: For Students

Concern: Class, it would be nice if we all showed concern for each other. I will show concern for you and you for me and each other. But what does concern mean? What would you see me doing if I showed concern for you? What would I see you doing if you showed concern for me and your classmates?

1. Brainstorm the attributes and characteristics of a person who shows concern for others.
2. Group them into categories and label each category. Remove duplicates.
3. Try to get an agreement.
4. Publish agreements so all can see.

Here is one version of the attributes and characteristics of a person who shows concern. It is important to develop your own with your students. *You show concern for another person when you:*

- Include and accept everyone in all activities and discussions. No one is excluded.
- Listen to what others are saying.
- Show you understand what is being said.
- Show you are not judgmental of ideas while you are trying to gain a better understanding.
- Allow and encourage others the freedom to present diverse ideas.
- Respect others' differences and find a common ground.

When we are concerned about all children, then all students are included in all activities, whenever this is possible. No one is excluded, not even those with special needs. Excluding any child, either physically or in our minds, violates the basic need of belonging, love, connecting, and fitting in. There are exceptions, such as a hostile student intimidating other students. But such exceptions are rare and not the rule, and we must strive to include everyone.

Before I recommend guidelines for maximum inclusion, I want to discuss what "special needs" means to me and then discuss the Federal Education of All Handicapped Act (Public Law 94-142, 1975).

All children have special needs. Some are shy and quiet, others are restless and antsy, and still others seem to know what the teacher is going to teach before it is taught. Some children need glasses, some have trouble controlling their emotions, and others daydream a lot. Some don't get love at home and need some in school. Some even need a safe place called school. Some students have special talents in mathematics and are ready to start algebra by sixth grade or earlier. But some of these same students may have difficulty in other areas.

Everyone has special gifts and special needs. When we begin to think that every child has gifts and needs instead of labeling students, we are on our way to creating the most inclusive ideal school.

For the sake of discussion, I will use the phrase "special needs" in its traditional sense even though I would be delighted to have the words "special needs" abolished. I would rather use the words "diverse needs."

In the mid-1970s, the Federal Education of All Handicapped Act (PL94-142) was passed. This law gave rise to many new labels. Throughout the history of education, we had groupings and labels such as Blue Birds and Red Birds and by any other name, Buzzards. With this new law, more labels emerged: autistic, attention deficit disorder, emotionally disturbed, mentally retarded, multiple handicapped, speech impaired, deaf, etc. Schools responded with their own labels: overachiever, underachiever, gifted, talented, average, etc.

When will we learn that labeling a child or anyone is a very dangerous process? Labels add negative thoughts into the minds of students, their families, and even their teachers. Labeling a child may be the most destructive practice facing our schools. As soon as a child is labeled, perceptions, expectations, beliefs, and actions accompany the label, causing a negative self-fulfilling prophecy.

Why can't we bring needed services to children without labeling them? School districts and schools label children since funding accompanies the labels and categories. Also, some parents demand labeling as they feel this ensures their children the special services needed.

If we must label, then do it, get the funding and promptly forget or downplay the labels. Wouldn't it be nice if a brave legislator, who really wanted to be known as an education legislator, proposed legislation to provide funding for special-needs students based on educational criteria, not labeling criteria? It is important to note that when the PL94-142 was being drafted, a group of educational leaders almost won the battle to get funding without using categories and labels but educational criteria.

At the time PL94-142 became law, I was the assistant superintendent for instruction and was handed the responsibility for its implementation even though a special education coordinator was hired. Early on, when we were trying to understand the implications of the law, few students were classified. We then cooperated with other districts to share services and special-needs teachers. We, in fact, sent these children away to be "fixed." I remember saying—and I am not proud of it—how will "these students" benefit by being in the regular classroom? As my knowledge increased and my inclusion beliefs began to take form, I realized that all children would benefit with a total inclusive classroom.

By cooperating with the University of Binghamton and Syracuse University we gained much knowledge about total inclusion and began returning all of our special-needs students to our classrooms. It wasn't easy, but we knew it would get better. It did. By this time I was superintendent of the Johnson City public schools. During my remarks to the entire school faculty, I reminded them about our shared vision and the latest knowledge. I also told them that if I were not practicing our shared beliefs, they should be gentle and remind me.

Sue, a primary teacher, informed me that I was not living our beliefs. She asked me one question to illustrate her point. Where are our severely disabled children—the ones who can't walk or talk well—the ones confined to wheelchairs? They were housed in a state development center in our district. Sue was absolutely right. We had the belief of inclusion, but not the practice. These students were not included. Our new dilemma was knowing that we should return these students to the regular classroom, but not knowing how to do it successfully.

The first job was to find a primary team of second-, third-, and fourth-grade teachers who would volunteer to get training and to be the first to include these children in their classrooms. With any new idea, we always had teachers volunteer to identify, solve, and develop the model. With our team of teachers in place, we began to implement our vision of total inclusion. Thankfully, the University of Binghamton and Syracuse University came to our aid. After a year of gathering knowledge and training, we were ready to include the profoundly disabled children into the regular classroom. It was a difficult year for everyone, but we learned a great deal and began the improvement process. We continued to get much-needed help from professors at the two universities. They practically lived in our building coaching the teachers and doing their own research. We also relied on related services, including one aide for each child.

Including special-needs students, even those with severe needs, is never easy, but it is rewarding. However, when a child was dangerous to himself, or others, and was more than the teachers and other students could handle, that child was excluded until everyone was prepared for the return.

The board of education was also put under some pressure when we announced that severely disabled children were returning to the district. I remember a parent of a faster learner coming to a board meeting and asking the board of education, "Why are you bringing 'them' back?" I asked the parent to explain what she meant by "them." After some discussion and when our board was assured that we were prepared and ready to do so, they affirmed our beliefs of inclusion and agreed with the action plan.

I also remember a tenth-grade girl with a physical disability coming to see me. She walked into my office using two walking devices, one for each arm. She asked if it were possible for her to be a cheerleader, even though she couldn't walk unassisted. My quick response was "you bet." We ordered a special uniform, talked to the other cheerleaders, and this girl became a cheerleader. She was readily accepted by her peers. I soon received a note from the county's athletic association reminding me that cheerleading was a sport and according to the byelaws, only eleven girls could be on the sidelines cheering at any time. We had a bench of fifty-seven cheerleaders and we substituted freely. The girl mentioned above is now a special educator.

One year the senior class voted two special-needs students as their homecoming King and Queen. One year the "star" basketball player had an autistic student sitting on the bench next to him during the games. The band director, Ken, had children with disabilities in the band both as players and flag carriers. The lead flag carrier was both a physically challenged and learning-disabled child. One year when she led the band carrying the lead flag in the competition, it won the New York State's governor's trophy.

While there are many such stories, I will conclude with a story about Stacy, a child who used a wheelchair and who couldn't walk or talk. She was a member of a teaching team of teachers and students who all worked together.

Stacy's team invited me to observe its assessment of expected learning. They informed me that Stacy was learning quite well and they devised a way of demonstrating this. They would ask questions about what they were studying that could be answered with a yes or a no. Stacy could not speak but she would blink her eyes when the answer was yes and not blink when the answer was no.

One day Stacy's mom called my office to tell me that Stacy was now invited to parties outside the school, something she thought would never happen. A few years later Stacy died, but her mom said that Stacy never experienced more happiness than when she was included at school. I had come a long way from asking "How could they benefit?" to being a total believer in the value of including every child.

The teachers who began the inclusion process for the severely disabled children confessed that they never worked so hard or cried so much, but that they also never experienced such rewards.

TEN GUIDELINES FOR MAXIMUM INCLUSION

The following guidelines are crucial prerequisites for responsible maximum inclusion of special-needs students and perhaps all students:

1. Create a School Where Everyone Learns Well

Create and operate a total systems model as presented in chapters 4 to 8. Many schools divide students into various groups such as average, honors, Title I, remedial, and special needs and hope to have maximum achievement. They also fragment their approach to improving education by adapting the buzzword or program of the year. When a school can't implement a process to get all students to learn well, what chance do they have of getting special-needs students to learn well? A school and its faculty must be committed to a process where all students learn well together in a common instructional setting even though it is possible to group some students for special purposes for a short period of time.

2. View Inclusion as an Attitude

View inclusion as an attitude and belief rather than a mere placement. When we view inclusion as a placement, we often behave and treat special-needs students according to their assigned categories. For example, what do you, your colleagues, and others think and perceive when you encounter students labeled learning disabled, emotionally disturbed, and so on? These categories and labels usually evoke feelings of negative expectations followed by self-fulfilling prophecies that confirm expectations. When our attitude is such that we value each child, perceive, believe, and expect all students to learn well, and then provide outstanding teaching, special-needs students will learn well alongside their peers.

3. Involve Everyone

Involve all students, parents, staff, administrators, board members, and other citizens groups with all the information and progress you are making. They must be shown that inclusion does not detract from or reduce other children's learning opportunities. Parents of special-needs students must also be shown that inclusion improves the quality of their child's individual educational progress.

4. Deal with Disruptive Students

Have a well-defined process to deal with disruptive and potentially dangerous students. When all students are actively engaged and a total systems process, as explained in chapters 4 to 8, is applied, discipline problems are greatly reduced and in many cases eliminated. However, even the best teachers encounter students whose emotional and/or social behavior is disruptive and sometimes dangerous. These students must not be allowed to remain in the regular classroom, but may return once their behavior is under control. When working with disruptive or dangerous students and their families, schools need a well-defined process with roles clearly defined. Many discipline policies and processes are vague and do not teach students to be responsible. As stated earlier, rewards or punishments have only short-term effect and then become counterproductive. Have the needs-satisfying conditions in place and a responsible discipline process understood by all and many problems will be eliminated.

5. Provide Necessary Resources

Bring related services and other needed resources into the inclusive classroom. When special-needs students are integrated into the regular classroom, failure to provide the necessary resources will doom the process. Including all students is labor intensive and expensive.

6. Provide a Continuum of Inclusion Options

Put in place a continuum of inclusion options. For example, at the high school, some severely handicapped students will require functional community-intensive orientation and training experiences. A small number of students may require temporary or longer-term programming and treatment in specialized settings. Others may require minimum separation from the class for specific targeted help. These children may spend most of their day in the classroom with outside interventions. One shoe does not fit all, but educational criteria will dictate needs and services. The mission and goal should always be to return all students to a normal, maximum-inclusive classroom.

7. Offer Continuing Education for Staff

Provide, as a top priority, adequate initial and continuing education for all staff involved in the placement and programming of special-needs students in the regular education classroom. Preinclusion training must be provided for those teachers and support staff who are affected. This is not an option. It is unprofessional and immoral to ask teachers to do something they are not trained to do. Training is crucial to the success of inclusion and must be provided by experts in the field. Remember, in my school district, we involved professors from two universities and spent an entire year training staff before including the severely handicapped children. The main reason maximum inclusion will succeed will be the training and continued training of staff.

8. Get Started

Start with teachers who volunteer and who have a sincere desire to include all students in their classroom. Some teachers will want to embark on these challenges, others want to wait and see, and still others do not want to include all students. This is a normal reaction, so be patient as the process starts. The majority of teachers will have a wait-and-see attitude. Make sure all teachers understand that they will be expected to have maximum inclusion in their classroom in the future. Encourage the volunteer teachers to inform all the other teachers about both the good practices and the problems they face as they lead the change. The key to all phases of maximum inclusion is for all staff to understand they will not be expected to make inclusion changes until they have received proper training. Also inform them that reasonable resources will accompany special-needs students.

9. Form Collaborative Teams

View special education teachers and specialized related services personnel as members of a collaborative team along with regular education teachers. It is important that all instructional team members share in the opportunities and responsibilities for educating all children in the inclusive classroom. All teachers are teachers of all children. All children involved are children and not special-needs and regular children. Whenever possible, form student learning teams, with the children intentionally mixed. Students are marvelous resources for each other. Everyone benefits both educationally and socially. It's a great way to model concern for each other.

10. Use the Five Key Questions

Always start and return to your stated vision, beliefs, dominant psychology, and compelling observations when planning and making decisions. This means using the five key questions stated earlier to plan or solve problems.

1. What is your vision?
2. What are your compelling observations?
3. What are your beliefs?
4. What is your dominant psychology?
5. Will your actions be consistent with the other four questions?

While there may be other guidelines, I believe these are necessary for a maximum-inclusion classroom and school. Violate any one of the ten guidelines and the process of full inclusion will not be as smooth and successful as it should be.

THE FASTER LEARNER

As stated earlier, "special needs" refers to everyone. This includes children who need to be challenged in more ways than doing very well on state and local tests. As a matter of fact, it is essential for these children and for our nation that in-depth learning is as important as doing well on tests.

Early on, I introduced the concept of *know* (information, facts, understanding) and *do* (connecting, communication, learning, life, and social skills). Faster learners should progress through the curriculum not just at the information and facts level but also in gaining a more thorough understanding of each subject. The concept of understanding a subject will be discussed in the next chapter.

Also, faster learners should be encouraged to participate more fully in the five skill areas of the *do* part of the curriculum. This concept will be discussed in the chapter on curriculum planning.

While we don't want any child to hit a glass wall, we also don't want any child to hit his or her head on a glass ceiling. Every child should be able to fly as high as he or she can without any fear of flying or trying.

Activity: Glass Ceilings

1. What are some glass ceilings some children hit in our classrooms? What causes them?
2. How can we remove them so all children can fly?

ESSENTIAL LEARNING CONDITIONS

To develop self-directed, responsible, and caring learners, there are two very important and essential conditions that must be present in every classroom: (1) high expectations of all students and (2) a caring teacher and class. These two conditions are intertwined and both must be in place and achieved.

Having high expectations and a classroom that is not caring will produce little student success, and having a caring classroom where the expectations are low will produce little student success too. In other words, high expectations and teacher caring go hand in hand. With proper balance of these two conditions, most students will learn well and their basic psychological needs will be satisfied.

High Expectations

The first condition is to have high expectations for all. This does not mean everyone will learn the same things the same way and at the same rate. But the quickest way to destroy a child's self-worth is to expect little of that child. Expectations must be high but appropriate.

Caring

In a caring classroom, all students are encouraged to explore, question, discover, investigate, and be creative with the use of knowledge. In a caring classroom, students will not fear failure for there is none—perhaps they haven't learned yet what you want them to learn. Furthermore, in a caring class, what all students are asked to learn is relevant, interesting, and personally meaningful, and not just preparation for a high-stakes test. Remember, in a caring classroom, everyone listens to each other and everyone knows they are valued. Ideas are encouraged and everyone's ideas are considered. In a caring classroom, there are no put-downs or judgments. Contrary to some educators' opinions, no one ever gave us the authority or skill to judge someone else. We can judge the learning but not the learner. In a caring classroom, there is no sarcasm, humiliation, yelling, or blaming.

CONCLUSION

A child is a child is a child. Every child has the same basic physiological and psychological needs, including the need to be part of the class. Naturally, they also need to feel worthwhile, to have some choice, and to experience some joy in school. As educators, it is our job to meet these basic needs.

Chapter Ten

Teaching, Learning, and the Teacher

Children will choose to learn when they have a teacher they trust.

Focus Questions

1. Why is it that some students will choose to learn for one teacher and not for another?
2. What are some characteristics of all successful and admired teachers?
3. How would you, as a teacher, like to be remembered?
4. Think of three people who have had a profound, positive influence on your life. Was one of them a teacher? If so, what did this teacher say or do to influence you positively?
5. Think of three people who have had a profoundly negative influence on your life. Was one of them a teacher? If so, what did this teacher say or do to influence you negatively?
6. Did you ever take a class and walk away discouraged because you didn't understand the teaching? Without blaming yourself, did you ever analyze why? Did you learn the way you were being taught? Did you understand what you were supposed to learn? Can you give advice to the teacher about how to plan and teach the lesson so that you would learn well?
7. You are the CEO of a major business and are asked by your local school to give advice on ways to revamp the curriculum so that students will eventually be able to get and keep a job. What kind of *knowledge* and *understanding* would you like students to get from any course? What should students be able to do with their knowledge?

Would they be able to communicate effectively in each subject, work as members of a team, respect themselves, think creatively, and solve problems?

8. If students really understood what you wanted them to know and learn, how would they demonstrate this? What would they demonstrate? How do you plan your curriculum for students to understand it? How do you plan to get students to use their knowledge?
9. You are to give a lecture to prospective teachers. Describe a teaching–learning process they would understand. What can you do as a teacher that someone not trained as a teacher can't do?

THREE LETTERS FROM TEDDY

Janet, a physical education teacher at the Johnson City High School, gave me a copy of a story entitled "Three Letters from Teddy" by Elizabeth Silance Ballard (1976). I became very emotional while reading the story because my own childhood experience made me identify closely with Teddy.

The story may be fiction, but it powerfully illustrates the profound influence of educators. Educators can have a very positive influence on the lives of children. They can also have quite a negative one. I remember asking a fifth-grade student why he liked using the computer to learn. He responded, "The computer never yells at me or makes me feel stupid."

Negative influences are highly publicized, although, in actuality, they are far outweighed by positive influences. However, negative influences are real and damaging, and they must be identified and eliminated. Take, for example, verbal and emotional abuse of children, which are forms of child abuse.

There is overwhelming evidence that most teachers enter the profession for the right reasons, namely, to make a difference in the lives of children. And they, in fact, do. Most educators make a wonderful difference in the lives of children.

As you read the following story, be proud of the teaching profession. This story will change your life, validate it, and make educators beam with pride.

Teddy's letter came today and now that I've read it, I will place it in my cedar chest with the other things that are important to my life.

"I wanted you to be the first to know."

I smiled as I read the words he had written and my heart swelled with a pride that I had no right to feel. *Teddy Stallard*—I have not seen Teddy Stallard since he was a student in my fifth-grade class, which was fifteen years ago.

I'm ashamed to say that from the first day he stepped into my classroom, I disliked Teddy. Teachers try hard not to have favorites in a class, but we try even harder not to show dislike for a child, any child.

Nevertheless, every year there are one or two children that one cannot help but be attached to, for teachers are human, and it is human nature to like bright, pretty, intelligent people, whether they are ten years old or twenty-five. And sometimes, not too often fortunately, there will be one or two students to whom the teacher just can't seem to relate.

I had thought myself quite capable of handling my personal feelings along that line until Teddy walked into my life. There wasn't a child I particularly liked that year, but Teddy was most assuredly one I disliked.

He was a dirty little boy. Not just occasionally, but all the time. His hair hung low over his ears and he actually had to hold it out of his eyes as he wrote his papers in class. (And this was before it was fashionable to do so!) Too, he had a peculiar odor about him that I could never identify.

Yes, his physical faults were many but his intellect left a lot to be desired. By the end of the first week I knew he was hopelessly behind the others. Not only was he behind, he was just plain slow! I began to withdraw from him immediately.

Any teacher will tell you that it's more of a pleasure to teach a bright child. It is definitely more rewarding for one's ego. But any teacher worth his or her credentials can channel work to the bright child, keeping that child challenged and learning, while the major effort is with the slower ones. Any teacher *can* do this. Most teachers *do*, but I didn't. Not that year.

In fact, I concentrated on my best students and let the others follow along as best they could. Ashamed as I am to admit it, I took perverse pleasure in using my red pen, and each time I came to Teddy's papers, the cross marks (and they were many) were always a little larger and a little redder than necessary.

"Poor work!" I would write with a flourish.

While I did not actually ridicule the boy, my attitude was obviously quite apparent to the class, for he quickly became the class "goat," the outcast—the unlovable and the unloved.

He knew I didn't like him, but he didn't know why. Nor did I know—then or now—why I felt such an intense dislike for him. All I know is that he was a little boy no one cared about, and I made no effort on his behalf.

The days rolled by and we made it through the Fall Festival, the Thanksgiving holidays, and I continued marking happily with my red pen. As our Christmas break approached, I knew that Teddy would never catch up in time to be promoted to the sixth-grade level. He would be a repeater.

To justify myself, I went to his cumulative folder from time to time. He had very low grades for the first four years, but no grade failure. How he had made it, I didn't know. I closed my mind to the personal remarks:

First grade: "Teddy shows promise by work and attitude, but he has a poor home situation."

Second grade: "Teddy could do better. Mother terminally ill. He receives little help at home."

Third grade: "Teddy is a pleasant boy. Helpful, but too serious. Slow learner. Mother passed away end of the year."

Fourth grade: "Very slow but well behaved. Father shows no interest."

"Well, they passed him four times, but he will certainly repeat fifth grade! Do him good!" I said to myself.

And then the last day before the holidays arrived. Our little tree on the reading table sported paper and popcorn chains. Many gifts were heaped underneath, waiting for the big moment.

Teachers always get several gifts at Christmas, but mine that year seemed bigger and more elaborate than ever. There was not a student who had not brought me one. Each unwrapping brought squeals of delight and the proud giver would receive effusive thank-yous. His gift wasn't the last one I picked up. In fact it was in the middle of the pile.

Its wrapping was a brown paper bag and he had colored Christmas trees and red bells all over it. It was stuck together with masking tape. "For Miss Thompson—From Teddy."

The group was completely silent and I felt conspicuous, embarrassed because they all stood watching me unwrap that gift. As I removed the last bit of masking tape, two items fell to my desk. A gaudy rhinestone bracelet with several stones missing and a small bottle of dime-store cologne—half empty. I could hear the snickers and whispers and I wasn't sure I could look at Teddy.

"Isn't this lovely?" I asked, placing the bracelet on my wrist. "Teddy, would you help me fasten it?"

He smiled shyly as he fixed the clasp and I held up my wrist for all of them to admire. There were a few hesitant oohs and ahhs, but, as I dabbed the cologne behind my ears, all the little girls lined up for a dab behind their ears.

I continued to open the gifts until I reached the bottom of the pile. We ate our refreshments until the bell rang. The children filed out with shouts of "See you next year!" and "Merry Christmas!" but Teddy waited at his desk.

When they had all left, he walked towards me clutching his gift and books to his chest.

"You smell just like Mom," he said softly. "Her bracelet looks real pretty on you, too. I'm glad you liked it."

He left quickly and I locked the door, sat down at my desk and wept, resolving to make up to Teddy what I had deliberately deprived him of—a teacher who cared.

I stayed every afternoon with Teddy from the day class resumed on January 2 until the last day of school. Sometimes we worked together. Sometimes he worked alone while I drew up lesson plans or graded papers. Slowly but surely he caught up with the rest of the class. Gradually there was a definite upward curve in his grades.

He did not have to repeat the fifth grade. In fact, his final averages were among the highest in the class, and although I knew he would be moving out of the state when school was out, I was not worried for him. Teddy had reached a level that would stand him in good stead the following year, no matter where he went. He had enjoyed a measure of success and as we were taught in our education courses, "Success builds success."

I did not hear from Teddy until several years later when his first letter appeared in my mailbox.

Dear Miss Thompson,

I just wanted you to be the first to know. I will be graduating second in my class on May 25 from E____________ High School.

Very truly yours,
Teddy Stallard

I sent him a card of congratulations and a small package, a pen-and-pencil set. I wondered what he would do after graduation. I found out four years later when Teddy's second letter came.

> Dear Miss Thompson,
>
> I was just informed today that I'll be graduating first in my class. The university has been a little tough but I'll miss it.
>
> Very truly yours,
> Teddy Stallard

I sent him a good pair of sterling silver monogrammed cuff links and a card, so proud of him I could burst! And now—today—Teddy's third letter:

> Dear Miss Thompson,
>
> I wanted you to be the first to know. As of today I am Theodore J. Stallard, MD. How about that???!!!
>
> I'm going to be married on July 27 and I'm hoping you to come and sit where Mom would sit if she were here. I'll have no family there as Dad died last year.
>
> Very truly yours,
> Teddy Stallard

I'm not sure what kind of gift one sends to a doctor on completion of medical school. Maybe I'll just wait and take a wedding gift, but the note can't wait.

> Dear Ted,
>
> Congratulations! You made it and you did it yourself! In spite of those like me and not because of us, this day has come for you. God bless you. I'll be at that wedding with bells on!!!

The influence Miss Thompson had on Teddy is very well stated. Although she said in her last letter to Teddy, "in spite of those like me and not because of us," I believe, it was because of Miss Thompson and teachers like her that many students do in fact make it. I did.

The influence Miss Thompson had on Teddy is repeated in tens of thousands of classrooms. When teachers believe in students and act on that belief, students eventually believe in themselves.

Activity: A Teacher's Perception

1. Describe how Miss Thompson initially perceived Teddy and how those perceptions influenced her attitude, beliefs, expectations, and actions toward him.
2. Describe how Miss Thompson's perceptions, attitudes, beliefs, expectations, and actions changed after she received his Christmas present.
3. How will this story influence you?

After I finished reading this touching story, I remembered some of my own behaviors as a "new to the profession" teacher. My own initial teaching was similar to the way I was taught. I repeated mistakes that my teachers had made when I was a student.

I soon learned that my style of teaching was producing poor results both for my students and for me. When I changed my perceptions, as Miss Thompson did about Teddy, I became happier, and found teaching rewarding and enjoyable. My students did also. I realize that new teachers often learn to teach in one of these ways:

1. They teach the way they were taught with all the perceptions, beliefs, attitudes, and teaching practices.
2. They learn to teach during their student teaching experience. They model their teaching after their supervising teacher's style with its various teaching techniques and "tricks."
3. They observe what is valued in the halls and faculty lounge during their first teaching job. They observe the culture of the school and classrooms and what is practiced and not practiced, which greatly influences them.

SCHOOL CLIMATE AND CULTURE

Recently I had a conversation with my good friend Bill, a retired bank president and CEO, about education. He asked, "Why when you have a good principal or teacher, does magic seem to happen?" I told him that a good principal values his or her teachers and lets them know this. This results in better teacher performance. The same is true for teachers and students. With a good teacher, students get excited and perform better, for they also know they are valued.

We then discussed leadership—in schools, in banks, and in other settings—and we both agreed that the climate and culture a leader establishes is an incredibly important component of a successful organization. Sound knowledge and practices are necessary as well, but without a positive climate and culture, an organization cannot thrive. And for an organization to be truly successful, other components are necessary as well. A total framework must be in place, as well as solid underpinnings to ensure its structure.

The conditions necessary to create an effective school can be described by returning to the five key concepts discussed in chapter 8. In a school with a good culture:

- Everyone knows, understands, and is actively involved in achieving the school's *vision* and *mission*.
- Everyone knows and understands, and not only lives the school's beliefs but defends and achieves them.
- Educators create psychological needs–satisfying conditions for each other and for students. No one tolerates verbal abuse.
- Everyone acts professionally, and makes good decisions based on knowledge and compelling observations, and not merely on opinions.
- Everyone feels valued, respected, cared for, and trusted.
- Everyone is involved in making decisions, and problem-solving techniques are understood and used. When a problem exists, everyone works cooperatively to solve it and then respects the solution.

In a school with a good climate, the following climate factors are understood, implemented, and continually assessed for improvement:

Respect. Everyone in the school is respected and proud to be there. Staff would rather work in this school than anywhere else.

Caring. This school is a nice place to be for staff and students. They know they are cared about.

Involvement. There are procedures in place to involve all staff in the important decisions of the school. Everyone is involved in solving conflicts. Recall the exercise on setting the rules of the classroom with the students. See the last chapter.

Trust. Staff trusts administration and administration trusts staff. There is mutual trust and respect. Students trust their teachers to help them learn and students can be trusted to do the right thing.

Communication. There are effective communication procedures in place and no one feels slighted or left out. Everyone feels free to voice opinions without fear of reprisals. All students feel they can communicate effectively with their teachers and share their thoughts and ideas openly.

Morale. Everyone in this school feels enthusiastic and supportive of colleagues, students, the school, and its reputation. Everyone defends the school and shares openly in its accomplishments.

Activity: A Visit to Your School

If you invited me to visit your school or classroom, I would ask the following question: "What would you hope I would see and hear in your classroom, faculty lounge, and halls?" Perhaps you might say:

- I hope you will see children helping each other learn and not competing against each other for grades.
- I hope you will see teachers, administrators, and students trusting each other.
- I hope you will see and hear teachers in the faculty lounge talking positively about their school and their students.
- I hope you will see everyone respecting each other, involved in the decision making, and enthusiastic about their classroom and school.
- I hope you will see high expectations of all students and yet a caring teacher.
- I hope you will never see anyone being embarrassed or humiliated.
- I hope you will see good teaching and planning.

Here are two additional questions:

1. Will I see these in your school? If yes, provide evidence.
2. What else would you like me to see?

During the years I was superintendent of the Johnson City schools, thousands of educators and parents visited our schools each year. Visitors were always welcome and encouraged to visit any school and to talk to any teacher, student, and support staff. There were no restrictions. Each visitor had choices. We asked that they not disrupt class time while observing, but to wait until later to ask questions.

We were pleased to open our schools to observation and to explain what we were trying to accomplish. We explained our beliefs, our psychology, our knowledge base, and our teaching and classroom practices. These exercises were good for everyone. It made us better. If you think you know something, try explaining it to others.

We also reminded our visitors that no school or classroom is perfect and that they shouldn't expect perfection. They might observe faulty practices. They might see students misbehaving or even encounter some teachers who disagree with the direction of the district. We reminded them that they would see a real live school district and all of its strengths and weaknesses. They would see a school district always striving to be better. Improvement was our continuing emphasis.

We also pointed out some aspects of our district and its 2,800 students that visitors might want to observe. These included:

- Observe the culture of each school—what each school and its staff values.
- Observe students trusting their teachers by living within the boundaries of the mutually established rules. Observe teachers helping all students, especially those who have not yet achieved the expected learning outcomes.
- Observe teachers expecting their students to learn well and having high but achievable learning outcomes for all.
- Observe our stated beliefs in action. See, for example, if all students are included in the class activities.
- Observe that all major practices are based on best knowledge and compelling observations.
- Observe the psychological needs–satisfying conditions present in every classroom and in the school.
- Observe much joy and freedom present, with teachers happy to be there.
- Observe teachers using their own styles, personality, and ideas while still achieving the vision of the school.

- Observe the involvement of the support staff in creating the total culture of their school.
- Observe that most children are learning well and that students with special needs and students who often have difficulty learning do not stand out.
- Observe children volunteering freely, exploring ideas, and taking risks.
- Finally, observe teachers using well-defined teaching methods while still maintaining their individuality.

At the end of the day we would ask visitors to tell us their observations, to critique the time that they spent with us, and we would answer any questions not yet answered.

Having visitors was not easy. It took a great deal of our time. But the benefits of being so open and laying bare our thoughts, our beliefs, and our practices outweighed any inconvenience. If you think you understand something, talk about it. It is only when you try to articulate something that it becomes apparent how comfortable and familiar you are with the subject and how well you understand it. This happened to every member of our district. Having our school culture, schools, and staff assessed every week kept all of us focused and searching for ways to improve. It also validated what we were trying to accomplish.

Most visitors were a joy to have and we all learned from the visitation experiences. Some visitors, however, came to find fault or to look for dissent among staff members. We would tell these visitors that we would happily identify teachers who were not happy with our current practices. We were also more than willing to share our faults and weaknesses.

Art, a businessman from Ohio, called and asked if it was OK for him to visit our schools. The answer was obviously yes. He did. He chose the school he wanted to visit and was given freedom to roam and talk unescorted. At the end of his day-long visit, he returned to my office.

Art said that he asked the very first teacher he encountered the following question, "You don't want those kids with severe handicaps in your classroom, do you?" Art said the teacher quickly responded with, "Sir, I don't know who you are, but let me tell you, when we don't have these students in our class, we request them." Art observed the inclusion of all students including those assigned full-time to wheelchairs and those who couldn't walk or talk. He saw that they were treated like all other students.

With tears in his eyes, he told me that his reason for coming to Johnson City was to see the inclusion program in action. He couldn't believe what he was reading or hearing about our program. He confessed that his grandchild had severe multiple handicaps and had to leave the state of Ohio to get the necessary services that we were providing in our public schools.

For the climate and culture to be good and continue to get better, students must be learning well. These things go together. As the character Forrest Gump said, in the 1994 movie by the same name, "They go together like peas and carrots." They must be mixed. When students are learning well, the climate and culture get better. When the climate and culture are good, students learn better. As one gets better, the other also gets better. A spiral occurs, with the diameter of each spiral circle getting larger each time the spiral returns. Remember, most students will learn well when they have enough time, the climate and culture supports them and the staff, and high quality teaching occurs.

TEACHING AND LEARNING

Activity: Calculus for Educators

What if your state passed a new law that stated that all teachers and administrators must take and successfully pass Calculus 1 to continue employment? Our increasingly technological world was cited as the reason for this new emphasis on calculus.

That is the bad news. Now there is some good news. I will be your teacher and I want you to influence my teaching, practices, and attitude toward you. Tell me how I should teach this class so that you will:

1. Learn calculus.
2. Feel more comfortable.
3. Have less anxiety.

I have done this activity with teachers and administrators both here and abroad. Following are some of the answers I received:

- Don't make me feel stupid.
- Give me the time I need to succeed.
- Don't compare me with other students.

- Give me extra help when I need it.
- Be sure to review the math I need to be successful each day.
- Assure me that you will try to understand how scared I am to take this course and that you will do what is necessary for me to succeed.
- Don't let me fail but understand I will try.
- Use language I understand. I am not going to major in or teach math.
- Teach me the way I learn.
- I need to know why I should study calculus when I'll ever use it.
- I learn when a hands-on approach is employed.
- I need to see many examples because that is the best way to learn math.
- I need to discuss what I learn and even try to explain it to someone else.
- I learn by reading and listening.
- I need to have you be sure I learn before I try the homework. Do you give homework?
- Will you use assessment to help me learn? Provide correctives to my learning errors? Only give a grade after I learned well?
- I hope you will never embarrass me or be sarcastic.
- Finally, I hope you understand that I am scared and any feeling of failure will lead me to quit.

These are just some of the many comments I heard. All of them are fair and manageable. Some variables in teaching and managing we can control. Some are out of our control and while we may influence them, we can't control them. Don't spend most of your time trying to manage variables you can't control. Spend your time on variables that you can control.

Activity: Teachers' Feelings about Studying Calculus

Reflect on the comments in the previous activity and think of a course you are now teaching or would like to teach.

1. How might your students' feelings be similar to yours when they encounter difficult subject matter or are fearful of what you are teaching?
2. How might you use the advice you gave me as your teacher of calculus to help your students succeed?

Activity: Teaching as a Profession

Madeline Hunter, a respected educator, once posed a very interesting question to teachers: "What can you do as a teacher that someone not trained as a teacher can't do? What is unique about your profession?" (Hunter, 2004).

Imagine that you are asked to give a lecture to a class of twenty-five student teachers who are new to the profession about the process or science of teaching and learning. Your job is to tell them how to teach. Naturally, you should remind them about high expectations, proper perceptions, and caring about each student. You should also remind them about beliefs and choice theory psychology. With this in mind, describe an intentional instructional process that is rooted in the best educational knowledge and compelling observations.

Following is a brief but important discussion about those variables that a teacher is trained to influence and manage, but are not manageable by someone not trained as a teacher. This is not intended as a full discussion of the variables or science of teaching, but rather as a foundation designed to encourage you to take the ideas and build on them, on your own or as a team.

A well-defined instructional-process and curriculum-planning model will serve as a major and important guide in your teaching. One purpose of having an instructional process is to optimize students' learning. However, we must also be sure that we are intentionally aligning our curriculum, our teaching, and our assessment. An instructional process allows teachers to use all knowledge bases, as appropriate, within the process. A teacher can, and should, take knowledge bases like team teaching, cooperative learning, or teaching to different learning styles, and incorporate these bases into their instructional process.

My experience has shown me that wonderful knowledge bases have been developed by practitioners and university professors, but not one of them on its own is sufficient to get all students to learn well. That is the teacher's responsibility.

Staff creativity abounds within a well-defined, intentional instructional process because it not only provides direction but also allows individuals the freedom to use their creativity without compromising the freedom to create their own course learning goals, to decide on teaching materials, or to determine the outline of the curriculum. Academic freedom does not mean that teachers act independent of an instructional process. Teachers will discover that their freedom is enhanced when they have a framework and a process for instruction.

For the sake of discussion the instructional process is divided into six stages. While each stage will be discussed separately, they are not mutually exclusive.

AN INSTRUCTIONAL PROCESS

Stage One: Preparation for Success

This stage prepares all students for success, both in their attitude to learn and in their academic preparation to learn. As such, this stage is divided into two parts—attitudinal and academic readiness.

Attitudinal Readiness

Some students come to class with feelings ranging from extreme confidence to total despair. Think of how you felt when you thought that you would be required to take and pass a calculus course. For those with a math background, you probably felt extreme confidence. Others may have felt extreme despair. Feelings of students who were unsuccessful in previous learning situations must be considered, for previous failure or difficulty may cause fear of future failure.

Look at the advice you offered earlier on how to teach so that you would learn calculus, feel more comfortable, and have less anxiety. You said it was important to create a welcoming, supportive, and caring environment so you would be assured that your experience would be a positive one.

What if the teacher welcomes each student into the classroom every day, greets each one at the door, calls each one by name, and connects with each one personally? This will go a long way in setting the right conditions for students to have a positive attitude to learn. To further create a welcoming classroom and get students ready and willing to learn, the teacher should also be reassuring. Perhaps the teacher could offer some of the following comments:

- Everyone in this classroom will do well and I will provide enough time and explanation for that to happen.

- While you are gaining an understanding of new concepts and learning new skills, my assessments of how you are doing will be used only to help you get better and not for grading.
- I will guide your learning and act like an academic coach to ensure you learn. At this point no grades will be given.
- Speaking of grades, as long as you work hard, try to improve, and be responsible, you will not get low or failing grades. Under these conditions, no grade will be assigned until you earn a good grade. It's your call.
- If you take a test and don't do well, I will give you a second chance if you show evidence of work and effort. You must earn this privilege.
- In this class it is possible for everyone to do well since you will be competing with yourself for grades and no one else.
- In this classroom there is usually no one way or one answer. I would like you to try new ideas and take risks. This is a nonjudgmental classroom.
- Everyone in my class is accepted unconditionally and your self-worth is never in question. We are here to learn and succeed. My job is to help you.
- I encourage you to assess how well you are doing. You can even demonstrate to me you have learned using your own assessment technique. We will negotiate this.
- You will help create the rules of this classroom and all of us will live by those rules.
- There will never be sarcasm, humiliation, or blame. No one will ever fear failure for there will be none unless you choose it.
- In this classroom you will be actively involved in learning and I hope you find learning enjoyable.
- It will be my job to help you and guide your learning. It will be your job to study, learn, and be responsible because ultimately learning well is up to you.

Academic Readiness

Students cannot be expected to learn what the teacher is trying to teach if they are not academically ready. We can always blame previous teachers, the student's intelligence, or the student's lack of reading skills; however, none of these are acceptable as true reasons why some students aren't learning.

It is important for a child to be a good reader, but having said that, some students will have difficulty reading. A child may not see the letters or words others might see. There may be a neurological problem. A child may have a vision problem or in some cases be legally blind. There may be other reasons as well. But even so, all these children are quite capable of learning well. It may be that we have to use various nonreading methods, including nonreading tests, to compensate for these problems. Don't make reading the prerequisite for success. Teach using other methods so you can compensate for this problem, while still teaching the child to read.

Another nonacceptable reason I've heard elementary teachers use is "the child does not know his or her multiplication tables." While this may be true and the child can't remember the tables, we as teachers, must not wait until the child does. Compensate for this child. Give him or her a copy of the tables while you continue with the new lesson.

This is not to minimize the importance of learning multiplication tables. But some children, even "very bright" children, have difficulty with memorization. One of my good friends, a PhD chemist, with a very responsible, respected position in a major corporation always had difficulty retaining the multiplication tables. Compensate for a student's shortcomings while still working hard to teach them and make them into successful learners.

In spite of all the excuses we might hear, the major reason some students can't learn a lesson is that they don't remember the necessary academic prerequisites to be successful in the lesson that day. In this situation, there are three options that a teacher can employ to achieve success.

1. The teacher can spend several weeks reviewing what he or she thinks students should already know. This approach has limited impact and effectiveness because it happens too far in advance of when students will need to use or know those skills. After weeks of review, students may still forget this prerequisite material and will still not be prepared to learn each day's lesson. There are some benefits to this approach, but its long-term effectiveness is limited.
2. Remedial programs are another option, including remedial teachers, tutors, and/or after-school help, summer school, or repeating an entire course or year. All of these approaches have limited success and in many ways are ineffective. Some of these approaches may work for a limited number of students but they rarely solve the long-term problems. Just think of how you would view yourself as a learner if you were placed in a remedial class, had to go to summer school, were assigned a remedial

teacher, or repeated a course, or year. Think of how you would feel if you consistently didn't understand your teacher and then had to get remediation.

3. The third, and best, option is when teachers place their emphasis on the prevention of learning problems. They ask themselves how they can prepare students for success each day, for each lesson. They ask how they can give those students in need of correctives a head start in the next lesson. For example, perhaps in their after-school help sessions, they could preteach tomorrow's lesson going over that which is crucial for success. Perhaps special-needs students can have their teacher or aide prepare them for success tomorrow. Perhaps remedial teachers can become prevention teachers, preparing students for success each day.

All of this implies that a teacher has planned each lesson with specific learning criteria. This also implies that the teacher has determined the specific skills students need to succeed each day.

Ask yourself before you teach a lesson, what students must be able to recall, relearn, or learn before they can understand what is going to be taught. Oftentimes, this will occur to you while you are teaching. If so, make a note and be sure to use it in the future.

Activity

Answer the following questions:

1. How can you give those students who frequently need remediation a head start for the next lesson?
2. How can you preteach a lesson so students will be ready and prepared to learn?
3. What specific examples can you use that will help students who are encountering new material? Think of a learning outcome and then provide specific examples of prerequisites that students need in order to be successful. Perhaps using different examples, reviewing new vocabulary, reading the story ahead of time, or solving preliminary problems may be necessary to ensure success.

Following are comments from individual teachers about preparing students for success:

Jane. This was an area I never considered before. The prerequisite skills are a much better predictor of success than IQ or a student's ability to read. If students are ready to learn what you are going to teach them, they will learn. I am very intentional about deciding what kids need to know before I start teaching them.

Nancy. Make opportunities for students to review, relearn, or sometimes learn those prerequisite skills, especially in first grade. Before I begin to teach students how to tell time on the hour, I review recognizing numbers 1 to 12. This is crucial to understanding time. All teachers build time into their daily lesson for a short review of the necessary skills for students to be successful that day.

Cheryl. Assessing prerequisites is a great vehicle to review your planning and to be sure it is aligned. As an English teacher, I learned there were interdependencies of units that I initially didn't consider. For example, in writing, I ask students to be able to write a cause-and-effect pattern or a compare-and-contrast pattern. If they had already studied short stories that were written in this pattern, that would serve as a prerequisite for new learning with a little review.

Tim. I think there are numerous times that you can intentionally plan for prerequisites. During class, I build time for review. I am not talking large blocks of time, perhaps five or ten minutes. But this is a valuable five or ten minutes. Doing this has saved much time later.

Dan. Before I teach students how to add two algebraic fractions with unlike denominators, I review how to add two fractions with like denominators. I review how to factor whole numbers, how to find lowest common denominators, and how to add two numerical fractions with unlike denominators like $\frac{1}{2} + \frac{1}{3}$.

The prerequisite preinstructional stage prepares all students for success. Success is predictable if teachers really do a good job at this stage. When teachers get all students ready academically and attitudinally, teachers will teach more successfully, students will learn more successfully, and the need for remediation will be diminished.

This stage also creates an opportunity to mix students of various aptitudes (rate) and diverse learning needs. Students who need more time, are behind grade level in reading and math, or have special needs can be part of an age-appropriate classroom if this stage is handled effectively.

Students cannot be expected to learn well unless they possess the necessary prerequisites of the lesson. Therefore:

- Anticipate any learning problems students might encounter.
- Provide assistance and opportunities for students to recall, review, and relearn what they previously learned and perhaps forgot.
- Prepare students for success each day and assure them they will succeed if they put forth the effort.

Additional Prerequisites

Some students come to school from abusive homes where parents themselves have lost control. Some come from homes where parents are involved in a separation or a divorce and may be arguing. Some students come to school hungry. Some come with inadequate clothing or lack of sleep and with no one to help with homework. Some come to school without their basic psychological needs satisfied and are groping for survival.

While we must understand and even report gross negligence or abuse to authorities, we must also do what we can to help. These situations are quite difficult for educators, who realize how limited they often are in what they can do. One thing we can do is to do our very best to get these students to learn. School can serve as a stable place in their lives and also provide hope for their future. We must have high expectations for these students and we must help them to set high expectations for themselves. Getting them to learn well and succeed is a necessary first step.

We must also create a culture that allows these children to feel loved and accepted at school. When home is sometimes unsafe, schools can always be safe both physically and psychologically.

Stage Two: Student Attention

Madeline Hunter once said you can lead a horse to water but you can't make it drink. But you can sure salt the oats (Hunter, 2004). Stage two is dedicated to "salting the oats" so students will want to drink from the teacher's learning well.

This stage of the instructional process allows for as much imagination and creativity as the teacher wishes. This stage can be exciting or dull. It can hook children into wanting to learn or it can turn them off to learning. It can be active or passive. If this stage is conducted effectively, you will have students' attention and they will want to stick around for the lesson.

Have you ever walked out of a lecture or a class when you were a student and asked yourself or someone else, what was that all about? What were we supposed to learn? What should we know? This happened to me many times when I was studying graduate-school mathematics. I remember one course in particular. I attended the lecture, sat there quietly, and listened intently while a well-published professor lectured. He talked; I took notes, and then spent the next four days trying to determine what he said and what I should have learned.

I had few teachers or professors who ever captured my attention, helped me focus on what I was to learn, or told me how my learning was useful. They frequently left me wondering and spending much energy and time trying to determine what I should know.

Since many of my teachers did not provide enough focus, I tried to study everything in order to do well on tests. Once the tests were over, I promptly forgot everything I'd studied. I wasn't motivated to learn and I wasn't excited about the lesson. I also had teachers who would start every lesson with phrases like:

- Now listen up.
- Pay attention, this is important.
- Take your seats and take out your notebook.
- This will be on the test.

Did they think that these instructions were sufficient to get me ready to learn? Did they think I was motivated to learn or focus my attention on their lessons just because they told me to pay attention?

Activity: Focusing Student Attention

1. What can you do as a teacher to get students ready to learn, focus their attention, and get them interested and eager to learn what you are going to teach?

2. Choose a lesson you are expected to teach and come up with some ideas that will help focus student attention with one of your colleagues. Get some constructive comments.

To get the attention of students, you need to be clear about what they are expected to learn, why they need to learn it, and how well they are doing along the way. This approach helps remove any mystery from the learning process. Many teachers do this for every lesson while some do it for units or the course as a whole. Some teachers actually put the overview of the course on poster board so students can always determine where they are and where they are going. This approach not only shows students what is expected but also serves as a review. Once you get the attention of your students, you can expect the following benefits:

- Time will not be wasted.
- Everyone will get involved quickly and immerse themselves in the lesson.
- Students' imaginations will be captured.

Students will know the answers to the following questions:

- What am I going to learn?
- Why is this important to learn?
- How am I going to learn it?
- How will I know if I know it?
- What will come next?

I hope you'll notice that I employed this strategy throughout this book as I introduced each chapter. As I began each chapter, one of my main goals was to get and focus your attention. Following are comments from teachers about focusing and getting student attention:

Frank. When I first began to teach social studies, I did what my teachers did to me. Everything was a mystery. I had to guess what it was I was supposed to learn and what would be tested. Now I try to take the mystery out of learning and make everything very, very clear.

Cindy. When I wanted to get and focus student attention on learning the adjective unit, I put students' jackets and other personal belongings in a large plastic bag when the students were out of the room. When they returned, they were concerned when they didn't see their belongings. I soon told them that I found all the missing belongings in a plastic bag but I didn't know which ones were theirs. I asked them to please tell me what was missing. "My coat is missing." one student said. So, I took a coat from the bag and gave it to her. She said, "No, my coat is pink." So I gave her a pink coat. She said, "You still gave me the wrong coat." I told her to just take it. After all students had the wrong items, I asked, "What is the problem here? I gave you a jacket, a lunch pail, or your missing item." They then began to explain in detail a description of their missing items. I wrote all the descriptors on the board. They soon realized that they could get what they wanted if they described their possessions in detail. They now had a reason for learning about adjectives. They were now focused on the unit, and had a list of adjectives on the board. This was more effective than simply saying, "Today we will study adjectives."

Tim. I think focusing student attention may be the most creative part of teaching. This is a transition stage. First you get their attention, show them what is to be learned, perhaps for the lesson, unit, or even the course, then use this to show students where they are in the learning process and where they are going. While teaching American history, I did something that was unexpected. I got dressed up as a typical nineteenth-century farmer and showed tools and artifacts of that period. Many students identified the tools and artifacts since their parents or grandparents had collected some of these antiques. Much discussion took place about the economics of farming. Students realized how difficult it would be to till their own garden with those tools, let alone plow many acres. They came to realize how difficult it was to support a family with small farms. They verbalized how farm work was transformed from manual to machine labor. They were even able to make the connection between computers and technology replacing workers and large farm equipment replacing farmers.

Cheryl. While teaching a twelfth-grade elective on expository writing, I needed to find a way to get students motivated for the entire course and not just the unit. Before the students entered the room, I placed the names of different types of writing on the board: narrative, descriptive, expository, and comparisons and contrasts. I informed the students that we were going to start by seeing how many writing ideas they had using the different types of writing. They moaned. I said that we were going to do this as a group. They gave a sigh of relief. I said that we were going to brainstorm ideas for topics they could write about. I said there are no wrong answers, so let your mind be open. Most students came to class feeling they didn't have anything they could write about and had no ideas. After our brainstorming activity, twenty-four students filled two boards with ideas. It was a phenomenal list with some good ideas and some not so good. But no judgments were made. From this list, each student checked those ideas that might be of interest to him or her. By doing this exercise, students became involved and knew where they were going. They were excited because they now had good ideas for topics to write about.

Stage Three: Initial Instruction

> *If the teacher is indeed wise, he does not bid you enter the house of wisdom, but rather leads you to the threshold of your mind.*
>
> —Kahlil Gibran

If the teacher is wise, he or she does not treat students as vessels to be filled or as zipper heads to be unzipped and filled with knowledge.

If the teacher is wise, he or she becomes the academic coach, guiding, directing, and helping students make the necessary adjustments so learning takes place. The teacher does not do the learning for the students but engages them as a team member in the learning process.

As long as students view the teacher as the one responsible for their learning and not themselves, little "real" learning will take place. Students will only study to pass a test.

But when students are involved in and responsible for their learning, when they participate in discussions, use their intended learnings, and apply these immediately, they will remember. When they explain what they have learned and teach others, they will learn in depth, gain a better understanding, and be able to retain their knowledge longer.

In short, most students don't remember much from what they hear. They do remember when they participate in their learning and when their teacher employs many and varied learning modes.

Activity

Take a moment and reflect on your own best way or ways to learn. Do you learn best when you hear a lecture? When you read? When you participate with others? When you discover and explore on your own? When you use your knowledge in a practical way? Or when you use some combination of the above? Record your thoughts as a reminder of how you learn.

When we understand that there are faster learners, slower learners, and different learners and we teach to accommodate all kinds of learners, then all students will learn well. This assumes that you've prepared all students for success by considering varied learning rates and styles.

I have asked many teachers when they successfully learned what they are now teaching. I thought I had a good understanding of mathematics when I first began to teach. However, as I explained some difficult concepts to my students, I got new insights that I didn't have before. I realized that I was learning as I was teaching and that perhaps I should structure my lessons so students could engage in small-group or team discussions and be given opportunities to teach and learn from each other. If I learned when I explained, why not let them explain and learn that way as well?

Let's pretend that you are now ready to teach a lesson. You have only one chance to maximize student understanding and learning of new material. How can you design your instruction to get it?

Think of how you learn best. Think of students in your school or students you knew when you were in school. Look at all the different types of learners. Some of them learn best when the work is practical. These are the students who like to tinker, build, and create with their hands. They like to experiment and explore. Teachers would sometimes say of these students, "They are good with their hands," implying that they are not good with their minds. But how can hands create without a wonderful mind directing them? Many students who learn this way have been convinced that they can't learn and some give up and drop out of school.

Then there are those students who like to learn in small groups in which all students contribute and learn with and from each other. If team learning is well structured and students don't just socialize and share ignorance, this approach is very effective and appeals to many students.

Still other students like to perform in front of their peers and be the center of attention. This is how they learn best. They like to write, direct, and perform. Others like to see the whole picture before learning the parts while others like to generalize from the parts. Many in the teaching profession liked to listen to a good lecture, take notes, perhaps read the text, study hard, and perform well on written tests. They were successful this way, so they, in turn, employed this approach in their own teaching. These teachers must remember, however, that not all students learn this way.

Some Teaching Strategies

During the initial instruction stage, a teacher should design and execute teaching strategies that appeal to a variety of learning modes. Some well-crafted lectures or explanations are very important, as are some well-structured small-group and team learning strategies as well as some well-planned practical hands-on applications. And, where appropriate, some activities where students can demonstrate their learning are also important.

Focusing on how students learn is far more important than concentrating on how teachers teach, although teaching and learning are best served when considered in tandem. Furthermore, by being exposed to different modes of learning, students may develop new learning preferences.

But thinking of placing all those learning modes into a single lesson is not practical or even possible. Instead, think of how you can get some of these approaches into a lesson and then vary the approaches in subsequent lessons. Try to get two different approaches in every lesson. Do your best but be sensible.

A solid, concise, clear, and complete lecture is very effective. However, lectures are even more effective if followed by other approaches. Remember, those in the classroom who are most active will probably do the most learning. Learning is not a spectator sport. It is a dynamic process. Following are comments from teachers about initial instruction:

Cheryl. During initial instruction we have to pretend that we have one chance to maximize student understanding. How can we best get our points across to our students? It is easy to get involved in what we call bird walking. Have you ever noticed how birds walk in the snow? They never go in a straight line. During the initial instruction, get as close to that straight line of instruction as possible and avoid bird walking. Not every lesson is going to have many and varied approaches but being aware that students learn differently and trying to include these different styles in our teaching approach will result in a much greater chance of reaching more of our students.

Paul. In a unit on poetry, I explain how poets make use of the technique of repeating sounds to make their poems more interesting or to enhance the mood of a poem. I define alliteration. Students then read examples of poetry that emphasizes alliteration, such as "Ickle Me, Pickle Me, Tickle Me Too" by Shel Silverstein (Silverstein, 2004). Individual students have an opportunity to read the poem aloud and perform it. In small groups, students discuss the repeating sounds of various other poems using alliteration. Then each group will determine if it was effective or not. If they like it, they tell why. If they don't, they also tell why. Each of the small learning teams creates a simple alliteration story to share with the entire class. They do this by brainstorming a list of words that are composed of repeating sounds.

Jane. Every time I get to initial instruction, I think of how I can get all students involved and use various learning modes. I was determined not to be totally teacher directed. I may get a lot of satisfaction from being the main star of the show, but not a lot of learning is going on. I found that the more students participate, talk, and are involved, the more they learn and retain. Every single day I make sure students have opportunities to discuss what they are learning rather than just listening. In my class all students have partners to discuss what they think they heard me saying and what it means. This is where students learn a great deal. It's here where adjustments are made and any misinterpretations or misunderstandings of the lesson are corrected.

Cheryl. It is so hard to break my old habit of dispensing information—to go as fast as I could. I was always watching the clock tick away and I was trying to beat the clock with information. But then I decided to make students work at least as hard as I do each day. I always say that to myself and it helps me make my initial instruction more diverse. I have workshops for my students, but in my classroom, workshop means the students do the work.

Summary of Student Involvement Activities

1. Create small learning teams.
2. Form student partners.
3. Have students teach and explain to other students.
4. Implement brainstorming sessions.
5. Initiate role-playing.
6. Have students read aloud.
7. Have students create examples.
8. Form student debate teams.
9. Structure event-, theme-, and issue-driven learning. Students can work in learning teams, individually, or with partners.
10. Encourage student-directed investigations.

In conclusion, pay attention to the following issues for initial instruction:

- Maximize students' understanding of new ideas and concepts during the initial instruction.
- Take the opportunity to get most students to learn well in the least amount of time.
- Vary how you teach by considering the various ways students learn. Use at least two modes of instruction.
- Intentionally align teaching, learning goals, and assessment.
- Plan well.
- Involve students actively in the learning process.
- Use team learning strategies.

Stage Four: Guided Practice and Adjustments

Much time and energy is wasted when students go home and don't know what they have learned and are not sure how to do their homework. Even more time is wasted when the teacher waits until students take a test to assess how well they have learned.

When students do their homework and practice incorrectly, they are reinforcing mistakes. They then have to unlearn. When students don't do well on a test, teachers correct the learning errors and retest. Most teachers would say this is a difficult and even unproductive process.

While the previous stages of the instructional process will help avoid many problems, it is in stage four that the teacher sees firsthand what students have learned and can identify those students who still need further explanation. All of this is done quite informally during guided practice activities. The teacher circulates, observes, listens, asks questions, and then makes the necessary adjustments and corrections to any misconceptions.

During this stage, students are also helping other students to make adjustments and corrections. While doing this, students are reinforcing their own learning and making their own adjustments. Remember how much you learned the first time you taught. All of this learning, practicing, and adjusting are done in a nonthreatening environment.

There are a few guidelines that must be followed during this guided practice and adjustment stage:

1. Guided practice and adjustments are an integral part of initial instruction and not a separate activity. They are intertwined continuously throughout the instructional process.
2. All instructional stages, including this stage, are aligned to what teachers want students to *know* and *do*.
3. This stage is crucial because this is when teachers can determine how successful the previous stages have been. Do students really know and understand? Have they learned what the teacher expected? Has the teacher done a good job in preparing students for success, getting and focusing their attention, and providing initial instruction?
4. The guided practice and adjustments stage must be short, intense, and interactive. It is in this stage of the instructional process that the teacher reinforces initial instruction and corrects any misunderstandings. The teacher ensures that any independent practice and learning will be done correctly. The teacher ensures that all students will do well on formal tests.

Following are comments from teachers about guided practice and adjustment:

Nancy. I look at the guided practice and adjustment stage as an evaluation of my initial instruction. How well did I do? Have my students learned what I want them to learn? Have my learning and practice strategies been effective or must I revise my planning and teaching? I think the guided practice and adjustment stage was frequently overlooked. I went from initial instruction directly to independent practice and homework without knowing whether or not students had in fact really learned what I wanted them to learn.

Tim. I view this stage as one of participation and intervention. I think it's a time when the teacher is very intentional and deliberate in planning the lesson. It's a time for students to share their ideas and verbalize their learnings. There are many ways to have guided practice. Students can practice some skill you just taught. This would be a very short activity. This can be done independently, with a partner, or small group. In math, for example, let's say you just taught how to factor numbers and you want to see if they know it. You give them a problem or two to do and you can check their knowledge immediately.

Cheryl. The simplest example is a teacher who is using a textbook lesson and a textbook exercise. I am thinking like an English teacher teaching a grammar lesson, where there are twenty questions. Instead of finishing the lesson and sending students home to do the twenty, I do the first five with them so we can correct any misunderstandings. I then have a large group discussion before we proceed. The students do the next five at their seats. I monitor by walking around the room to see how they are doing. I am now correcting their mistakes and guiding them to success. Students are letting me know if they need any help or clarification. Independent practice at home should not be any more difficult than the guided practice that was done in class. Guided practice must be short and intense and must complement the lesson. Guided practice gives students a head start for independent practice and homework. Students go home knowing they can do the homework successfully and have some of it done before going home.

Tim. The guided practice and adjustment stage allows both the teachers and students time to self-assess. Students question whether they have an understanding of what was taught. Teachers question whether they provided an adequate explanation. Lots of trust is needed in this stage. Students must trust their teacher and confess when they need help or have questions. Teachers must trust students to ask when they don't know something, to work with their peers, and to make good use of this time. In this stage, teachers and students are assessing the teaching and the learning.

Did students learn and did the teacher give good explanations? Correcting both teaching and learning is done in this stage. It is a cooperative and trusting stage. All are committed to the same purpose—student learning.

In conclusion, students must be given the opportunity to practice both the content and skills they have learned. During guided practice, the following should take place:

Conduct informal assessment. Determine whether students have learned.
Reteach students in need. Vary teaching style.
Create group or independent guided practice experiences.
Assess teaching and planning.

Stage Five: Summary and Closure

Before students leave the classroom each day, have them provide a summary and closure of the lesson or unit. If students do the talking and provide the summary, they will remember what they have learned longer.

Get the students' attention, focus their learning, get them involved during initial instruction where they do a great deal of work, make adjustments during guided practice, and then have them verbalize or write about what they have learned. Perhaps you can ask your students, "What did you learn today in this class?" Make a list of their responses on the board. Perhaps you want your students to keep journals containing and summarizing what they have learned. Perhaps you want your students to share their understandings with other students. Perhaps you want them to react to what they learned and to share their observations and feelings in a well-structured way.

Closure and summary can be done individually, in small groups, or as an entire class, but the key is having the students provide the summary.

Closure summaries do not occur only at the end, they can also occur at the beginning of a lesson or during a lesson. It is good to summarize many times during the course of a lesson or unit. It calls attention to what students should be learning. If they missed something during initial instruction or guided practice, they can get it during closure. This is a good instructional technique.

Encourage students to share their journals or their summary with their parents. This is a good home activity to keep parents informed and involved in what students are learning. Not only will a summary and closure activity reinforce learning or be used to introduce the new lesson, but, hopefully, when parents ask their children, "What did you learn today?" the children won't reply, "Nothing."

In summary, it is important and essential to summarize and bring closure to each lesson and unit. You may want your students to do some of the following:

- Keep a journal and summarize what they have learned.
- Share their learning with other students.
- Share their learning with the entire class.
- Summarize the previous day's learning at the beginning of a new lesson.

Stage Six: Assessments and Testing

All assessments must be intentionally aligned with what the teacher expects students to *know* and be able to *do*. This learning criteria must be clear to all students. There must be no surprises.

Teachers then need to use the instructional process to teach what is expected and stated. Teachers should not teach one concept and test something else. If they teach a concept, they must test whether students have learned that concept. If the teacher expects students to learn a body of information and skills, they must teach and test those skills.

The alignment of learning criteria, instruction, guided practice, and testing are critical in getting all students to learn. There is ample evidence that alignment will help all students to learn well.

Some educators do not align but there are no good reasons for this. Learning will only improve with alignment. A pilot is taught how to fly a plane and the test is to see if he or she can fly it. Pilots expect to be tested on what was taught and not on something else. Only in education do we think that alignment is cheating. Even with state-mandated tests, many times teachers have to guess what will be tested. Students in our schools should be provided the courtesy of alignment.

This is not a recommendation for teaching the test. It is a recommendation to design your curriculum using the know-and-do planning process. List your learning criteria, expect your students to learn it, teach it, and then test to see if they do. This is what is really meant by teaching to the test—teach the learning criteria and test it.

With alignment your results will be rewarding. This is especially true when students are involved in understanding and skills. Perhaps you must differentiate your expectations and tests. I expect some students to learn more quickly than others and have a greater depth of understanding. As I said earlier, faster learners need to have opportunities to explore in greater depth the skills outlined in the *do* section of the know-and-do model.

Perhaps you can also differentiate ways to assess the depth of understanding of faster learners, not so much to get a grade, but to let students know how well they are doing. Use the descriptors of each skill area to assess the learning. This type of learning and testing will be expected of students when they go to college. They need these experiences.

I know that not all professors will align the expected learnings, their instruction, and their testing. Some even want their students to guess what will be tested. However, this is not a good reason for us not to be helpful to all of our students. We won't prepare students for college by making learning and testing a mystery. We must do our job well and the rest will take care of itself.

Some students who have experienced the alignment process report that they are able to influence this practice with their college professors. One example comes to mind. A professor at a local university gave a test where almost everyone did poorly. Naturally, he should have known this before he gave the test, but he didn't. He gave the test papers back to the class and said, "None of you did well on this test and if I were to give you the grade you earned, you would all get Cs, Ds, and Fs." He continued, "Don't worry, I'll mark on the curve." One of his students, he reported, asked, "Does that mean we now know it?"

The professor, a friend of mine, said that this insightful question changed his thinking and that he soon began to align his curriculum, instruction, and testing.

In an ideal school, all assessments and tests are aligned to a predetermined set of learning criteria derived from the know-and-do model. There are no surprises when students take a test. They know that the teachers followed all the stages of the instructional process and that they are prepared to be successful.

In an ideal school, there are many varied and different forms of testing. While the traditional paper-and-pencil test can be used to measure performance, alternative modes of testing including more natural or creative ones are encouraged. Projects, reports, small learning team reports, discussions, speeches, and written papers are just a few of the ways students can demonstrate their understanding and skills. With your permission and guidance, students can be given the responsibility to create their own assessments.

Also, consider not allowing students to take a test before you think they are ready. Perhaps you can use homework as a condition to take the test. But in any event, it is the students' responsibility to provide evidence that they are ready to take the test. This approach also reduces the need for retesting later on. This is a good message to send to students. It is your responsibility to prepare yourself and to show evidence of readiness to be tested.

But before a student who has not taken the test with the rest of the class or who needs to take a retest is given it, he or she must provide evidence of work. An oral exam, completed homework with a demonstration of understanding, or another type of evidence must be provided. Following are comments from teachers about assessments and testing:

Elaine. I feel that if we have done our job well in the previous stages of the instructional process, it is now that we certify that learning has taken place. This is the stage where students get the results that they are successful. If we do not get good results, I will look at how well I did as a teacher. I will be asking myself questions about the previous stages:

- Did I align my teaching to the learning criteria and assessment?
- Did I prepare students adequately for success?
- Did I provide for many ways of learning in the initial instruction?
- Did I have good guided practice and did I make the necessary adjustments?

Gene. I try to never give a test until I am as sure as I can be that every student in my class can get 100%. They know what to study and they know what will be tested. They also know that I have done everything and they have done everything possible to learn. For me, the test is just the icing on the cake. It's all baked, all ready, and all we have to do is put the icing on it.

Sandy. Sometimes a student will come to me and say I am not ready to take the test. I have had students who "bluffed" their way through the instructional process. I thought I was assessing well in guided practice but sometimes a student gives the impression that he or she understands, and

I believe it. But when a student comes to me and says I am not ready, I ask them, why not? I won't just accept "I'm not ready." When I was new to the process, I got the excuse, "Well, I was busy last night and I didn't have a chance to study so I think I'll take the test later." I thought, at first, it was my responsibility to allow students to do this. I was creating a mess for myself. I was giving the students a license to be irresponsible. I do not accept these types of excuses anymore. Sometimes students will let me know when they are not ready and I have observed that they haven't learned yet. They don't take the test. Sometimes I say to one or two students in my class, "You are not ready and let me tell you why. You were absent a great deal and I have no evidence that you are prepared. Perhaps you just need a little more time." I make the judgment. I always let students know that I am assessing the learning that's taking place and not them. I always remind students of this.

Larry. Basically, there is a mutual understanding that before a student takes a test, certain understandings are in place. Traditionally, teachers have tested students to see if they have learned or not. That doesn't work because several weeks have already passed before the teacher knows that students aren't learning. I know how well students are learning and most of the time the test is just a validation of their learning for them and me.

Paul. If a student simply refuses to do the work, including homework, he or she is not afforded an opportunity to take a test. Students must demonstrate a responsibility. Don't wait until you give a test to address the problem; do it right away. If the problem is not resolved quickly and the student continues to be irresponsible, notify the parents quickly and seek their help. Distinguish between an attitudinal problem and an academic problem. If it's an academic problem, then it's a matter of working with these students on a daily basis to try to resolve the lack of knowledge. If it's an attitudinal problem and you have done all that is possible using choice theory ideas, and the student simply refuses to do the work, then why in the world would you give the student the right to take the test?

Elaine. If students know exactly what is expected of them throughout the unit, and we provide a sound instructional process as presented, and we are consistent with our practices and requirements of the unit, I think most problems will disappear.

Pat. As a parent, I have had a child who decided not to learn the first time the test was given even though the stages of instruction were followed. He soon learned that it was lots of extra work to take the retest. He learned that it was easier to do it right the first time. Sometimes you have to learn the hard way. It was a valuable lesson.

In summary, many students will have learned well what is expected by the time they get to the test. Some will not. Therefore:

- Determine how well these students have learned.
- Correct any misunderstandings.
- Reteach those not doing well using different teaching–learning strategies.
- As a last resort, alter your expectations for those who continue to have difficulty, but never for those who won't or choose not to learn.
- Give tests and retests to those who earn the privilege of taking them.

CONCLUSION

Very good instruction and learning will occur when teachers:

1. Create a positive climate and culture in their classroom and school.
2. Provide the proper amount of time students need to learn (aptitude).
3. Review, recall, or reteach knowledge students have previously learned and perhaps forgotten. This is necessary if students are to learn. Prepare students for success each day.
4. Get and focus student attention on what is to be learned.
5. Align all instruction with stated and expected course or subject, unit or chapter, and lesson learning criteria.
6. Provide the initial instruction to maximize student understanding. Ensure that this instruction includes various teaching and learning modes.
7. Make the necessary adjustments and correctives during guided practice. Assess and correct all learning errors.
8. Align tests to the stated learning criteria. Be sure students are ready to do well on the tests before they are given.
9. Manage time in such a way that most students can learn at least at the competent level within a prescribed time frame.
10. Carefully plan curriculum so that course or subject, unit or chapter, and lesson learning criteria are clear and measurable.

Chapter Eleven

Curriculum Planning

If we fail to plan, then we plan to fail.

Focus Questions

1. What advice would you give a new-to-the-profession teacher about how to plan a unit and lesson so that most students will learn?
2. What advice would you give so that most students will be challenged, and even the faster learners will be studying in depth?
3. If students "understood" what you wanted them to learn, how would you plan your subject's curriculum? How would students demonstrate their understanding? How would students use their knowledge?

Planning is the most essential element in the teaching and learning process. Only when teachers plan with a clear vision of what students should *know* and *do* can they intentionally create the conditions for success.

Seven planning tools and corresponding examples are presented in this chapter, in addition to two planning supplements. The planning tools are:

- Acquiring knowledge
- Creating course learning goals
- Outlining course by units
- Planning units
- Acquiring skills
- Determining lesson learning goals
- Writing lesson plans

And the planning supplements are:

- Planning for your substitute
- Using student record forms

Planning is a process and a journey that takes much time and effort. It will become overwhelming if you try to do all of your planning for the year at one time or if you have more than two or three preparations. But to be effective as a teacher you still must plan. The better the planning, the more effective the teaching and learning.

You can do only so much planning without burning yourself out. But with a format and planning tools, you can start the process and continue to build over time. Use the tools in this chapter to personalize your own planning and curriculum as well as to plan for the state and local standards. Use the tools to meet your own needs. Feel free to modify any of the planning tools to make them more useful for you and the subjects you are teaching.

Using the know-and-do model presented earlier will yield some immediate results when applied to even one part of a course, unit, or lesson. When you use the process to map out the entire course, you will experience dramatic results. Record your best thinking and revise your planning on a continual basis as new and better ideas occur. In a few years you will have your course(s) well thought out and only minor revisions will be needed.

The tools presented in this chapter will guide the planning for your course, chapters, units, and for your daily lessons. The tools will also help you manage your time, plan for students with diverse needs, for your substitute, and for the teaching process.

You can start with your course, unit, or lesson—the choice is yours. However, the know-and-do model ties all the pieces together. It gives clear direction for planning by providing a detailed framework for that which all students are expected to know (content) and to be able to do (skills). It brings a continuity of planning from the course learning goals to the daily lesson plan. It integrates content and skills within and across different courses. It intentionally prepares students to have a comprehensive understanding of each subject and for success in school, further education, and a productive life.

The planning tools will help you plan effectively, intentionally, and efficiently to incorporate national, state, and local standards into all lessons. This process will cut your planning time and help you to manage time.

Finally, the key word in the teaching, learning, and planning process is alignment. Align your teaching and student learning to what you want your students to know and do. Align your planning to include all desired learning goals and standards. Align your goals across disciplines and teachers. Align your attention and efforts to what is required and important. Don't wander; be intentional.

When planning, teaching, and assessment are carefully aligned to the desired learning goals, slower learners will learn very well and even approach the rate of learning of faster learners. This will result in better time and class management.

While you must align your planning, teaching, and assessments to the standards of your school and state, this does not mean that only these standards are included in your planning and teaching. This does mean, however, that the required standards must be included. National standards exist in virtually every discipline and were created by the National Councils. They serve as learning guidelines for our nation. These national standards provide a broad view of what all students should know and be able to do upon graduation. It is important for all K–12 teachers, and even higher education educators, to become familiar with these standards in order to understand the long-term goals for their students.

Activity: National Standards

Obtain copies of the national standards for each of the subjects you are teaching. These are provided by the National Councils for each subject. Get familiar with them.

State standards and assessments have been created using the national standards as a guide. The state standards are the blueprint from which teachers plan their courses, units, and daily lessons. Across our country, teachers are faced with the job of aligning their curriculum to their state and local standards to ensure all standards are taught. Teachers in every grade level and in every subject play a role in the performance of students on state and local assessments.

Activity: State and Local Standards

Obtain copies and review your state and local standards and assessments. This will help you improve your understanding of what is required for all students to be successful.

State and national standards are often presented in the language of what students should know and do. Therefore, this chapter will help you make sense of these standards, plan to incorporate all of them into your units and lessons, plan for teaching and learning, and plan for special circumstances. I have taken the liberty of presenting some state standards and some of the language used in them. Notice the similarities of the words from different subjects and try to see where they align with the know-and-do model.

Art. Students will respond critically to a variety of works in the arts, connecting the individual work to other work and to aspects of human endeavor and thought. Students will actively engage in. . . . Students will develop an understanding of. . . .

Social Studies. Students will use a variety of intellectual skills to demonstrate their understanding of major ideas, eras, themes, developments, and turning points in world history and examine the broad sweep of history from various perspectives. Students will use a variety of intellectual skills to demonstrate their understanding of. . . . (This statement is repeated many times.)

Mathematics, Science, and Technology: Analysis, Inquiry, and Design. Students will use mathematical analysis, scientific inquiry, and engineering design, as appropriate, to pose questions, seek answers, and develop solutions.

Mathematics. Students will understand mathematics and become mathematically confident by communicating and reasoning mathematically, by applying mathematics in real-world settings, and by solving problems through the integrated study of number systems, geometry, algebra, data analysis, probability, and trigonometry.

Science. Students will understand. . . .

Technology. Students will apply technological knowledge and skills to design, construct, use, and evaluate. . . .

English Language Arts. Students will listen, speak, read, and write for information and understanding. Students will read and listen to oral, written, and electronically produced texts and performances from American and world literature; relate texts and performances to their own lives; and develop an understanding of the diverse social, historical, and cultural dimensions of the texts and performances represented by speakers and writers. Students will use oral and written language for self-expression and artistic creation. Students will listen, speak, read, and write for critical analysis and evaluation. As listeners and readers, students will analyze experiences, ideas, information, and issues presented by others using a variety of established criteria.

Career Development and Occupational Studies. Students will demonstrate how academic knowledge and skills are applied in the workplace and other settings. Students will be knowledgeable about the world of work. . . .

As you can see, the standards in all subjects place a great deal of emphasis on students' understanding the subjects they are studying as well as students' demonstrating that they can use these understandings. What is lacking however are discussions of what is acceptable to show understanding, how to plan for it, and how to include the skills into units and lessons.

It is important to have standards and these must be assessed. But it is equally important and critical to develop the means to translate standards into action. An abundance of assessments will not do it.

A COMPREHENSIVE FORMAT: ACQUIRING KNOWLEDGE AND SKILLS

With a comprehensive format and with all teachers in all disciplines using this format as a guide, time will be conserved, teaching will be more effective and efficient, and all teachers will contribute to students' learning what is required. Students will get a comprehensive education instead of learning isolated information. Planning becomes less overwhelming and teachers get a better understanding of how to get all students prepared to understand and do well with the standards.

Equally important, the vision, discussed in chapter 5, will be achieved and students will be prepared for either the world of work or for further education.

While the basic ideas of the know-and-do model were presented earlier, a review and extension are important.

Acquiring Knowledge *(Know)*

The continuing debate of what is important for students to know has been raging for a long time. Some educators place a great deal of emphasis on students' learning information and facts. They are right. Some educators place a great deal of emphasis on students' using and applying their knowledge. They are right. Still some educators place a great deal of emphasis on students' understanding the content. They are also right.

Why do we even have this debate or the vast swings in emphasis? To be fully educated and be prepared for a bright future with much knowledge, students need information and facts. By themselves, however, what does one do with them? On the other hand, one cannot think well or create without them.

Students, except in rare cases, should be able to use their information and facts in applied situations. While some students may be interested only in theory and not how their subject is used, most students want to use their knowledge. Most advances in society are obtained by using knowledge.

For really educated people, it is important that they have a conceptual framework and an understanding of the subjects they are studying. Students will remember content longer when it is taught conceptually and for understanding. With an understanding, new ideas and knowledge are developed. But what does it mean to teach a subject for understanding? Most educators I have talked to seem to avoid the very difficult question of what it means to understand the subject they are teaching. They might say, "I want my students to explain it to me, to use it, to compare and contrast ideas, to write a paper, give a speech, or to solve some problems." These are all skills, and very important ones, but they avoid the question of what it means to understand the subject and to have students learn their subject completely.

Teachers often confuse understanding a concept with using or applying the concept. They want their students to explain, write, or even give a presentation of some concept. This shows what students will do with the concept. It does not answer the understanding of the concept question; it answers the skill question.

Activity: Attributes of Understanding a Concept

Take your subject and some concept or idea from the subject and ask, "If I taught this concept for understanding, what would I teach?" For example, what does it mean to understand a social problem, an economic issue, fractions, or a novel? What are the parts that contribute to an understanding? What are the attributes or components of understanding the particular concept?

When conducting a series of seminars for elementary teachers, I asked, how many of them knew what a fraction was? All raised their hand. I then asked, "If you taught students to understand fractions so they would get a comprehensive knowledge of fractions, what are all the parts, attributes, or components that contribute to their understanding?" No one volunteered. No one said they could explain what understanding fractions means even though many of them were teaching fractions. I suggested that we develop the concepts of fractions by brainstorming, and grouping and labeling all ideas associated with fractions that came to our minds. I asked them to tell me any word that came to their mind when they thought of the word *fraction*. I said there were no wrong answers and no judgments would be made. Another teacher recorded the responses.

We ended the brainstorming session with over eighty words and ideas. We then grouped these words and ideas in like categories and then labeled each category. The following six structures or parts emerged. There may be others or you may wish to create your own "understanding" framework. There is no one way. The following structures, attributes, or indicators emerged from our discussions.

1. Meaning
    A. Vocabulary
        1. Numerator
        2. Denominator
        3. Proper fractions
        4. Improper fractions
        5. Mixed fractions
    B. Part of a whole
    C. Part of a set
    D. Division
    E. Ratio
    F. Symbols
2. Procedures
    A. Operations
        1. Addition
        2. Subtraction
        3. Multiplication
        4. Division
    B. Finding equivalent fractions
    C. Comparing fractions
    D. Finding least common denominators
    E. Finding greatest common factors
    F. Finding least common multiples
3. Applications
    A. Problem solving
    B. Probability
    C. Measurement
    D. Ratio
    E. Proportion
4. Interrelationships
    A. To other real numbers
    B. To equivalent fractions
    C. To decimals
5. Properties
    A. Closure
    B. Identity
    C. Cumulative

   D. Associative
   E. Distributive
6. Automaticity
   A. Mental drill
   B. Drill and practice
   C. Cumulative reviews

This is a brief discussion of what it means to understand fractions. All six categories are important, but not all students need to know all within the categories. Some students, for example, may study the properties of the real number system while others will spend more time on the operations. It is a good way to challenge the faster learner while others may be concentrating on the required curriculum. Some math and science teachers use the six structures developed for fractions to teach any math or science concept.

STRUCTURES OF DISCIPLINES

All subjects, like the one above, have structure and that structure should be developed by you and your colleagues. This is crucial if your students are going to learn how to study your discipline. Remember as you do this, there is no one structure and the structures can vary by teachers and discipline.

My good friend and colleague Dr. Frank Alessi was asked about the structures of the social sciences. He followed the brainstorming, grouping, and labeling process and formed some of its structures. He arrived at five critical attributes of a political system. Following is a brief discussion and activity questions to guide you.

Political Decision Makers

These are the people who make, interpret, and enforce the rules of political systems.

- Who are they in your school?
- Who are they in your local government?
- What are their personal characteristics?
- Who are the leaders?
- How do they get and keep their position?

Political Decision Making

This is the process by which a political system makes, enforces, and interprets rules.

- What formal or informal rules govern decision making?
- How is information gathered?
- How are decisions carried out?
- How are they enforced?

Political Institutions

These are the organizations and ways of handling political decisions.

- What are the political institutions?
- What are their functions?
- What authority, officially or unofficially, does each have?
- How do they influence the decision-making process?

Political Culture

This is made up of the benefits, attitudes, values, and skills of the people who are part of a political system.

- How are citizens aware of the role of government in their lives?
- What influence does a citizen have in decision making?
- How do people learn of political systems in their environment?
- To what extent can the people participate in the political process?

Citizenship

This is the part played by an individual in a political system.

- What influence does a citizen have on government?
- What is a citizen's role in decision making?
- How does the government affect the life of a citizen?
- What are the citizen's responsibilities in the political system?

Although only two structures are presented here, it would be helpful for students to have structures to guide their study of every discipline. Having a structure gives them a way to study each discipline in a comprehensive manner, instead of learning isolated information. It gives them a way of truly understanding a subject.

No structure is perfect or complete, but if we waited for the optimum structure we would not take any action. Some structure is better than no structure. You can always make the structure more complete and better.

Recently, I ran into a former student who was just finishing his college studies. I asked him what was most important for him when he entered college from high school. He, without hesitating, said it was learning the structures of various disciplines that helped him do well in college. He said he had a way of studying and making sense of every subject that other students didn't. A structure helps answer the question "What does it mean to understand?"

Activity: The Structure of Your Discipline

Return to an earlier activity in this chapter on understanding a concept and try to determine the structure of a subject you are now teaching or are going to teach. Brainstorm, group, and label. It would be helpful to do this with other teachers.

Each planning tool includes a detailed example, followed by a planning tool. Study the following example before you plan:

PLANNING TOOL 1: ACQUIRING KNOWLEDGE

Example 1: Fractions

1. Information and Facts

What information, facts, or vocabulary should students know when studying fractions?

____

____

Vocabulary

numerator	denominator
proper fractions	improper fractions
mixed fractions	decimal fractions

2. Skills and Procedures

What operations, procedures, skills, or applications should students use when studying fractions?

____

____

Operations	**Procedures**
addition	finding equivalent fractions
subtraction	GCF, LCM, LCD
multiplication	
division	

Applications

solving problems	measurement
probability	proportions

3. Concepts and Understandings

What are the key meanings and understandings students should know when studying fractions?

____

____

Meaning	**Properties**
ratio	closure
division	commutative
part of a set	associative
part of a whole	identify, distributive

Interrelationships

to other real numbers
to equivalent fractions
to decimals

Example 2: Blank Planning Tool

1. Information and Facts

What information, facts, or vocabulary should students know when studying ____________? ______________________________________

____

2. Skills and Procedures

What operations, procedures, skills, or applications should students use when studying ____________? ______________________________

____

3. Concepts and Understandings

What are the key meanings and understandings students should know when studying ____________? ______________________________

____

* * *

When you analyze your content, try using the planning process for acquiring knowledge discussed here. It will make student learning more complete and students will have a better understanding of your subject. You don't need to have or use the structure of your subjects to plan but it can be quite helpful.

There is little doubt that having an abundance of knowledge is critical to applying that knowledge. One cannot make connections, communicate effectively, or have life or learning skills without much knowledge. One cannot think clearly, understand, or be creative without knowledge. It is the cornerstone of education and must not be minimized. Information and facts, skills and procedures, and concepts and understanding are absolutely necessary for every subject and for every educated person. Don't ask anyone to be creative, think with some depth, or apply skills without knowledge.

Let us examine further the visions and the five skills discussed in chapter 5.

Acquiring Skills

Once teachers ensure that students have knowledge, they should turn their attention to the five doing skills. These skills are not discrete; they overlap and influence each other. The five skills are: connecting skills, communication skills, life skills, learning skills, and social skills.

When planning a unit (event, theme, etc.), include one or more from each of the following five skills. Once you include one or more in your unit, place an X next to the attribute of that skill to keep a record of what you've taught. You will then be able to teach those not previously assigned. This will help you maximize your skill coverage during the course. Refer to the following list of skills of what students should do when planning your unit or lesson.

The Connecting Skills

The connecting skills develop a student's ability to think critically about texts, models, theories, experiments, hypotheses, concepts, constructs, and so on. In addition to learning and understanding particular course information, procedures, and concepts, students must learn, for example, to compare one idea to another, to evaluate the validity of an idea, to see how one piece of information is different from another and why. Some connecting skills are:

construct ______ create ______ develop ______
explain ______ synthesize ______ apply ______
analyze ______ evaluate ______ justify ______

Find:

examples ______ nonexamples ______ differences ______
patterns ______ similarities ______

Others:

__________ __________ __________

The Communication Skills

The communication skills allow a student to share ideas with others. When a student can read, write, and speak clearly about a concept, idea, or theory, the student will likely develop a better understanding of that concept, idea, or theory. Some communication skills are:

read ______ write ______ speak ______
listen ______ illustrate ______ view ______

Others:

______________ ______________ ______________

The Life Skills

The life skills, like other skills, make a particular course or unit's learning goals relevant not only to that course or unit, but to a student's entire life. Using technology, competently working with others in a team, and being responsible for one's time and quality of work are skills every student needs to succeed both in and out of school. Some life skills are:

use technology ______
create hypotheses ______
test hypotheses ______
use problem-solving skills ______
build team skills ______
self-motivate ______
take initiative ______
pay attention to detail ______
be honest and have integrity ______
know how to make decisions _____

Others:

______________ ______________ ______________

The Learning Skills

The learning skills are a foundation for all learning. One component of very good teaching is being able to give students the skills for learning the content of our courses and, at the same time, for life-long learning. Students need to learn how to use the tools of the disciplines and what makes the structure of each discipline unique. They must also learn to be creative thinkers without fear of failure. They need to learn study skills and to apply structures of learning from one context to another. Some learning skills are:

be a self-directed learner ______
carry on investigations ______
use the tools of the disciplines ______
make learning connections ______

use the structures of the disciplines ______

learn how to study and learn each discipline ______

Others:

______________ ______________ ______________

The Social Skills

The social skills, along with other skills, are the hallmark of living together in a free and concerned society. Students need to be aware and learn what it means to interact in a positive way with others. Some social skills are:

respond to others ______
listen attentively ______
listen to ideas ______
understand diverse points of view ______
show compassion ______
be sensitive ______
be cooperative ______
be encouraging ______
be empowering ______

Others:

______________ ______________ ______________

To be successful in achieving standards, all teachers in every grade and in every subject must intentionally plan and teach the five skills stated above. There are many benefits in doing so. Students will be better prepared for any state or local assessment. Faster learners will be challenged in depth instead of skimming the surface of a subject. Various learning preferences will be accommodated, whether reading in depth, writing creatively, giving speeches, acting out ideas, or investigating an event or concept alone or in a team-learning situation.

Examples of Five Skills

The following are some examples of using the five skills with fractions:

1. Find the following patterns:

   A. $\frac{1}{2}, \frac{2}{4}, \frac{3}{6}, \frac{4}{8}$, ______, ______,
   B. $\frac{3}{1}, \frac{6}{2}, \frac{9}{3}, \frac{12}{4}, \frac{15}{5}$, ______, ______,

2. Investigate the meanings and derivations of the word *fraction*. Give examples. Also determine the derivation of the word *decimal* and its relationship to fractions. How do they differ? How are they the same?
3. Find similarities and differences between the meaning of the word *fraction* and each of the following. Explain your answers in writing and include examples of each.
   A. whole numbers
   B. integers
   C. natural numbers
   D. rational numbers
   E. irrational numbers
   F. real numbers
   G. imaginary numbers
4. Explain why, when adding decimals, one must align the decimal points. The explanation can be done in writing or orally.

Later in this chapter a planning tool for acquiring skills *(do)* will be presented.

Activity: Learning Goals for the Five Skills

Take any concept you are now teaching, or will teach, and write learning goals that include some of the five skill areas.

Overlapping Standards

When examining the standards of the various disciplines, many of the standards overlap. Overlapping standards often use words like *compare, contrast, create*, or *develop*. All disciplines want their students to express themselves clearly, create, analyze, explain, read, write, use technology, solve problems, and make learning connections, to name a few.

When all teachers participate, for example, in having their students become good writers in their subject, everyone benefits. This assumes, of course, that all teachers have good writing skills themselves. This may or may not be true and some teachers may feel uncomfortable having to examine a paper for the writing process.

I recommend that as part of a staff's in-service or continuing education program, a writing process be presented. If every teacher emphasized this skill, along with other skills, students would know what is expected. Overlapping expectations by the entire staff will convince students how important the five skill areas are. Determine if any other skill processes need to be included in your continuing education program.

Activity: Overlapping Standards

Examine the standards for all subjects in your school and determine which ones overlap. Determine how teachers can achieve consistency and efficiency by including common ones in their planning.

Activity: Defining Common Terms

Take words like *compare, contrast, create, develop*, and others contained in overlapping standards and, along with your colleagues, find common meaning.

A discussion of the meaning of each term will lead to greater clarity. This will result in greater student expectations, the reduction of teaching and learning time, and making standards more meaningful for students. Teaching students how to achieve with the attributes of the five skill areas is very important. Many times students want to achieve but simply don't know what is expected by the use of certain words. Meanings must be carefully and intentionally taught.

Course Learning Goals

Depending on what you are teaching, course learning goals can be either specific or global in nature. The right balance between being too specific or too global must be determined. When teaching, for example, a fourth-grade arithmetic course, the course learning goals are often determined mainly by the textbook. While these texts often contain the national, state, and even local standards, you may have to supplement or modify them. These text goals are usually quite specific.

Most textbooks contain approximately 140 lessons since there are approximately 180 school days in most states. Forty days are reserved for review and testing. Most lessons have approximately three objectives for students to learn. Now 140×3 is 420 objectives. I defy most people to remember or state all 420 objectives. There are too many to remember. The objectives are often fragmented, and students don't see the whole picture.

During a trip to Australia, I was asked to comment on a state's written learning goals for all subjects. Volumes of learning goals were prepared for each subject. If you are an elementary teacher trying to teach multiple courses with each course having hundreds of learning goals, what chances are there to teach them or for students to learn them? The challenge was impossible to meet. I told the state curriculum committees that their expectations were unrealistic in the format presented. I asked, "Can you help your teachers make sense of all the learning goals?"

After some discussion and a presentation of the know-and-do process, I departed with the hope that they would combine expectations across disciplines and reduce the number of learning goals to a more manageable number. Many of the subjects had overlapping learning goals. After we worked together, they recognized that most of their goals were expressed in the five skill areas of acquiring skills.

Fragmented curriculum learning goals and standards won't yield better learning results. Applying a more comprehensive process will.

On the other hand, as you will see below, in a philosophy of education course, Dr. Anne Mamary stated her course learning goals quite globally. This is acceptable as long as you align your teaching and assessment to the standards. Here are Anne's course learning goals:

1. To read, discuss, understand, and critique a range of philosophies of education.
2. To consider how these philosophies apply to our room practices as students and teachers.
3. To explore how philosophies of education both shape and reflect societal values.

4. To examine how these philosophies of education, put into practice, shape students and teachers, either to support and/or to challenge societal norms.
5. To consider how philosophies of education might be used to enhance our work as students and teachers.

Notice that these more global course learning goals reflect knowledge, understanding, and a variety of skills.

Once course learning goals are known, you should then determine and plan your course units (chapters, themes, events, issues) and the approximate time allocated for you to teach and for students to learn them. You must manage time carefully for you and your students to be successful.

Managing Your Time

Planning and time management are intertwined and must be done simultaneously. You only have so much time to teach a course or unit and to achieve your course learning goals. Don't meander.

Paul, a middle-school social studies teacher who loved to teach a unit on immigration, developed a good unit with good learning activities. The unit was highly successful and his students loved finding out about their grandparents and great-grandparents who had immigrated to America. There was a major problem, however, because the unit was no longer part of the local or state curriculum and was not part of the state's assessment program. Paul didn't have time to teach both the required curriculum and the unit on immigration. Paul was disappointed when he was told that he had to be sure the state mandates took precedence over his lessons. His immigration unit soon became one for students to investigate on their own. It became an extension of the other units but had to be done individually or in small learning teams.

As curriculum mandates changed, many favored teaching activities were no longer included. Many teachers were unhappy with the changes, but instead of discarding all their efforts they had the faster learners conduct investigations in these units.

Dave, a science teacher, was proud of the units that he developed but didn't have unlimited time to develop all of his units. He had a family, children, and many other responsibilities. He had a life outside the classroom. Dave used his textbook as a guide when he was developing his own unit and lesson plans. He let the authors guide him until he had time. He used their examples, activities, and problems. He also used their learning goals as a basis for his course learning goals, modifying them to include the required ones. As time went by, Dave developed his units and the textbook became less important.

No matter where you start, you must begin with the end in mind. That is, it is important to plan backwards from your course learning goals. These must include national, state, and local standards. After determining your course learning goals, you must then place them deliberately into your units, chapters, required readings, themes, events, lessons, and into all of your planning. Know where your course learning goals are, where they are placed, and then be sure all are included.

To hope that you have included all course learning goals in your unit and not be sure is not acceptable. To hope that you taught all course learning goals and assessed whether students learned them and not be sure is also not acceptable. Hoping but not being sure is a disservice to you, your school, and above all to your students.

If time permits, you can include the units and activities that you like to teach. With good course management, alignment of your curriculum with your teaching, and using the instructional process shown in the last chapter, you can be sure students will learn at least the required standards and still have time for a deeper understanding and skill acquisition.

Six Steps for Planning Course Learning Goals

1. Analyze national, state, and local standards for your subject.
   A. Identify what students need to *know* and understand. Include the three parts of acquiring knowledge outlined in this chapter.
   B. Identify what students need to be able to *do*. Include the five acquiring skills outlined in this chapter.
2. Determine what students will be learning in your subject or course. If your district has already determined the learning goals, it is not necessary to rewrite them. If not, you as a teacher must create the learning goals for the course.

3. When creating the actual learning goals:
   A. Identify the content in the *know* category.
   B. Identify the skills to be learned in the *do* category.
   C. Match content and skills that have a natural connection to create meaningful learning experiences.
4. Throughout the course try to incorporate as many of the skills as possible, intentionally focusing on the ones mandated.
5. Course learning goals can be written in two ways:
   A. Specifically identify both content and skills in a single statement. For example, a high-school algebra course goal could be "Students will graph linear equations using the slope–intercept method."
   B. Identify both content and skills in separate statements, for example, middle-school science course goals. By the end of sixth grade, students will understand that matter is made up of particles whose properties determine the observable characteristics of matter and its reactivity. Here is a sample:
      - Students will observe and describe properties of materials such as density, conductivity, and solubility.
      - Students will construct models of atoms and molecules.
      - Students will find similarities and differences between physical and chemical changes.
      - Students will learn to hypothesize following the scientific method.
      - Students will learn to use the tools of science while experimenting throughout the learning process.
6. When creating course learning goals:
   A. It is important to vary the skills throughout the school year.
   B. Create learning goals with the know-and-do model, ensuring that a variety of learning styles will be practiced throughout the learning experience.
   C. When students apply their learning of a skill integrated with content, a demonstration of learning becomes a natural consequence of the experience. True authentic assessment is produced.
   D. Collaboration in and among grade levels will give all students the skills to perform well on any assessment and to be successful in life.

PLANNING TOOL 2: CREATING COURSE LEARNING GOALS

National Standards

List the national standards for your course if they exist. Include in your plans.

____

____

____

State Standards

List the state standards for your course if they exist. Include in your plans.

____

____

____

Local Standards

List the local standards for your course if they exist. Include in your plans.

____

____

____

Your Standards

List your own standards for your course and include them if there is time.

____

____

____

Course Learning Goals

Compile your course learning goals. Check for inclusion of all mandated standards. Ensure none are omitted.

1. ______________________________
2. ______________________________
3. ______________________________
4. ______________________________
5. ______________________________
6. ______________________________
7. ______________________________
8. ______________________________
9. ______________________________
10. ______________________________

Examples of Course Learning Goals

Example of an Integrated Algebra 1 Course Goal

Students will solve systems of linear equations and inequalities both graphically and algebraically and will apply these procedures to represent situations and solve problems.

Examples of an Intermediate-Grade Science Course Goal

Course Learning Goal #1:

Know: By the end of the sixth grade, students will understand that matter is made up of particles whose properties determine the observable characteristics of matter and its reactivity.

Do: (1) Students will observe and describe properties of materials, such as density, conductivity, and solubility. (2) Students will construct models of atoms and molecules. (3) Students will find similarities and differences between physical and chemical changes. (4) Students will learn to hypothesize following the scientific method. (5) Students will learn to use the tools of the discipline while experimenting throughout the learning process.

Course Learning Goal #2:

Know: By the end of sixth grade, students will understand that energy and matter interact through forces that cause a change in motion.

Do: (1) Students will carry on an investigation of physics in a real-life situation, such as an amusement park, playground, or athletic arena. (2) Students will apply their knowledge of simple machines to use pulleys, levers, and gears to make work easier and to explain through writing and illustration how each machine transforms the force applied to it. (3) Students will build the team skills of cooperation, consensus, decision making, and accountability while constructing a "Rube Goldberg" type of machine and explain through writing and illustration the energy transformations evident in them.

Unit Planning: Course Outline by Units

You have analyzed national, state, and local standards by identifying what students need to *know* and be able to *do* and identifying the district and local curriculum. You have analyzed state and local assessments by determining how students are expected to demonstrate their knowledge and skills on state and local assessments.

You are now ready to write unit learning goals. This phase of the planning process is designed to give structure to curriculum planning. Each course or subject must be outlined by units. There are two parts of the unit planning process:

1. "Chunking" content and skills into units.
2. Determining time approximations.

You as a curriculum planner must determine a way to group content and skills into a meaningful, well-organized curriculum. All course learning goals must be carefully placed into units of study, taught intentionally, and above all learned by your students. If done effectively, students will naturally become more successful in their learning.

The course outline can be organized through one or more of the following formats: units, chapters, themes, events, issues.

The second critical part of the unit planning process is to determine the amount of time necessary to teach and learn each unit. As practitioners, we know these will be approximations. Many factors affect the teaching and learning process. Begin by determining the anticipated amount of time needed to teach each unit. Then find the total amount of time for all units. You may now have to revisit each unit and adjust both content and time to stay within the predetermined teaching days. As the year progresses, record the actual days spent teaching each unit. Compare this with the anticipated time. Adjust the following year.

Creative and careful planning of the units will help ensure that all content and skills will be successfully taught and learned.

The following example of a course outline by units, including time management, was determined by a ninth-grade algebra teacher using her textbook as a guide. All the units stated in the example are aligned with the national, state, and local standards.

Not all learning goals within each unit are essential and some may be eliminated by the teacher as she manages allocated time. Since this teacher has to prepare students for the state assessments, she allocated 10 days for review and state tests. This teacher was well prepared, she was able to teach this course for understanding and with good skill acquisition. She still had time to prepare students for the state assessments.

For ten years I taught high-school math courses that had state exams at their conclusion. As I gained experience and became better prepared, I was able to teach a meaningful course and still have my students prepared for the state tests.

PLANNING TOOL 3: COURSE OUTLINE BY UNITS

Example 1: Algebra 1

Course/Subject: Algebra 1
School Year: 2006–2007
Grade: 9

Units (Chapters, Themes, Events, Issues)	Approximate Number of Days	Actual Days Spent
Term or Semester: 1		
1. Getting Started	4	4
2. Logic	14	12
3. Algebraic Expressions	15	14
4. Monomials and Polynomials	20	21
5. Equations and Inequalities	15	14
6. Geometry	13	14
7. Ratio and Proportion	13	10
8. Midterm Review and Test	3	3
9. ______	______	______
10. ______	______	______
Totals	97	92

Term or Semester: 2		
1. Factoring	10	11
2. Fractions	10	8
3. Systems of Equations and Inequalities	20	18
4. Operations with Radicals	9	11
5. Quadratics	12	12
6. Probability and Statistics	15	15
7. State Review and Tests	10	10
8. ______________	_____	_____
9. ______________	_____	_____
10. ______________	_____	_____
Totals	86	85
Totals both semesters	183	177

Example 2: Blank Planning Tool

To help you manage your time, use the following planning tool. It will also help you decide what is nice to teach and what is necessary to teach.

Course/Subject: _______
School Year: ______
Grade: ______

Units (Chapters, Themes, Events, Issues)	**Approximate Number of Days**	**Actual Days Spent**
Term or Semester: 1		
1. ______________	_____	_____
2. ______________	_____	_____
3. ______________	_____	_____
4. ______________	_____	_____
5. ______________	_____	_____
6. ______________	_____	_____
7. ______________	_____	_____
8. ______________	_____	_____
9. ______________	_____	_____
10. ______________	_____	_____
Totals	_____	_____

Unit Learning Goals

Now that you have determined the units and time approximations for each unit, it is time to be sure that the content of each unit is aligned to the national, state, and local standards.

In the previous example, this teacher had enough experience to know the approximate amount of time needed for each unit and the content that was to be placed within each unit. She still had to make time adjustments. Without that experience or when starting a new course, you may have to make many more time and content adjustments.

Let's take a look at a specific unit that can either be part of some text or stand alone. This is a unit on poetry.

Note: When you use a textbook as a guide, as in the previous example, have a list of the state and local standards. Refer to these lists as you plan each unit. Begin by writing the learning goals stated in each chapter or unit. Then be sure each of the state and local learning goals are included. If any are not, then you must position them in the appropriate chapters or units.

After you are sure all required learning goals are included, return to each unit or place an "x" next to each required standard. This will remind you which ones may be tested. You may want to emphasize these when teaching them.

In the following poetry example, the unit learning goals are derived from the course learning goals. While you should review your national standards, the state standards are shown because they are used to determine the unit goals.

State Curriculum and Assessments for English

Standard 2: Language for Literacy Response and Expression

Students must:

- Read a variety of literature of different genres.
- Recognize some features that distinguish the genres.
- Read aloud carefully and fluently.
- Present personal responses to literature.
- Explain the meaning of literary works, with some attention to meanings beyond the literal level.
- Create poems using the elements of literature.

Course Learning Goals for English

1. Students will be able to recognize the importance of poetic format and punctuation in order to identify, understand, and create effective poetry.
2. Students will interact with a wide variety of texts to develop as enthusiastic, independent, and reflective readers.
3. Students will write for a variety of purposes and audiences, and in a variety of forms, developing, organizing, and communicating ideas.
4. Students will use the writing process to produce written products.
5. Students will prepare and deliver a presentation, effectively using elements of communication.

Begin by determining the approximate amount of time allocated for this unit. Estimate a date to start and a date to finish. Then determine the actual starting date and finishing date. Finally, record the actual number of days to complete the unit. All of this will help in future planning. Then write your unit learning goals based on your course learning goals. Determine the assessments you will use.

PLANNING TOOL 4: UNIT PLANNING

Example 1: Poetry

Name of Unit: Poetry

Anticipated number of days to complete unit: 25

Estimated date to start: 5/1
Estimated date to finish: 6/5

Actual date to start: 5/2
Actual date to finish: 6/8

Actual number of days to complete unit: 28

Unit Learning Goals

List the unit learning goals in the space provided. A unit learning goals statement should include both what students will *know* and be able to *do*.

1. Students will create a variety of poetic pieces using a writing process that includes narrative and lyric by using the techniques of alliteration, repetition, rhyme, and onomatopoeia.

2. Students will read and interpret poet's meaning and verbalize this in own words to do a written explanation.
3. Students will identify poet's use of poetic devices (i.e., alliteration, rhyme scheme, and repetition).
4. Students will make an oral presentation of a poem of choice for the purpose of becoming an interesting speaker.
5. With the use of technology, students will be creative in illustrating and publishing one of their poems.
6. Students will develop creative thinking and writing through daily journal entries.
7. Students will find examples of modern-day ballads to discuss and share with the class.

Assessments

List both formal and informal assessments to be used to determine what students *know* and are able to *do*. Refer to the course and unit learning goals for your assessments. Assessments include natural products that arise from the learning goals. Demonstrations of learning are a natural consequence of students' applying content through the skills learned. Assessments may also include other methods such as tests, self-assessment, and standardized tests.

1. Final copy of each of the following will be assessed: narrative, ballad, and lyrics (Final copies may be accompanied by a recording or an oral presentation of the above.)
2. Summative exam on content learned
3. Oral presentation
4. Published piece of poetry using digital imaging for illustration
5. Informal assessment of ongoing journal entries

Before planning your lesson goals, check to determine which skills *(do)* are being taught. Remember it is important to vary the skills in a unit so students get a comprehensive exposure to all of them. This will take time, so don't try to include them in a few lessons. Again, if every teacher in every subject planned to include the skills in their units and lessons, everyone would benefit. Everyone's job would be easier.

Example 2: Matter and Chemistry

Name of Unit: Matter and Chemistry

Anticipated number of days to complete unit: 37 days

Estimated date to start: 9/15
Estimated date to finish: 10/28

Actual date to start: 9/15
Actual date to finish: 11/1

Actual number of days to complete unit: 40

Unit Learning Goals

List the unit learning goals in the space provided. A unit learning goal statement should include both what students will *know* and be able to *do*.

Connecting Skills

1. Students will find similarities and differences between the various characteristics of physical and chemical change.
2. Students will find similarities and differences within the structure of the states of matter.
3. Students will construct models of an element existing in three states of matter.

Communication Skills

1. Various modes of learning include engaging students in active reading from the text to gain knowledge and understanding of content.
2. Students will illustrate through diagrams and models their understanding of the states of matter.

Life Skills

1. Students will solve problems following the scientific method. They will identify the problem, hypothesize, and carry out an experiment to test their hypotheses.
2. Students will become more responsible for their learning. Teacher and students will set criteria and performance standards for laboratory work,

thus allowing students to self-assess individual performance and written work.

Learning Skills

Students will become better self-directed learners. They will learn to use a variety of tools of the discipline. The scientific method, experimentation, and many laboratory rules will be implemented.

Social Skills

Students will be given opportunities to practice their listening skills and how to respond to others. This will be done in learning teams where each student shares information and conclusions. A team report will follow.

Assessments

List both formal and informal assessment to be used to determine what students *know* and are able to *do*. Refer to the course and unit learning goals for your assessment. Assessments include natural products that arise from the learning goals. Demonstrations of learning are a natural consequence of students' applying content through the skills learned. Assessments may also include other methods such as tests, self-assessment, and standardized tests.

1. Students will be responsible for submitting an informal and formal written exam on the content learned.
2. Students will be expected to demonstrate their understanding of outlined conceptual learning; this should include the similarities and differences among the states of matter and in physical and chemical changes.
3. Students will solve a scientific problem based on chemical and physical change. They will demonstrate their ability to problem-solve using the scientific method and other tools of the discipline.
4. Students are expected to construct a model of an atom for a particular element and a molecule for a given compound.
5. Students will use a diagram to illustrate their understanding of the structure of the four states of matter.

Course Learning Goal

The following course learning goal was achieved in this unit: students will discover that matter is made up of particles whose properties determine the observable characteristics of matter and its reactivity. Use the following planning tool to help you manage your learning goals.

Example 3: Blank Planning Tool

Name of Unit
Anticipated number of days to complete unit:

Estimated date to start: ________ Actual date to start:________
Estimated date to finish: ________ Actual date to finish: ________

Actual number of days to complete unit: ________

State Learning Goals

List the state learning goals in the space provided.

____
____
____

Course Learning Goals

List the course learning goals in the space provided.

____
____
____

Unit Learning Goals

List the unit learning goals in the space provided. A unit learning goals statement should include both what students will *know* and be able to *do*.

____
____
____

Assessment

List both formal and informal assessments to be used to determine what students *know* and are able to *do*. Refer to the course and unit learning goals for your assessments. Assessments include natural products that arise from the learning goals. Demonstrations of learning are a natural consequence of students' applying content through the skills learned. Assessments may also include other methods such as tests, self-assessment, and standardized tests.

____
____
____
____
____

Earlier in this chapter the five learning skills were discussed. To ensure that these skills are taught and learned, plan to include them in your unit planning. This will also serve as a record of the included skills.

From the two examples just presented, you can see that these skills are included in a natural way. Don't force inclusion of these skills in the unit, they must occur naturally.

Following are a continuation of the poetry and chemistry examples and how to plan for acquiring skills.

PLANNING TOOL 5: ACQUIRING SKILLS

Example 1: Poetry

A unit learning goal must indicate what students should *know* and be able to *do* at the end of a unit of learning. To create a unit learning goal, integrate the identified content with skills from the know-and-do model. Refer to the following list of what students should be able to do when writing unit learning goals. Place a check next to those used. See the examples in the unit plans given.

Connection

Construct _____ Explain _____
Analyze _____ Discover _____

Create __X__ Synthesize _____
Evaluate _____ Develop _____
Apply _____ Justify _____

Find:

Examples _X_ Similarities ____
Differences ____ Patterns ____
Other ____

Communication

Read __X__ Write __X__
Speak _____ Listen _____
Illustrate __X__ View _____

Life

Use technology __X__ Solve problems _____ Hypothesize _____
Create _____ Identify _____ Use procedures _____
Build team skills _____ Promote cooperation _____ Build consensus _____
Teach decision making _____ Ensure accountability _____ Inculcate responsibility ____
Teach time management _____ Do quality work _____ Self-assess _____
Develop attitude _____ Encourage learning _____

Learning

Be a self-directed learner _____ Use the tools of the discipline _____
Carry on investigations _____ Make connections __X__
Be creative _____ Learn how to study and learn _____
Use key concepts _____ Use structures _____

Social

Response to others _____ Listen attentively _____
Listen to ideas _____ Understand diverse points of view _____

Show compassion _____
Share ideas _____
Be empowering _____
Be cooperative _____
Be encouraging _____
Be sensitive _____

Example 2: Matter and Chemistry

A unit learning goal must indicate what students should *know* and be able to *do* at the end of a unit of learning. To create a unit learning goal, integrate the identified content with skills from the know-and-do model. Refer to the following list of what students should be able to *do* when writing unit learning goals. Place a check next to those used.

Connection

Construct _____
Analyze _____
Create __X__
Evaluate _____
Apply _____
Explain _____
Discover _____
Synthesize _____
Develop _____
Justify _____

Find:

Examples _X_
Differences ____
Other ____
Similarities ____
Patterns ____

Communication

Read __X__
Speak _____
Illustrate __X__
Write __X__
Listen _____
View _____

Life

Use technology __X__
Create _____
Build team skills _____
Solve problems _____
Identify _____
Promote cooperation _____
Hypothesize _____
Use procedures _____
Build consensus _____

Teach decision making _____
Teach time management _____
Develop attitude _____
Ensure accountability _____
Do quality work _____
Encourage learning _____
Inculcate responsibility ____
Self-assess _____

Learning

Be a self-directed learner _____
Carry on investigations _____
Be creative _____
Use key concepts _____
Use the tools of the discipline _____
Make connections __X__
Learn how to study and learn _____
Use structures _____

Social

Respond to others _____
Listen to ideas _____
Show compassion _____
Share ideas _____
Be empowering _____
Listen attentively _____
Understand diverse points of view _____
Be cooperative _____
Be encouraging _____
Be sensitive _____

Example 3: Blank Planning Tool

Refer to the following list of what students should be able to *do* when writing unit learning goals. Place an X next to those used.

Connection

Construct _____
Analyze _____
Create _____
Evaluate _____
Apply _____
Explain _____
Discover _____
Synthesize _____
Develop _____
Justify _____

Find:

Examples _____
Differences ____
Other ____
Similarities ____
Patterns ____

Communication

Read _____
Write _____
Speak _____
Listen _____
Illustrate _____
View _____

Life

Use technology _____
Solve problems _____
Hypothesize _____
Create _____
Identify _____
Use procedures _____
Build team skills _____
Promote cooperation _____
Build consensus _____
Teach decision making _____
Ensure accountability _____
Inculcate responsibility ____
Teach time management _____
Do quality work _____
Self-assess _____
Develop attitude _____
Encourage learning _____

Learning

Be a self-directed learner _____
Use the tools of the discipline _____
Carry on investigations _____
Make connections _____
Be creative _____
Learn how to study and learn _____
Use key concepts _____
Use structures _____

Social

Response to others _____
Listen attentively _____
Listen to ideas _____
Understand diverse points of view _____
Show compassion _____
Be cooperative _____
Share ideas _____
Be encouraging _____
Be empowering _____
Be sensitive _____

Lesson Planning

Once the course learning goals have been completed, the course outlined by units with the unit learning goals derived, and time approximations determined, it is time to plan each lesson. Be sure to refer to the unit learning goals and time approximations when planning each lesson. Align your lesson learning goals to the unit goals and manage your time for each lesson so that you stay on schedule. It is easy to wander, so be careful.

The following examples of lesson goals are a continuation of the poetry unit example.

PLANNING TOOL 6: LESSON LEARNING GOALS

Example 1: Poetry Lessons

For each lesson, determine what students should *know* and be able to *do*. Align these lesson goals to the unit and course learning goals.

Lesson #1: Journals

Know and do:

1. Students discover the meaning and purpose of keeping a creative journal. Students begin creating personal journal entries.
2. Students create chain poem.

Notes: ____

Lesson #2: Defining Poetry

Know and do: Students focus on senses to create a definition poem.
Notes: Journal entry #2; read poem aloud, ask for interpretation.

Lesson #3: Reading Poetry

Know and do: Students will learn strategies for reading poetry effectively to enhance comprehension and interest.
Notes: Journal entry #3; students practice strategy with peer, then with large group.

Lesson #4: Rhyming Schemes

Know and do:

1. Students identify three different types of rhyming schemes.
2. Students create a poem using one of the rhyming schemes learned.

Notes: Journal entry #4; when reading examples of rhyming schemes, also discuss meaning.

Lesson #5: Creative Illustration

Know and do: Students will illustrate and publish using digital camera and word processor or creative writing program.
Notes: Journal entry #5; read poem together, answer comprehension questions.

Lesson #6: Alliteration

Know and do: Students create a story using the alliteration technique.
Notes: Journal entry #6; read poem independently, answer comprehension questions.

Lesson #7: Onomatopoeia

Know and do: Students create a poem using onomatopoeia.
Notes: Journal entry #7; students find two examples, then create one of their own.

Lesson #8: Narrative

Know and do:

1. Using a familiar story, students will rewrite using a rhyming scheme.
2. Using an alliteration poem from the previous lesson, students will rewrite using a rhyming scheme.

Notes: Journal entry #8; read a narrative, discuss meaning, and do a comprehension check.

Lesson #9: Ballad

Know and do: Students find examples of modern-day ballads to share with class.
Notes: Journal entry #9; students find two examples and create one of their own.

Lesson #10: Lyrics

Know and do: Students create own lyrics to fit with a well-known melody.
Notes: Journal entry #10; teacher shares a lyrical poem of her own.

Lesson #11: Presentation

Know and do: Students present poem of choice to large group during a "Poetry Read."
Notes: Journal entry #11; teacher shares favorite poem with students to begin Poetry Read event.

Lesson #12: Blank

Know and Do: ____
Notes: ____

Example 2: Blank Planning Tool

For each lesson determine what students should know and be able to do. Align these lesson goals to the unit and course learning goals.

Lesson #1: ______________

Know and Do: ____
Notes: ____

Lesson #2: ______________

Know and Do: ____
Notes: ____

Lesson #3: ______________

Know and Do: ____
Notes: ____

Lesson #4: ______________

Know and Do: ____
Notes: ____

Lesson #5: ______________

Know and Do: ____
Notes: ____

Lesson #6: ______________

Know and Do: ____
Notes: ____

Lesson #7: ______________

Know and Do: ____
Notes: ____

Planning for the Instructional Process

This is the stage when educators of all levels consider the critical question: What constitutes an ideal lesson in which the conditions are present for all students to learn well? The answers, which are clear and consistent, were presented in the previous chapter.

Alignment to the standards, clear learning goals, understanding and checking both attitudinal and academic readiness, focusing student attention, active student participation, addressing various learning modes, guided practice and adjustments, independent practice, ongoing assessment and feedback, and summary and closure are all integral parts of a most effective teaching/learning experience.

When teachers include all of these components in their instructional process, student achievement will dramatically increase for all students. The following are questions to ask when planning for each phase of the instructional process:

Aligning to the Standards

1. What standard or goal will be addressed in this lesson?
2. What do students need to *know* and be able to *do*?
3. How will students be formally and informally assessed?

Preparing for Success

1. What knowledge and skills must students possess to be successful with the lesson learning goals?
2. How can teacher and students revisit previous learning that is connected to the new learning?
3. How can students be prepared for success?

Focusing Student Attention

1. How can we get students ready to learn?
2. How will students be focused on what they will *know* and be able to *do* by the end of the lesson?

Initial Instruction

1. How can you engage students to ensure that they will learn more adequately the first time they learn something?
2. How can you engage students in experiences that will address various learning styles?
3. How can you engage students in experiences that are directly aligned to the standards and assessments (what students should *know* and be able to *do*)?

Guided Practice and Adjustments

1. How can students be engaged in practicing the content and/or skills that they have learned?
2. How can you formally or informally assess their understanding in content?
3. How can you formally or informally assess their proficiency in the new skill?
4. How can you address interventions?

Summary and Closure

1. How can teacher and students summarize the lesson?
2. How can teacher and students review the lesson?

Assessments and Testing

1. How will students be formally and informally assessed on the new learning?
2. Is this assessment aligned to the lesson goals and standards?
3. How will students be held accountable for their learning?

Lesson Plan for the Instructional Process

The following lesson plan design is to assist the teacher in the instructional process. It includes the identified components of a very good lesson that intentionally provides necessary learning experiences for all students to become proficient in both content and skills.

Within this instructional and planning process, you have the freedom to incorporate all practices of teaching–learning strategies that are appropriate for your students. Within these well-defined processes, there are ample opportunities for your creativity and individuality. Using the instructional and planning process will result in very good lessons and instruction on a regular basis. Following are two examples of a lesson plan. Again, modify for your own style.

PLANNING TOOL 7: LESSON PLAN

Example 1: Convection Currents

Align to the Standards or Unit Goals

What standard or unit goal will be addressed in this lesson? Science Standard 4, The Physical Setting. 2.2a. The interior of the earth is hot. Heat flow and movement within the earth causes sections of the earth to move. This results in earthquakes, volcanic eruptions, and ocean basins.

What will students *know* and be able to *do* by the end of this lesson? Students will use the tools of the discipline and the scientific method to investigate how the heat from the earth's core affects the earth's crust.

Materials

Hot plates, syrup, trays, puzzle pieces, beaker, Bunsen burner, water, sawdust, stirring rod.

Preparation for Success: Academic Readiness

Structure of the earth, the core is hot, convection currents in mantle. Will check prerequisites during cue set.

Focusing Student Attention

Put the structure of the earth on the board. Ask for students to volunteer labeling. Wait for all to volunteer. Have them describe each part: crust, mantle, outer core, inner core. Review question from previous day's lab. How does the heat from the core affect the mantle? Demonstrate lab again and ask for conclusions (convection currents) today. You will learn how the heat from the core affects the crust. Refer back to the diagram on the board and ask for their hypothesis. Record hypothesis on new lab sheet.

Initial Instruction

In groups, students will complete experiment on lab sheet. Remind them what material represents. Hot plate, core, syrup, mantle, puzzle pieces, crust. Record observations and conclusions as illustrations and charts are analyzed.

Guided Practice: Informal Assessments and Adjustments

Answer the following question: My conclusions from today's experiment were correct or not because . . . . Refer to the reading for support. Give at least three supporting details.

Summary and Closure

Share answers and conclusions.

Assessments and Testing

1. Observations of experiments
2. Assignments
3. Unit Test—later date

Extensions

1. Students check the Internet for Volcano World.
2. Include current volcanic and earthquake activity. Share with class.

Example 2: Alliteration

Lesson Learning Goals

Students will create a poem/story utilizing the literary technique of alliteration.

Materials

story web plans
sentence strips
dictionary/thesaurus poems, such as *Ickle Me, Pickle Me, Tickle Me Too*

Preparation for Success: Academic Readiness

Using a web as a story planner. Knowledge of tongue twisters. Sharing my personal journal from middle-school years to establish relationships and a sense of security in writing what students think and feel.

Focusing Student Attention

1. Write a couple of tongue twisters on the board ("Sally sells sea shells . . . ," "Peter Piper . . .")
2. Read the twisters once aloud before asking for volunteers to read ten times fast to ensure full participation.
3. Ask, "What is it about these phrases that make them so hard to say?" (repeating sound)
4. Make tongue twister up with large group:
   a. Pick sound.
   b. Students brainstorm words beginning with sound-list on board.
   c. Make different sentences using words on board.
5. Explain lesson content—Repeating sounds in poetry.

Initial Instruction

1. Explain how poets make use of the technique of repeating sounds to make their poems more interesting or to enhance the mood of a poem.
2. Notes—Definition of Alliteration.
3. Share examples of poetry that emphasizes alliteration with students, for example, *Ickle Me, Pickle Me, Tickle Me Too* by Shel Silverstein.
4. Share an alliteration story.
5. Discuss the repeating sound "likes/dislikes"—question parts of the story.

Guided Practice: Informal Assessment and Adjustments

Break into groups of three to four. Using five to six sentence strips, groups are to create a simple alliteration story to share with large group. Students are given a story web to help guide creation of story.

Encourage students to pick a sound and brainstorm a list of words first (dictionaries may be used).

Summary and Closure

1. After 15 minutes, have groups share, putting strips on board.
2. Focus on one example, point out repeating sound and how it helps the mood of the story.
3. Go over the independent practice exercise.

Assessment and Testing

1. Homework: Write an alliteration story to include in poetry portfolio using a story web to assist with planning (same as guided practice).
2. Allow five minutes to start in class.
3. Assessment: Rough draft and final copy of independent practice.

Extensions

1. Illustrate story.
2. Rewrite previously written poem using alliteration technique.
3. Instead of a beginning sound, write a story using an ending sound or other blend, for example, *-tion*.
4. Using the Internet—find some poetry and share with the class.
5. Publish on the Internet.

Example 3: Blank

Lesson Name or Number: ______
Date: ______
Lesson Learning Goals: ____
____
Standard of Learning Addressed: ______________________________________
____
Materials: ____
____
Preparation for Success: Academic Readiness: __________________________
____
Focusing Student Attention: ____________________________________
____

Initial Instruction: ____

____

Guided Practice: Informal Assessments and Adjustments: ___________

____

Summary and Closure: ____

____

Assessments and Testing: ______________________________________

____

Extensions: ____

____

Planning Supplement 1: Substitute Plans

Lesson Plan for Course or Subject: _______
Date: _______
Course Name: _______
Time: _______
Room: _______
See Unit: _______
See Lesson: _______
See assignments in the lesson planner: ________
Additional suggestions for the lesson or alternate plans: _____________

____

____

General Information

1. My textbooks ____
2. The teacher's edition or answer keys ___________________________
3. Seating charts ____
4. School procedures ____
5. Classroom procedures _______________________________________
6. Grade book ____
7. Library and hall passes ______________________________________
8. Keys ____

My Schedule

Period	**Course**	**Room**	**Comments**
______	______	______	______________________________
______	______	______	______________________________
______	______	______	______________________________
______	______	______	______________________________

Special considerations for some students (medical, therapy, etc.): _______
____

Students and teacher who can help: ______________________________
____

Correspondence Journal Between Teacher and Substitute

Teacher's Name: ______
Date of Absence: ______
Teacher's observation of each class and any anticipated problems: ______
____

Substitute's Name: __________________
Phone # (optional): _________________
Substitute's Observations (Please include: What went well? What was accomplished? What problems were faced in the lesson? What feedback do you have for the next lesson? What problems did you face with any student? Who? What? Resolution?): ___________________________
____
____

Planning Supplement 2: Student Record Form

Student: Grade: Phone:
Address: Guardian: Relationship:
Call When/Where: Phone: Teacher Last Year:

Grades

1st: 2nd: 3rd: 4th: Final Grades:

Extra Help: ____
____

Dates/Notes: ____

____

Contacts (List any contact made with student, parent, guardian, counselor, or others. This can be for reasons of behavior, academic, or other): ______

____

Date: Contacts/Interventions: Comments:

CONCLUSION

The field of education has grown and changed tremendously over the last ten years. New and more rigorous state and national standards for student learning have resulted in an increasing focus on student achievement in our schools.

In order for all students to achieve the new standards of learning, changes need to take place. The curriculum must be clear for each grade level and content area. Teachers must understand exactly what all students should know and be able to do to be successful with the state standards and assessments. Many districts are creating curriculum planning and alignment committees consisting of teachers, administrators, and curriculum and subject specialists in order to bolster this effort.

Chapter Twelve

Classroom Practices

Since we can't always predict which students will become our next geniuses, we must treat all students as if they are the ones.

Focus Questions

1. Have you tried learning a new skill lately? Consider a skill like learning to play bridge or golf.
2. What do you think your instructor's goals were?
3. How were mistakes viewed by you and your instructor?
4. Did you get a grade?
5. If your instructor were to give you grades for your initial performance, would you have learned better?
6. Do you think you would have continued learning this skill if grades were given?
7. What motivated you to continue?
8. Did your instructor compare you to others in the class?
9. Was getting better a major goal?
10. Did your instructor vary his or her techniques?
11. How and when do testing and assessment help students learn better? How might they get in the way of student learning?
12. What role do grades play in improving student learning?
13. What are the differences between the concept of failure and making mistakes?

Everyone I know has an opinion about education and how classrooms, teaching, and schools ought to be managed. They have an opinion about how teachers should teach and about their testing, grading, and homework policies. They have an opinion about what should be taught and what should be emphasized in the classrooms. They have an opinion about who can learn and why some can't learn. Everyone has opinions about how to "fix" education. While opinions vary widely, I have observed that those who were successful in school want the same practices for every child. They want the educational system to stay the same. But for those who were unsuccessful in school, they blame their schools. They want the educational system to change.

Conversations of parents at parties often turn to education, how their children are learning and school practices. Opinions vary, with some more emphatic than others. At a recent birthday party for my friend and colleague, the topic of education was discussed. Most of those doing the discussing were noneducators. They had very strong opinions and recommendations about how teachers teach and manage their classrooms. As I listened to these opinions, I concluded that they were based on each person's own personal experiences as parents or students.

Tom, who attended a private school, recalled with fondness a statement made by his Jesuit teacher. It went something like this: "Don't expect anyone to get 100 on any of my math tests. You can't. If you did, that would mean you know everything about geometry and that is not possible." Tom excelled in math and he got the highest grade in his class, 86%. He said the other grades were scaled down from his 86 using the "bell curve." Tom thought this classroom practice was OK. Why not, for he was the one with the high grade and, after all, not everyone can learn math. He also thought the grades assigned should reflect class standing.

John recalled how his teacher always graded on the "curve." This teacher gave an equal number of As, Bs, Ds, and Fs. Naturally most students received Cs. He also thought that rewards ought to be reserved for the most talented, and other students should know they couldn't do as well. After all, he reasoned, that is the way life is. John went on to prestigious universities for both undergraduate and graduate study. He was pleased with his learning experiences and he was quite successful.

During another conversation with Jerry, one of the most caring people I know, he stated that he really didn't believe all students were capable of learning well. Jerry was a highly successful businessperson as well as a good learner. His grandchildren were also good learners but he knew many of their friends were choosing not to learn. Jerry's conclusion was that not all students can learn well and grades ought to reflect these expectations.

In all of these conversations no one said that grades should reflect whether students have learned the predetermined standards or not. What they said or implied was that testing and grading should be used to compare and sort students so those expected to learn get high grades and those not expected to learn get low grades. When I first started to teach, I designed my math test so some students could do most of the problems, some could do only a few, and only a few could do them all. I now know that it is possible for everyone to learn the skills necessary to do well on a test.

Recent conversations with business executives revealed some startling comments. Some told me that education should be designed to prepare students to be successful in a capitalistic society. They seem to forget that not everyone is going to participate in the system. They also seem to forget that the models, formulas, and practices that are used in business were established by theorists with advanced training and degrees. They also seem to forget that before one specializes it is important to have a broad range of learning. It is wrong to try to place students into a career path too early without a good education.

The know-and-do model was developed to provide all students with the necessary preparation to be successful either in further education or in the world of work. It is important for students to be flexible enough to deal with change. A good broad education that emphasizes knowledge and transferable skills will create this kind of flexibility.

I sometimes think that even if all students were learning well, we would still hear that our schools are failing or that they need improvement. In truth, most schools are not failing but there is always room to improve. As educators we must always strive to get better.

This chapter is dedicated to practices that help define our classrooms but are rarely discussed openly. Unless we examine each classroom practice against our stated mission of getting all students to learn well, the mission cannot be achieved. If we want all students to learn well and be prepared for a bright future, they must be encouraged to explore ideas, be creative, integrate knowledge, draw meaningful conclusions, and hypothesize. If we want all students to go well beyond the goal of just getting good grades to focus on meaningful learning and take risks in learning, then they should not fear testing and grading.

Here is the problem. Should students be given the freedom to demonstrate their creativity and ability to go beyond the norm or should they always try to give teachers what they want?

A few years ago my son James called about a dilemma he was facing while he was a student at the University of Pennsylvania. He said he was taking one of the most interesting courses he had ever taken and read every article on the suggested reading list. He said if he gave the professor what he believed the professor wanted and played it safe, he thought he would get an A or 4.0 for a grade. But he said if he took a risk by showing that he was able to analyze the readings, synthesize knowledge, and draw informed conclusions, he might not get a high grade. "What should I do?" he asked.

I know, as most parents do, that this was a loaded question. If I gave advice, he would probably have done the opposite. I said that I would respect and love him no matter what decision he made. Weeks later he told me he got a 4.0 on his test. He also told me that he took the risk of trying out new ideas. Because he took a risk, his professor secured him a full scholarship to continue his studies for a master's degree.

Why can't all students be free and encouraged to take risks, share ideas, and show how much they really know without any fear of not giving teachers what they want? They should. If they try something that doesn't work, an effective educator would simply correct the errors, and have students make the necessary adjustments. A grade should reflect the new learning, after competency is demonstrated.

The classroom practices of testing, assessment, retesting, and grading influence not only if students will learn but also if they will be prepared to become future leaders who can develop new and important ideas. We simply don't know when and where the best ideas will emerge. Many of the most famous inventions and discoveries were made by people not expected to make contributions to society. Since we can't always predict which students will become our next geniuses, we must treat all students as if they will be the ones.

The current overemphasis on standards, and corresponding testing, will result in long-term detriment to students and this nation. Yes, students and teachers must be held accountable, but we must go well beyond the limiting testing and grading that is now being employed in many schools. If we want our students to have the knowledge and skills outlined in this book, we must change our thinking about classroom practices and get away, far away, from testing and grading students for the purpose of comparing and sorting them. That is not our job. Our job is to get all students learning well.

This chapter will consider five classroom practices. There are others, but the five presented here will either encourage or discourage students from going above and beyond minimums or what is expected.

1. Testing and Assessment
2. Grading
3. Retesting and Managing Time
4. Homework
5. Discipline

You can accept these practices and you can add to them. You can accept the discussions provided but it would be more valuable to use the process suggested to develop your own. One word of advice, as you develop a process for each practice, keep parents informed and involved. For each practice consider the following four phases:

Phase 1: What should the purposes of this practice be?
Phase 2: What should the nonpurposes of this practice be?
Phase 3: What are the predominant current practices in your school?
Phase 4: What regulations or guidelines would you like to see implemented in your school?

All activities in this chapter will be most effective if done by the total faculty or by a committee representing the entire staff. Be sure to inform and keep all teachers involved in the process.

The discussions that follow each activity reflect the thinking of the Johnson City teachers during my tenure as superintendent, with some modifications and updating.

CLASSROOM PRACTICE 1: TESTING AND ASSESSMENT

Using the instructional process, you have prepared students for success. You taught using different teaching–learning modes, and provided an abundance of guided practice and informal assessments. Now students are ready to take a more formal assessment. By this time you should know whether your students are ready to demonstrate their understanding of their knowledge on a test. Doing well on a test, project, or written paper is an expectation for all students. It is a time for all students to celebrate their effort and achievement and to show their teacher and parents that they have performed well.

Activity: Determining the Purpose of Testing and Assessment

There are many ways to assess how well students are doing in a course. What should the purposes of assessment and testing of student performance be?

Discussion of the Purpose of Testing and Assessment

Testing and assessment should be used:

1. to determine what a student has learned and what he or she still needs to learn,
2. to help each student learn and use knowledge well,
3. to determine how effective the course or program is,
4. to determine how well the teacher applied the instructional process, and
5. to provide information to students, teachers, and parents.

Activity: Determining What Is Not the Purpose of Testing and Assessment

Sometimes teachers assess and test a student's performance for the wrong reasons. Perhaps it was the way it was done to them. Nevertheless, it is very important to examine some of the nonpurposes of testing and assessment so that they can be avoided. Inappropriate use of testing and assessment can actually interfere with student effort and learning. What are some practices that should never be used when assessing and testing student performance?

Discussion of What Is Not the Purpose of Testing and Assessment

Testing and assessment should not be used:

1. to label, sort, or compare students;
2. to discipline, control students, or "to get even";
3. to foster competitions;
4. to obtain enough grades for the grade book; or
5. to assess the learner.

Activity: Determining Some Guidelines for Testing and Assessment

It is appropriate to get faculty agreement on the purposes and nonpurposes of testing and assessment, but if action is not taken, the activity is useless. Based on the previous discussions, what are some guidelines you would like to see implemented?

Discussion of Some Guidelines of Testing and Assessment

1. Teachers will align all assessment and testing to the course, unit, and lesson learning goals.
2. Teachers will communicate to students what is to be learned and how they will demonstrate that learning.
3. Teachers will measure both knowledge and skills.
4. Teachers will design tests to reflect their instruction and various learning modes.
5. Teachers will give a student a test only when they have information that the student will achieve at least at a competent level. A student will be denied a test if the teacher believes the student is not adequately prepared.
6. Teachers will use both traditional and alternative assessments to measure what students should *know* and be able to *do*.

CLASSROOM PRACTICE 2: GRADING

Sometimes grades get in the way of learning. Students can get hooked on grades and study just to get good grades. There is nothing wrong with getting good grades, but good grades and learning well are not always connected. Studying solely to get a good grade usually has students trying to determine what will be on the test. Sometimes they guess right; sometimes they don't. Studying to learn and studying to get good grades are sometimes not the same. It would be nice if they were. Students could then study to learn, to apply their skills, to make connections within their learning, and to be able to communicate their knowledge and skills in a variety of ways.

Grades are part of our culture and our schools. However, it might be effective, in the long term, if grades were not given before fourth grade. This includes red ink markings, scores, and negative comments. Only comments about how to improve understanding should be used. Even when we give some form of grades to students, it would be useful to let them know what they can do to improve and get better.

We should encourage students to study to learn and to demonstrate their learning not only on more traditional tests but also on alternative forms of assessments. Allow students the freedom to take risks on tests and even the freedom to demonstrate what they have learned through various agreed-upon methods.

Alternative forms of testing have some risks. Students may try new ideas and not do well. But if teachers allow for flexible grading and corrections are made to learning outcomes and errors, then a grade can always be altered to reflect the learning. Teachers are encouraged to hold off on the grade until the learning is demonstrated in an acceptable manner.

A flexible grading system that allows students to learn well before a grade is given may cause some problems because some teachers feel that it is their job to compare and rank students using the grading system. This is *not* our job. We are not in the business of comparing and ranking students. We are in the business of teaching so all students will learn.

Sometimes parents are concerned about how well their children are doing in comparison to others. We should report to parents how well their children are doing with regard to the expected goals, but never how well they are doing with regards to others.

Some parents will complain when they see that their son or daughter did well more quickly than someone else and both got the same grade. With a flexible grading system, time is not a factor for grades; learning dictates the grades. Once most parents understand that you are not comparing students but that grades reflect what each student has learned, there will be less resistance.

Performance standards should be determined for each unit. Students should be informed of these standards and then be expected to accomplish them.

Activity: Determining What Grade Reflects Good Learning

1. How do you determine whether students have learned what you want them to learn?
2. If a student gets a grade of A or its equivalent, does that mean the student has learned well?
3. If a student gets a grade of B or its equivalent, does that mean the student has learned well?
4. How about grades of C, D, or F?

Every time I have done this activity with teachers I get the same basic reaction. They say grades of A or B represent good learning. They say a D or F doesn't. They hedge with a grade of C. Most say a grade of C does not represent good learning.

Many schools have chosen a minimum standard of C or 75% as the least acceptable grade. Still others have chosen a minimum standard of B or 80% as a minimum grade. The same schools argue that unless students get at least the equivalent of a C, with most students expected to achieve at least a B or A, real learning has not taken place.

After establishing a minimum acceptable grade, some schools have agreed not to assign a grade until a student has achieved the minimum acceptable grade. To do this and report to parents, these schools have devised a method to indicate the student is working to get a good grade but has not yet reached that grade. They sometimes will use a grade of "inc," representing incomplete learning. Still others use an "ny" grade, which means not yet, and indicates that the student hasn't yet achieved mastery.

Performance standards can vary from course to course. You and your colleagues should determine the performance standards that work for you and your students.

When you use "inc" or "ny" as a grade, however, it is important that you examine how you use it. The spirit of giving a student an inc or an ny must be done with care and understanding. Those teachers who use it as a stimulus response, a hammer over the student's head, will not have success. Do not use it as a threat or a way of trying to coerce students to learn. This is not the intent. Rather, the intent is to show caring and empathy and to foster students learning at reasonable performance levels.

When considering this alternate approach to traditional grading, do it slowly. Do not change the grading system too quickly, but let it develop gradually over time. Be sure parents are involved in the process so everyone can prepare for it. No one involved should be surprised. Once you have agreed to a change, be sure parents know early on if their child is getting an "inc" or an "ny" grade.

With an ny grade, you will need an aggressive plan to help the student reach the minimum established grade. This must be done promptly. The more time that passes, the more difficult it will be to achieve success.

If some students have no grade at the end of a unit while most do, simply go on to the next unit, while still requiring those not reaching the minimum acceptable grades to reach them. Students can seek extra help after school from their teachers or get help from another teacher after school or during the school day. Some schools have allocated the first two weeks during the long summer break to allowing students to get the help they need to remove any no grade and get full credit for a course. Still other schools have students come to school during other vacation times. Some schools have Saturday or evening help sessions. Again, never use these extra help sessions as a threat to any child, but as an opportunity for them to learn and get a good grade. Whenever teachers give a poor grade to a student and go on, it shows the students you don't care. Let us care enough to expect good grades.

When I was a graduate student at Stanford University studying mathematics, I asked my advisor what he would think if I took a graduate writing course to improve my writing skills. Having done most of my graduate work in mathematics, I realized that I needed to become a better writer. I was scared when I entered the class with all the language majors. I believed they were all good writers.

On the first day the professor said, "I want all of you to be good writers." He told us we would have to write a three- to four-page paper each week and that his comments on those papers would improve our writing. We were told that we could rewrite each paper and as long as we were putting forth the effort, we would not be assigned a grade until we wrote a good paper.

Following his wonderful suggestions I rewrote each paper many times while continuing to write the next paper. At any given time I was rewriting two papers and writing one new one. I had never worked so hard, but I loved it because I knew I would do well. That experience had a profound influence on me personally as well as educationally. Using his flexible grading system, this professor wanted us to learn. He helped all of his students learn well.

Activity: Determining the Purpose of Grading

While teachers receive suggestions and even school policy about grading, each teacher has his or her own grading system. What should the purposes of grading be?

Discussion of the Purpose of Grading

1. To certify that a student has achieved at competent or highly competent levels (There are a few exceptions such as students who have learned enough to go on but are not quite at the minimum competent level. This is a teacher's judgment. Never let lack of effort be one of the exceptions.)
2. To communicate an acceptable standard of performance to students, parents, and others

Activity: Determining What Is Not the Purpose of Grading

Sometimes teachers give grades for all the wrong reasons. They follow the same guidelines used when they were students. What are some nonpurposes of grading?

Discussion of What Is Not the Purpose of Grading

1. To promote competition or comparisons among students.
2. To produce a required number of grades for a grade book.
3. To control or punish students.
4. To inflate grades to pass students to the next grade level.

Activity: Determining Some Guidelines for Grading

Based on the previous discussions, what are some guidelines that you would like to see implemented for grading?

Discussion of Some Guidelines for Grading

1. A grade will always reflect achievement of what a student knows and is able to do. It will never reflect how long it took a student to learn or how students compare to one another.
2. A grade will reflect a predetermined agreed-upon standard of competence.
3. No low or failing grades will be given to a student who has not achieved the standard of competence. The exception to this is the student who shows no effort to learn when the teacher has made a significant effort.
4. A grade may be altered (not averaged) whenever a student can demonstrate new and better learning of the stated criteria—what they should *know* and *do*. Parameters for altering a grade will be determined and stated. Reasonable opportunities will be given.
5. Grades will not be given for effort but for demonstrated achievement.
6. Grades will reflect Individual Education Program (IEP) for students. The content *(know)* and the skills *(do)* may vary and the grades will reflect acceptable stated standards.

CLASSROOM PRACTICE 3: RETESTING AND MANAGING TIME

Consider the following:

- A student has not demonstrated he or she has learned well, at least to the stated acceptable competency.
- A student has not demonstrated he or she is ready to take the scheduled test.
- A student wants to demonstrate new and better learning in order to improve his or her grade.
- A student wants to demonstrate to the teacher that he or she has extended the expected learnings of the unit.

All of these considerations require some form of retesting, testing, or other forms of assessment. Naturally there are limitations for any of these considerations. Without guidelines clearly understood by everyone, the retesting procedures can get out of hand.

Begin with the premise that it is a privilege to be earned and not a student's right to take a retest or alter a grade. It is the student's responsibility to demonstrate that he or she has done the required work and can show competence through a brief, often oral, assessment. Not all retests should be conducted with paper and pencil, nor is it necessary to give the entire test again. Sometimes an oral test, a portion of a test, or an alternative method can be used to demonstrate competence.

Some teachers have all retesting done at the same time and usually this is after school. While this is an inconvenience for the teacher it is also an inconvenience for the student. Teachers should announce well ahead of time when the retesting will take place as well as the deadline to show required work for admission to the retesting sessions.

It is absolutely imperative that students be shown that taking a retest is a privilege and that it is their responsibility to demonstrate readiness to earn it. They must get the message, but not in a threatening way, that it is easier and wiser to do it right the first time. It will take time for students to realize this but don't give up, it will work.

The consequences of not giving retests are lower student performance and both teacher and student discouragement. When a teacher tests, and then moves on, with no opportunity to alter a poor grade, students get the message that they can't afford to make a mistake. While it can be argued that this happens in life and in further education, I don't think this is true or appropriate for our classrooms. Yes, students must prepare and be expected to achieve on the initial test. They are expected to have and feel some anxiety about demonstrating their knowledge and skills. They should also be able to take risks and know that it is possible, if all does not go well on the test, to be given another chance to demonstrate a better understanding. Let me emphasize that it is expected that all students will take the test at the completion of the unit and that taking a retest is an exception and not the norm.

Managing Time

From experience, teachers know the amount of time it takes for students to learn a particular unit of study. Try to get most students to learn in the time allotted, but be flexible to accommodate different student performance. Providing for both time-based and performance-based learning is a balancing act. Try to do both. Teachers must determine the approximate amount of time needed to learn a unit and to get all students to learn within the stated time parameters. Most students will learn what you want them to learn within the allocated time.

Some students, naturally, will need more time to learn, but if the entire instructional process is followed well, most will not. A word of caution: don't wait until everyone in the class learns the required learning criteria before moving on to the next unit of study. Teachers must control the amount of time needed to learn but with enough flexibility to alter or adjust the time. For those students having difficulty learning, you may want to alter the expectations to the necessary essential levels, that level which is a must for understanding the next lessons and units. Altering an expectation is a last-resort decision.

Expectations *must not* be altered for those students who choose not to do the work. These students must be held accountable to the desired level of expectations. When working with students who choose not to learn, reread the chapter on psychology and internal motivation. Also give these students a no grade rather than a low or failing grade. Emphasize that you want them to learn and that you will help them, but that it is their responsibility to do the work and to learn.

Oftentimes when teachers operate solely under a performance-based curriculum, time escapes them and soon the class becomes fragmented and unmanageable. It is virtually impossible for teachers to have many groups within the same classroom. By starting with group-based instruction, where the teacher sets time parameters for starting and ending a unit of study, and with the intent that all students will learn within this time, it has been found that most students do precisely that.

For those students who need additional help, provide it as suggested before, during, or after school. Small-group help sessions are quite appropriate. Some schools have a vacation time schedule and also hire teachers to provide additional help. It has been my experience that most students do not seem to mind giving up their free time to learn. This is possible if the teacher sets the proper climate and culture. This time must never be viewed as a punishment.

Some schools have study rooms for students to receive extra help and have teachers and peers available. For example, there might be a room where math teachers are available all day and where students who are good at math volunteer their time as well. This can happen for most disciplines.

Some Concluding Thoughts on Retesting and Time Management

Most students will have learned well what is expected by the time they get to the test. Some will not. Therefore:

1. Determine how well students have learned before taking the test.
2. Make the necessary adjustments and corrections. Correct any misunderstandings.
3. Reteach those students not doing well. Perhaps use a different teaching–learning mode.
4. Have approximate times for starting and ending a unit.
5. Try to get everyone to learn within the scheduled time.

6. For those who have repeated difficulty, use professional judgment and alter expectations. This is a last-resort process. Never alter expectations for those students who won't do the work.
7. Give retests to those who earn the privilege.

Activity: Determining the Purpose of Retesting

Retesting is necessary but if not done properly will cause many problems. When all teachers use the same process many problems will disappear. What is the purpose of retesting?

Discussion of the Purpose of Retesting

1. To have students demonstrate new and better learning
2. To promote student responsibility by having students prepare and demonstrate an attitude and readiness to take a retest (To take a retest is not a student's right, but an earned privilege and opportunity.)
3. To have students earn excellent achievement at the competent or highly competent levels
4. To have both teachers and students assess those learning goals not previously learned at the stated standard of performance
5. To assist teachers in determining what teaching modes and correctives needed to be incorporated in the unit or lesson plan

Activity: Determining the Nonpurposes of Retesting

Retests should never be given for the wrong reasons. If they are, students will not learn as well and the entire process becomes an adversarial one. What are some practices that should never be used for students to take a retest?

Discussion of What Is Not the Purpose of Retesting

1. Students must be encouraged to achieve well on the first test and to avoid taking a retest.

2. Taking a retest is a privilege and an opportunity and not a right.
3. All parameters for taking a retest will be determined and published, including estimated time deadlines.
4. Students must demonstrate additional preparation, learning, and readiness to take a retest. They must show evidence of work.
5. Only learning goals not achieved need to be retested.
6. If learning goals are measured in another unit, that test can serve as the retest.

CLASSROOM PRACTICE 4: HOMEWORK

Some parents say their lives are so hectic that there is little time for family activities. These parents prefer no or very little homework. They say, for example, that baseball, hockey, basketball, soccer, and other lessons occupy all their valuable time.

The bottom line for these parents is that their children's lives are so structured that there is little time for anything but their activities. Homework is viewed as a chore to get done and not a valuable learning experience. Some of these parents confess that they help more with homework than they should. Some even do the homework for their children. This is particularly true for parents of elementary-school children.

However, most parents of secondary students see homework as necessary. These parents believe students can get some, if not all, of their homework done in study halls during the school day. They believe that if their children don't have homework, they will fall behind and not be prepared for tests and may not get into the most competitive colleges and universities.

The need for homework varies from early elementary school through high school. Young children should get little or no homework. When they get homework, it must be modest, with the intent of getting young children to be responsible and perhaps to show their parents what they are doing. A little more homework is expected in the upper elementary grades.

For the most part, homework is necessary in middle and high school. It allows students to practice and apply their knowledge, explore ideas, become self-directed learners, determine what they still must learn, and reinforce and retain knowledge and skills. There is not enough time during the school day to prepare and practice. There is not enough time to develop their communication skills, use technology, solve problems, create hypotheses, or read and study the references associated with the lessons. There is not enough time during the school day to prepare for tougher, more advanced courses that require several hours of homework each night.

There is just too much to learn for it all to happen within the six- or seven-hour school day, 180 times a year. If these parameters are changed, the discussion of homework takes a different slant. Perhaps with a longer school day or an extended school year, students would be able to practice, retain, and extend their learning and do what is necessary without doing much extra work at home.

The truth is that the better the instructional process, the less the homework is needed. With the very best teaching, students want to continue their learning at home. They find homework an extension of the class and want to extend their understanding. In these instances, homework is not busy work but meaningful and desired by students.

Gabe was a high-school junior who averaged four hours of homework each day. It was his choice to be in the International Baccalaureate Program of his high school. Gabe is now a student at a prestigious college and is doing well. He knew the rewards of hard work.

When students have space assigned for study, no distractions, time parameters to study, and parental interest and support, students get their homework completed, study more, and learn more. Parents often ask their children, "Did you get your homework done?" This is an important question, but better questions would be, "What kind of homework did you have today? How was it related to what you learned in class?"

Is homework important? Can you imagine anyone who has achieved anything, who did not spend many hours practicing and extending his or her knowledge and skills? Fine piano players, hockey players, golfers, and scientists did not excel without practice. It takes a great deal of practice, dedication, responsibility, and study to become really good in any field. After primary school, homework plays an important part in children's education and this increases gradually as the years go on.

Activity: Determining the Purposes of Homework

The many purposes for homework vary from primary through high school. What are the many purposes for homework? After listing these purposes, make good decisions for your class and grade level.

Discussion of the Purpose of Homework

Homework can be given:

1. To provide independent practice
2. To promote retention of knowledge and skills
3. To provide cumulative practice and review
4. To practice and reinforce understanding and skills
5. To inform teachers if additional teaching strategies are necessary
6. To encourage self-assessment and correctives
7. To promote self-directed learning and investigations
8. To encourage responsibility
9. To enhance confidence
10. To communicate between school and home
11. To encourage creativity

Sometimes students get homework and neither parents nor students know why. Some teachers give homework because they think it is expected and not for a good purpose.

Activity: Determining What Is Not the Purpose of Homework

It is important to examine practices teachers should never use when assigning homework. What are some practices that should never be used when assigning homework to students?

Discussion of the Nonpurposes of Homework

Homework should not be used:

1. To provide busy work
2. To discipline or punish students
3. To foster competition
4. To show parents that you are a "good teacher"
5. To practice incorrectly when students don't understand
6. To show students that they don't know everything

Activity: Determining Some Guidelines for Giving Homework

It would be nice to get faculty agreement on some guidelines for giving homework. What are some guidelines concerning homework you would like to see implemented in your school?

Discussion of Some Guidelines for Homework

1. Teachers will publish the purposes and nonpurposes of homework and students' responsibilities. They will follow the purposes and refrain from using nonpurposes.
2. Homework will be given only when the teacher determines students can do it.
3. All homework should be relevant and aligned to the lessons and standards.
4. Teachers can assign different homework to different students. Some students need to spend more time on the five skills of testing and assessment, grading, retesting and managing time, homework, and discipline while others need to focus on the basic knowledge.
5. All homework should be realistic both in content and time needed to complete.
6. Completion of homework and short verbal assessment can be used to allow retests.

7. All homework should be monitored for completion but not necessarily graded.
8. Students should be given opportunities to begin homework in the classroom under the watchful eye of the teacher.

CLASSROOM PRACTICE 5: CLASSROOM DISCIPLINE

One of the first questions a beginning teacher asks is, "How can I get students to listen, pay attention, learn, and behave?" While most students will not misbehave, some come to class to disrupt, cause a scene, and get attention. The key is not to give them the stage to get it.

Activity: Students Who Misbehave

1. Why do some students misbehave for some teachers and not for others?
2. Determine what teachers are doing when their students are not misbehaving.
3. Determine what teachers are doing when their students are misbehaving.

Earlier I said that successful teachers, those whose students choose to learn instead of acting out, establish a wonderful relationship with each student. In these classrooms, blame, humiliation, yelling, or sarcasm do not exist. All students are valued, students know this, and are learning well.

In these classrooms, teachers are preparing all students for success each day both academically and attitudinally. Teachers are assuring all students that they will learn well. They get and focus attention on what is to be learned. They use their imagination and skills as a teacher to be creative in doing this. In these classrooms, teachers get students involved quickly in the learning process, teach to the many and varied ways students learn, and encourage all students to be responsible for their own learning. The teacher becomes the academic coach. They know whoever is the most active is learning the most.

Reviewing chapter 10, and its discussion of the climate, cultural factors and instructional process necessary for an ideal classroom without behavioral problems would be helpful as you read this chapter. Also, thinking back to chapter 8, which illustrates how choice theory helps us understand why we do what we do, and that all behavior, both good and bad, is chosen to satisfy one or more of our basic psychological needs would also be productive.

When children do not feel that they belong, fit in, or are part of the group, they might act out. When children do not feel that they are worthwhile or have no sense of being in control, they might act out. When children do not feel they have the freedom to state their opinions, think, create, take risks, or try new ideas, they might act out. And when children do not experience joy and fun, are not learning well, and think that what they are asked to learn is mindless and not useful, they might act out.

Students will act out when their needs are not being met. If you help students satisfy their needs more effectively, they will make better decisions and your classroom will become more productive.

Don't make the same mistakes I made during my first year of teaching. My perceptions were that some kids were going to misbehave, no matter what I did. I expected this to happen and it did. My perceptions were wrong. My expectations were wrong. My actions were wrong. Once I began to think and act differently, my students also began to change, and most, if not all, of my problems disappeared. (Review chapter 3 for more details.)

When students are learning well and are involved in their learning, when teachers are aligning their teaching, planning, and testing, when teachers are creating a positive and satisfying climate and culture, and when teachers' perceptions, expectations, and beliefs are encouraging, most students' basic psychological needs will be satisfied effectively.

The following conditions are necessary to prevent behavioral problems and to encourage students to learn.

1. Students must sense and know that you, as their teacher, are excited about teaching and being with them and you must show them that this is true. You are excited about the subjects you are teaching and this

shows. You are excited about learning and acquiring knowledge and skills and this is obvious to those around you.
2. You have much knowledge about teaching, and about the subjects you are teaching.
3. You, as their teacher, have high expectations and are caring of all students. Having high expectations and not caring will not get results. Being caring and not having high expectations of students will not get results.

It is very important that the teacher's very first class each year get off to a fast start. This will set the tone for the entire course. You can do this in many ways depending on the age of the children and their grade level. In the early grades you can have activities where all students are involved and successful. When this works, students are anxious to go home and tell their parents how excited they are about school.

In middle or high school you can start by actually teaching an interesting, well-prepared lesson. Use the instructional process and have students involved actively in the lesson. They will get the message that they can succeed and learn in this class and that learning is very important. That is why they are there.

Another good beginning activity is to establish mutual responsibilities through the "my job, your job, not my job, not your job" activity. This involvement in determining class rules and expectations will go a long way in preventing and solving behavior problems. After all, the students, along with you, created these rules. After an agreement is reached and published, everyone commits to live by it and everyone holds each other accountable.

When a child is not living by those agreements, put the child in conflict with the rules. Never put children in conflict with you. This would be a big mistake. Furthermore, never get into an argument with a child; you won't win and you won't get what you want. When either of you are emotionally upset, no resolution of the problem can be attained. It is much better to deal with the problem when everyone is calm.

When a child is not following the agreed-upon rules, never ask why. You will get the most marvelous creative reasons and most of the time they are fabrications. Ask three questions when a child is misbehaving:

1. What are you doing? This must be asked in a calm nonthreatening way. You want the child to identify the behavior. If he or she continues to say nothing, then tell the child, in a firm calm voice, what he or she is doing. This identifies the problem.
2. Ask if what he or she is doing is against the posted rules. Point to the rule or rules. You want the child to identify the rule or rules broken. If you get no answer, tell the child, in a calm voice, what he or she is doing and what rule he or she has broken.
3. Finally, ask the child what he or she is going to do about his or her behavior. You want the child to make a plan and to recognize that the behavior was unacceptable.

You may be thinking that this process is taking a lot of time. If done right, it will take only a minute or two. If it takes more time and either of you are getting upset, or the process is going nowhere, then wait a while and address the issue again later.

If the child is not able to manage himself or herself without disrupting the class, move that child to a predetermined location. This can be in the classroom or elsewhere. Some teachers have a time-out seat in the classroom where the child is sent until the problem can be solved. Although in the classroom, this child is not allowed to participate in any of the activities. This child can be asked the three questions and must answer them in order to regain his or her status as a participating member of the class.

Still other teachers have a time-out seat outside the classroom, perhaps in the hall or another teacher's classroom. Students, for obvious reasons, do not like to be separated from their class. Again the student and teacher must work out the problem before the student is allowed to return. Dr. William Glasser's book *Control Theory in the Classroom* provides more insight into the three questions and how to resolve behavioral issues (Glasser, 1986).

Remember that time-out space should not be viewed as a punishment space. If you want students to be responsible and to learn, punishment won't get it for you.

Another workable strategy is to let students know that they don't have to act out to get out. If for some reason the class is becoming intolerable for some students, they should know that they have alternatives to misbehaving. They can quietly get up and go to a predetermined quiet space in the classroom. With prior permission of the principal, the student may leave the classroom and go to another predetermined part of the building. One school that I visited in Australia had a quiet room near, but not in, the main office. Some children were allowed to go there, where some hands-on learning activities were present, to get settled. Most students who went there knew it was a temporary measure to get back in control. The quiet room is not good or bad. It is simply an alternative to acting out in the classroom. Some students who already knew the lesson were allowed to opt out and go to the quiet room or the library to do other work.

Finally, when trying to work out a problem with a child, never ask the question "Why did you do it?" or "Will you ever do it again?" This will only exacerbate the problem.

Everyone must be calm when trying to solve a problem. If you, or the student, are too upset, the problem will not get solved. Never argue with students. Be responsible and remember that you are the adult.

Activity: Determining the Purpose of Classroom Discipline

When students are learning, actively involved, and a positive culture has been established, most problems will never occur. What should be the purpose of classroom discipline?

The Purpose of the Classroom Practice of Discipline

Classroom discipline problems will be avoided and disappear when teachers:

1. Create an environment where all students learn.
2. Provide a process to promote self-discipline and responsibility.
3. Create a classroom that satisfies the basic psychological needs.
4. Encourage socially acceptable and effective behavior.
5. Provide a positive climate and culture.
6. Establish the classroom rules with students.

Activity: Determining What Is Not the Purpose of Classroom Discipline

Some classroom discipline practices created by teachers don't solve discipline problems, and at times even exacerbate difficult situations. What are some classroom discipline practices that should never be used?

What Is Not the Purpose of the Classroom Practice of Discipline

Teachers should never use classroom discipline:

1. To punish students
2. To humiliate students
3. To argue with students
4. To judge students rather than the behavior
5. To be sarcastic

Activity: Determining Some Guidelines for Classroom Discipline

Without good and effective classroom discipline practices, little learning will take place. Which comes first, good teaching with students learning or good practices so students can learn? It is probably a combination of both. When all teachers follow the same classroom discipline guidelines, students soon get the message that self-control as well as learning is important. What are some classroom discipline guidelines you would like to see implemented?

Guidelines for Classroom Discipline

1. Teachers will create procedures so that all students are physically and psychologically safe.
2. Rules and consequences for creating a positive classroom climate and culture will be developed by everyone.

3. All rules will be published and everyone agrees to be held accountable, with appropriate consequences.
4. Teachers will use a positive classroom discipline process to help children learn and become responsible every time there is a problem.
5. Everyone understands that prevention of discipline problems is the most effective classroom discipline practice.

Activity: Developing a Discipline Plan

After reading all ideas and reviewing the knowledge concerning classroom discipline, design a plan to prevent discipline problems and to solve them if they exist.

Classroom Practices: What Teachers Have to Say

Elaine. If we have done our job in the instructional process, then the test certifies that learning has taken place. If students don't do well on the test, we need to look at ourselves and make the necessary adjustments in our teaching. These are the questions I would ask myself:

1. Did I get the students ready to succeed?
2. Did I test what I was teaching?
3. Did I align my instruction with the desired outcomes?
4. Did I provide adequate guided practice and did I ensure the students understood?

Gene. I am expecting every student to get 100%. They know that when I pass out test papers I am expecting everyone to get as close to perfect as possible.

Larry. I used to test to find out if students have learned or not. That is much too late to find out. Now I am reasonably sure all will do well since I followed the instructional process. There are some exceptions but not many.

Paul. Homework must never be busy work but it should be so important that students know what they should be able to do. They then do their independent homework. If a student simply refuses to do homework, he or she is not afforded an opportunity to take the test. If they do not fulfill their requirements, they are not permitted to take the test. Address all problems when they occur and do not let them drag on. If a student has an attitudinal problem and refuses to do the work, why in the world would you give the student the right to take the test or retest? If students don't fulfill their obligation, why should they have the right to participate in the examination or retest? If a student has an academic problem, then it is a matter of working with the student on a daily basis to try to resolve the lack of knowledge and skills.

Elaine. If students know exactly what is expected of them throughout the unit, and we are consistent with the classroom practices, and if we are consistent with the requirements of the unit, I believe many problems will disappear. There must be no surprises. Students know what they must learn, what will be tested, how to earn good grades, what is expected during independent practice, and the requirements to take a retest. If for some reason a student did not do well enough on the test, he or she needs to know how to improve the grade.

Pat. As a parent I found that my daughter learned a simple lesson when she had to take a retest. She told me that it would have been better and easier to pay attention and do the work the first time. She confessed that there was a lot of extra hard work. Students must understand that partial or incomplete knowledge is not good enough anymore. They need complete and in-depth knowledge. Everyone must realize that teachers, students, and parents are on the same team, with the same goal of getting all students to learn well. In the past it seemed that teachers, students, and parents were adversaries, but not now.

Nancy. At the elementary level, children are not really given much, if any, homework. They need more time with their family once the school day is over. Since students have been on task all day, and their minds have been going all day, they need more unstructured time at home to relax, play, and be with friends and family. It allows them to be kids. It allows children to be children.

Elaine. With good communication, parents become valuable resources helping correct any problems their sons or daughters have. Make sure parents are aware of what is going on with all the classroom practices.

Gary. A few parents said that the grading and retesting practices were unfair. They said that their children got a high grade on the test the first time and didn't have to take a retest or alter the grade. But, some students took longer to learn and had to take retests, but got the same grade. After all, they said, our children did it right the first time and learned more quickly than others so they should get a higher grade. I informed them that we, all teachers in this school system, deal with students as individuals and they don't have to compete for learning. Since all teachers follow the guidelines for the classroom practices, most parents eventually supported the process.

Frank. We've really gotten away from equating the slow learner with the poor learner. I think that is tremendous because sometimes I think of two students reading the same book. Who is to say that the one student who reads it faster has achieved better than the one who takes longer to read it?

Al. Wouldn't it be nice if no grade was ever fixed and that any time, within reason, a student can demonstrate new and better learning, the grade would be altered to reflect that learning? Are we in the grading or learning business? Sometimes grading and learning do not complement each other. Wouldn't it be nice if schools could concentrate on students' learning instead of students' grades?

Paul. Assessment does not always have to be done with paper and pencil. You can tell by body language, the closure activity, and assessing throughout the lesson. You can actually reduce problems by having complete awareness of the teaching–learning process at all times. It takes a lot longer to read and grade a class of unsuccessful compositions, poorly written, than it does to read and grade successful compositions well written.

Larry. The traditional notion "if at first you don't succeed, flunk" is not a part of the testing, retesting, grading process. Students know that if they persevere and have the time and good instruction they need, they will succeed. With success comes further motivation. I really think this process is the kind with which all educators can agree. Who can disagree about earned success? A test under these circumstances is a validation process.

CONCLUSION

I have seen many students turn off to school when they knew that no matter how hard they tried they were still being compared to others for grades. When students don't do well on a test and there are no provisions for taking another test and getting a good grade, they will not try. Outdated discipline policies do not work and homework must be appropriate to the age and grade of the student. If you employ all the classroom practices presented in this chapter, you will be well on your way to creating an ideal school.

Chapter Thirteen

The Principal

There is no greater gift to a school than having a great principal.

Focus Questions

1. If you as a principal had the full cooperation of your staff, your board of education or community group, and a reasonable amount of money to affect change, what would be your hope, vision, plan, and design?
2. How will a principal set the conditions so that staff and community want to change and get better?
3. How will a principal manage change? Describe your change process.
4. How will a principal set the conditions so that staff will satisfy their basic psychological needs?
5. What are some characteristics of all successful principals?
6. What is the role of the principal in determining the culture and climate of a school?
7. You have observed some principals who have been very successful in the operation of their school. Why do you think they were successful? Describe some of their practices. What might you hear them saying?
8. You have observed some principals who have been less than successful in the operation of their schools. Why do you think they were unsuccessful? Describe some of their practices. What might you hear them saying?
9. How are problems solved and decisions made in your school? Describe a process. Are they accepted, effective, and used? Who is involved in problem solving and decision making?

10. How are tensions managed in your school?
11. How are staff members who do not want to improve or who kill every major idea that comes their way treated in your school?
12. What if every good idea that would improve your school and student learning is killed in the faculty room? How can a principal help change this so that teachers who want to change are not pulled back into the pack or influenced negatively?
13. How would you like to be remembered as a principal?
14. What are some barriers or inhibitors to change? How can a principal be the chief causal change agent? How could a principal direct change in a positive way? How does change begin? What are some reasons that even good change is eventually rejected by staff? When is change no longer a choice by staff, but is mandated?

A community was seeking a new principal for its elementary school and asked me to help them with the process. Involving the teachers, support staff, some parents, and some community leaders, I asked one question. What personal characteristics do you want a principal to possess? Here are some of their responses. We want a principal who:

1. stays focused on the real purpose of our school, which is "all students will learn well and achieve at high levels"
2. values every child, teacher, and all who work in the school
3. builds confidence in our school and will serve and lead and not coerce or command
4. creates a common vision and set of beliefs, shares and articulates them in the community, and acts to achieve them
5. manages our school on a sound theory of motivation and human development
6. understands teaching and learning and will never forget that he or she was once a teacher
7. inspires teachers and students through personal example of high expectations, intellectual pursuits, and accomplishments
8. values learning and has a constructive academic focus
9. is driven by and makes all-important decisions using the most compelling educational knowledge available

10. understands and acts on the concept that schools are in a people business and that people are its most important resource
11. takes the long-term view and perspective in making our school very good and avoids current fads
12. remains optimistic even during difficult periods
13. creates a climate and culture that encourages shared decisions, problem solving, respect, communication, empowerment, and high morale
14. creates absolute standards to measure success, including collecting data and writing plans to improve
15. cares about our school, students, and staff and has high expectations

All of the personal skills listed above are necessary and important. But your principal must possess many other skills if you are interested in creating an ideal school. While every educator has a difficult job, the principal's job is, perhaps, the most difficult. Sometimes it even seems impossible. A principal is like a juggler trying to keep numerous objects in the air and prevent them from falling and wobbling out of control. If all of these objects were dependent solely on the personal skills and characteristics of the principal, they, and your school, would eventually come falling down.

To prepare all students for a productive future a principal must also be adept at problem solving, decision making, communication, effecting change, curriculum planning, and instructional skills, to name just a few. Schools need highly skilled principals if our goal is to prepare students for a bright future. Principals are the key to improving our nation's schools.

If our nation would concentrate on improving the skills of teachers and principals, rather than on student testing and national standards, our educational system would be greatly improved. The greatest gift a school or nation can have are strong, effective principals who are focused on every aspect of their students' educational, social, and emotional growth and not consumed completely by state and national tests, especially when there is no evidence that these mandated tests prepare our students for the future they will encounter. Do these tests prepare students for an uncertain job market and economy? Do these tests prepare students to be leaders of our nation's economy? While some of these tests may ensure minimum knowledge and literacy, they do not guarantee the comprehensive skills and knowledge that students will need when they are out in the world.

A principal might be called successful when his or her students do well on state tests. This kind of success is narrow and good test scores, on their own, are not enough to make a school or its principal successful. We need principals who can nurture and lead schools well beyond these tests. Our schools need principals who can inspire teachers as they help their students understand concepts and ideas, and then apply them using the five skills mentioned earlier. Our schools need principals who will promote an environment in which students will become curious about learning, eager to seek new knowledge, and adept at using their imaginations in a creative and educational manner.

Our principals need the personal characteristics stated above as well as the following skills.

TOTAL-SYSTEMS LEADER

A principal should take a "top of the mountain" perspective, rather than concentrating solely on all the daily problems that eat up so much time. When a global, more holistic approach is utilized, many small problems will disappear. This is not to say that problems don't exist or should be ignored. It is to say, however, that when a more systemic approach is taken when managing a school, many problems will be minimized. The reason for this is that the time and effort of everyone associated with the school are dedicated to creating a positive climate and culture, achieving a compelling vision, living the school's beliefs, and making a concerted effort to get all students to learn. When students are learning well, fewer problems will arise and everyone connected with the school will feel satisfied. Students, themselves, will have little time to misbehave because stimulating learning and achievement will be occupying their time. There is no greater motivation than earned success and achievement after a challenge.

By taking a comprehensive systems approach, everyone sees the complete picture, has clear directions, and becomes dedicated to student achievement. When this happens, teachers feel like the professionals they are, can talk intelligently about the direction of their school, and feel a sense of pride in the role they play in the school's success.

Nothing turns teachers off quicker than the fix-of-the-day mentality to managing a school. When they view their principal as one who adapts the latest program, catches the latest fad, manages a school to just get by, makes no waves, offers no vision or direction, little respect is given to that principal. Teachers want a principal who can lead, see the total picture, keep his or her eye on the ball, and is not prone to knee-jerk reactions. They want a principal they can truly respect. They distrust a principal who is always bogged down in the day-to-day problems and is too busy to give them long-term direction and leadership. They want a principal who can make total-systems decisions rather than the isolated ones that negatively affect the entire staff and school.

The total-systems principal and thinker may be very difficult to find. Our nation's schools must seek and recruit principals from the teaching staff who are visionaries. Our best teachers have the potential to become our truly best principals. It is not hard to observe visionary teachers. All you have to do is watch how they manage their classroom. If they possess the personal characteristics stated earlier in the classroom and throughout observation, interviews, and discussions, there is a strong likelihood they have what it takes to be visionary leaders. There are far too many leaders who can manage a school and far too few who can lead. Visionary leaders are hard to come by. So they must be sought out, nurtured, and trained.

Along with being visionaries, principals must have process skills as well as personal skills. These can be learned. With good personal skills and style and knowledge and use of process skills, principals will be able to lead effectively and have a major influence on our nation's schools.

SCHOOL CULTURE, RELATIONSHIPS, AND THE PSYCHOLOGY OF LEADING A SCHOOL

Chapter 10 taught us that an ideal principal, one who is capable of going beyond maintaining the status quo, will motivate teachers to perform at high levels. An ideal principal will also get parents positively involved, who in turn will inspire their children to perform well.

The principal is the cultural relationship leader. The principal involves everyone in important decisions, establishes mutual respect, and creates an atmosphere of trust and cohesion. The principal builds a culture of learning, high expectations, and a caring environment.

It is the principal who creates an honest, open communicative relationship and sets the conditions of high morale. It is the principal who creates the psychological needs–satisfying conditions where everyone feels valued and connected. It is the principal who creates an environment of joy through accomplishments.

Activity: Positive Cultural Principal

Most of us have worked in a school where the principal nurtured a positive culture and relationships. Describe what this principal did.

Activity: Negative Cultural Principal

Most of us have worked in a school where the principal created a negative culture and relationships. Describe what this principal did.

In chapter 8 the discussion focused on relationships, culture, and dominant psychology. We looked at the reasons why human beings do what they do and discussed the limitations of the psychology of external motivation. Teachers and students do not respond well to rewards and punishment. This type of external motivation destroys the culture and relationships in a school.

The work that Dr. William Glasser has done on choice theory is extremely useful in understanding why people do what they do. Choice theory illustrates that building positive and productive cultures and relationships in a school are essential and necessary to having an ideal school. Choice theory focuses on our psychological needs and the fact that all of our actions and behaviors are chosen to satisfy these needs. This theory posits that every human being is born with five basic needs—one physiological and four psychological. The four psychological needs follow:

1. Everyone has the need to belong, connect, fit in, and relate positively with others. Everyone has the need to care for and be cared for, to be

involved and to avoid isolation and loneliness. It is too easy for a principal to call on the same teachers to be on committees, to get advice, and to represent the school at various functions. A principal must ensure that all teachers are asked for their opinions and are involved in representing the school. When the principal creates conditions that allow teachers to feel as though they belong and fit in, this psychological need will be satisfied.

2. Everyone has the need to have a sense of power, to be in control of one's own life, and to feel worthwhile. When the principal creates and uses a shared decision-making process, listens to what each teacher says, values teachers' knowledge, information, and contributions, everyone can feel worthwhile. When the principal creates conditions that allow teachers to experience a sense of power, this psychological need will be satisfied.
3. Everyone has the need to have some freedom and choice. When the principal encourages an honest, open discussion of issues and when teachers feel free to express themselves without any intimidation or humiliation, this psychological need will be satisfied. When the principal creates a free and open school society where all ideas are considered and given a fair chance in debates and decisions, this need will be satisfied. And when a principal creates conditions that allow teachers to have some freedom and choice to participate in all important decisions, this need will be satisfied. Being involved in the decision-making process does not ensure that every individual's ideas will be implemented. It does, however, ensure that their ideas will be considered and will make a difference in the overall decision-making process. As mentioned earlier, academic freedom does not mean that each teacher or principal does his or her own thing. With freedom comes responsibility—the responsibility to achieve the vision and mission of the school, live and defend the shared beliefs, make all decisions based on knowledge and compelling observations and not just opinions, and to create a psychologically safe and nurturing environment for everyone.
4. Everyone has the need for fun and contentment. When the principal creates an atmosphere where teachers and students work hard and achieve, everyone has contentment and fun. When the principal creates a congenial supportive environment, school can be fun and teachers and students will be happy. When students are challenged and learning well, they and their parents will find the school experience enjoyable. Nothing is more fun than earning success. Fun in the classroom does

> not mean engaging in meaningless activities or each person doing what he or she likes. It does mean having high expectations, a demanding curriculum, and teachers and principals who care. Fun in the classroom does not mean tasteless humor or humor at the expense of anyone else. It does mean students are content and happy to be there nurturing each other through the difficult as well as the happy times. It is no fun to live in a fearful, coercive, and controlling classroom or school. It is fun to live in a friendly, trusting, nurturing, and respectful classroom.

Choice theory also helps us understand that all behavior and actions, both good and bad, are an attempt to satisfy one or more of these basic psychological needs. Even when students or teachers express themselves in a negative, sarcastic way, it is their best attempt to satisfy one or more of these basic needs, even though, at times, these attempts might be ineffective and socially unacceptable.

In an ideal school, the principal creates the conditions that make it possible for everyone who works and learns in the school to have their basic psychological needs satisfied—effectively and in a socially acceptable manner. An ideal principal exhibits the following three characteristics:

1. creates the conditions, climate, and culture that are conducive to satisfying the basic needs of everyone in the school
2. understands the theory of internal motivation and human behavior and rejects external motivation psychology and all attempts at the control that is associated with it
3. empowers staff to be involved and responsible

Personal skills are very important in establishing the culture of a school, but process skills are crucial as well. When a problem arises, how is it solved? If it is solved by relying on personal characteristics and desires, solutions will not be consistent and will vary greatly. How are decisions made? How are conflicts resolved? How are policies screened and changed? How are visions created? How are beliefs and values determined? How does one use compelling observations and knowledge to plan? How are recalcitrant teachers and employees managed? How does one communicate and show concern? How is change managed? How does a school continually plan to get better? These are just a few of the process questions we should be asking about our school leaders.

Focusing on standardized tests will yield some results. But focusing on the process of instruction, planning, and classroom practices will yield even greater results.

Focusing on the vision of the school will yield some results. But focusing on the process to achieve the vision will yield even greater results. Focusing on students' learning information and facts will yield some results. But focusing on the process of understanding each subject will yield even greater results.

A teacher may have natural talent and good personal skills. But a teacher who has natural talent along with the process of instruction, curriculum planning, and classroom practices will get even better student results. Similarly, principals may have a natural talent to lead. But a principal who has this natural talent along with the following process skills will get even better results.

PROCESS SKILLS

Communication Skills

During a "conversation" over dinner with a person who is always thinking about what she wants to say instead of having a real conversation, I conducted a little experiment. She asked me a question about education. I knew she didn't care what I thought and was not going to listen to my answer. I decided to quit talking in the middle of a statement. Her response was "very good" and then she proceeded to change the subject to a topic of more interest to her.

How many of us have been in the principal's office to have a conversation and he or she was not the least bit interested in what we had to say, and may even have been reading papers on his or her desk, taking phone calls, and seeming generally distracted during the meeting?

Activity: Insensitive Conversations

Make a list of behaviors that would be deemed insensitive if exhibited during a conversation or meeting. This list should include body language behavior.

Insensitive conversations create a negative, nontrusting, toxic relationship. These kinds of conversations can destroy friendships and can greatly damage a school culture. However, there is more to communicating than simply avoiding insensitive behaviors during conversations and meetings. A principal must have strong, comprehensive process skills in the area of communication. For example, how do you show a person you heard what they said? How do you show you understand?

Activity: Sensitive Conversations

Make a list of behaviors that would be deemed sensitive if exhibited during a conversation or meeting. This list should include body language behavior.

Following are some commonsense communication skills that principals should possess:

When communicating:

- Listen intentionally and attentively to what others are saying and meaning.
- Show you understand what they are saying and meaning.
- Show you are not judging their ideas but that you are trying to understand.
- Show they have your full, undivided attention.
- Encourage the conversation and be sensitive to their ideas and feelings.
- Show you understand and if necessary seek clarification and further explanation, all without judgment.
- Show, using body language, that you are positive, encouraging, and a good listener.
- Never use body language to show disagreement, rejection, concern, or dismissal.
- Never use body language to show you are too busy, saying no, or killing their ideas.
- Make sure full discussions take place after listening to the ideas that have been presented, so that meaningful results are obtained.

All conversations should be:

- meaningful
- inviting
- involving
- knowledge, rather than opinion, based

Using Knowledge

Getting the best knowledge, educational observations, research literature, and data used in your school may be a daunting task. The use of educational knowledge defines the goodness and quality of a school. Without using it, decisions are random, opinions dominate discussions, and planning is compromised. Using knowledge influences our vision, creates our beliefs, determines our psychology, and drives our actions. Knowledge should be used to influence all actions and it is the basis for communicating, making decisions, and planning programs.

Chapter 6 outlined my most compelling observations, based on educational research concerning students, teachers, psychology, beliefs, vision, classroom practices, the principal, renewal, and continuing education for staff. This is a good time to review some of those points.

Students. A student's aptitude to learn a skill is not his or her capacity to learn but the amount of time needed to learn. With high expectations, a caring teacher, and quality teaching, most students will learn well.

Teachers. When teachers align their learning goals, teaching, and assessments, all learners benefit greatly. When teachers teach for understanding along with basic information, all learners benefit greatly.

Psychology. When the basic psychological needs are satisfied, teachers perform well and students learn better. External motivation is an ineffective way to get students to learn. Earned success is a very effective motivator.

Philosophy and Beliefs. When teachers believe students can learn well, students will more likely achieve. When students see their teachers excited and optimistic about teaching and about the subject they are teaching, students will be excited and optimistic about learning.

Vision. Having knowledge and understanding of a subject is important, but having life, learning, social, and communicating skills as well as being able to make connections in learning is even more important. This is a necessity for all students.

Classroom Practices. It should be certified that students have learned well only after they demonstrate it. All assessments should be used to help students learn and after they learn well, a grade will be assigned.

Principal. It is the principal's job to establish a climate and culture so that basic human needs can be satisfied by all who work and learn in the school.

Continuous Assessment. When assessment is measured against predetermined outcomes and is used as a basis for self- and co-assessment, performance will get better.

Continuous Staff Development. Only when schools provide continuous training and time for teachers to learn and plan will our nation's schools get significantly better.

Let's also review some of the implementing steps in using knowledge:

1. Gather information and data from a variety of sources. A summary of some important information is provided in chapter 6.
2. Get agreement with staff on a set of knowledge-driven observations. Remember there is no perfect research but there are compelling observations.
3. Compare all current practices with your compelling observations list.
4. Create a plan to implement knowledge that is not currently being implemented.
5. Determine which items on the list can't currently be implemented, but provide a timeline for their implementation.
6. Involve everyone in the implementation of the compelling observations.

It is easy to ignore knowledge when planning and making decisions. But using knowledge and research is what makes us professionals. Sure, we also need a degree and certification, but our practices and behavior are what really matter. We will get the respect we need and want as educators when we demonstrate that our planning and decisions are made according to the best compelling observations. This distinguishes us from noneducators and nonprofessionals.

Creating a Vision and Mission

Chapter 5 asserted that a vision is both a personal and professional hope of what a school should be. A vision is your dream of the ideal school. A vision is who and what you are as a school leader. Earlier in this book, a vision was created for all students in your school. This was a necessary step in making your school an ideal school. It defined what you want for all your students, provided a clear picture of what you want to accomplish, and aligned all your actions.

It is now time to create a vision for all those who work in the school. If you were creating a vision with your staff, what would it be? Would it portray a staff that wants to come to work every day, is involved in all major decisions, shows caring and respect for each other, and is dedicated to achieving the vision and beliefs of the school? Would it portray a staff that follows the agreed-upon instructional process and uses a well-defined curriculum planning process to ensure that all students will gain knowledge and skills?

Would it portray a staff that follows the agreed-upon processes for testing, retesting, grading, homework, and discipline? Would it portray a staff that shares and determines mutual responsibilities for making your school an ideal school? Would it portray a staff that creates a positive culture in which basic psychological needs are satisfied? Would it portray a school culture in which the lines of authority are purposefully blurred and yet each member of the organization is doing his or her job effectively?

Activity: Creating a Vision for Staff

Determine and visualize what all staff wants for each other so that their basic needs are satisfied in their ideal school:

- Brainstorm a composite list.
- Remove duplicates.
- Combine similarities.
- Get agreement for a consensus list.
- Define what each statement means.

- Determine mutual responsibilities: what are the responsibilities of the teachers and the principal, and what are not the responsibility of the teachers or the principal.

This process can be exciting and the conclusion and actions can be even more exciting.

Many schools have a vision and mission for students but it is extremely rare for a school to have a well-defined, published vision and mission for staff. If schools develop positive, supportive visions and missions for teachers, principals, and educational leaders, our nation will achieve significant educational gains.

A vision starts with the principal. A visionary principal can create a vision. A principal who has never had a vision can't.

Activity: Visionary Leaders

Name three great noneducation leaders who were dreamers and visionaries. Can you name one "great leader" who didn't have a vision?

Don't be afraid to dream and to have a vision of what can be, even if at the time it doesn't seem realistic. A dream can't come true if you don't have one. Even if your dreams don't all become a reality, they are an important step in improvement and growth.

Generating Beliefs

Beliefs influence everything we do. They control our ideas, drive our actions, and help us get what we want. Chapter 7 illustrated that there are often competing beliefs present in schools. When this is the case, the staff is not always united, decisions can be compromised, actions won't be consistent, and students will get mixed messages.

Some teachers believe that competition in the classroom is healthy. When competition exists, some students will succeed and others will not.

Some teachers argue that this mirrors real life and schools should not shelter students from failure.

Other teachers believe that cooperation in the classroom is healthy and that a healthy cooperative environment will allow all students to succeed. They argue that student failure leads to a difficult, often under-employed life.

Two activities were presented in chapter 7 to help develop the beliefs of a school. The first activity was to list what one might observe in a classroom with competing beliefs. For example what might you see in a classroom with high expectations for all? What might you see in a classroom with high expectations for a few? The second activity was to brainstorm statements about competing beliefs, then list, display, and draw conclusions and consensus. For example, complete the following sentences as they affect students and their learning:

I believe that when students trust their teacher to help them learn, then ________________.

I believe that when students don't trust their teacher to help them learn, then ________________.

Review these activities and choose one or both to help you develop your beliefs. You can choose to develop your own activities, but developing a set of beliefs for your school should not be a choice. It should be mandatory. Every very good school has them, and everyone in these schools lives by them.

Review the knowledge-driven observations presented in chapter 6 and use them to screen your own generated beliefs. Knowledge, not opinions, is important in developing school beliefs.

Remember, the entire staff must be involved in developing school beliefs. The principal must be the leader in constructing the beliefs and then ensuring these beliefs are modeled and practiced, but everyone associated with the school should play a part in the process.

Activity: The Principal's Job Is Implementing Beliefs

How would the principal and teachers act if staff was expected to be:

- cooperative
- inclusive

- talented
- high-performing
- able to align vision, beliefs, and knowledge
- involved in continuing education
- trusting
- successful
- optimistic

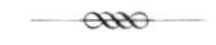

Managing the Instructional Process, Curriculum Planning, and Classroom Practices

It is often said that the principal is the instructional leader of the school. Following that premise, the teacher should then be the instructional leader of the class. It is the teacher's job to organize what is to be learned, and to implement classroom practices. However, it is the principal's job to ensure that the practices are clearly in place. It is the principal's job to understand the instructional process and to observe and determine whether the teacher is effective. The principal must understand the complex planning process and monitor how successfully teachers are implementing that process.

Strong classroom practices are essential in improving the culture of a classroom and a school. A principal must ensure that these practices are not optional, but required.

To monitor these processes, principals must have more than a passing knowledge of them. They must understand them, be able to articulate them, and know how to implement them effectively. When a teacher is not utilizing classroom practices effectively, the principal must help them to do so. Following is a review of the instructional process.

Stage 1: Prepare All Students for Success Attitudinally and Academically

To prepare students for success academically for each lesson, each day you can:

1. Spend the first few minutes of every lesson reviewing what is necessary for success in the lesson.

2. For those students who always need extra help after school, use this time to get them ready for tomorrow's lesson.
3. Convert remedial teachers to prevention teachers. Let them prepare students for success in the next lesson or unit.
4. Special-needs teachers should prepare their students for success with the classroom teacher.

To prepare students attitudinally for success each day you can:

1. Consider why they have a negative attitude.
2. Assure them that you are on their side and are there to help them learn and give them the time they need for it.
3. Assure them of the following: If they work hard, no grade will be given until they learn well. If they don't do well on a test, they will get a second chance. They do not have to compete for a grade; it is possible for everyone to get good grades. You will be their academic coach.

Stage 2: Getting and Focusing Student Attention

Focusing students to learn each day's lesson or unit may be the most creative part of teaching. Sometimes doing the unexpected and getting students involved in what is to be learned can get students' attention. When students know what they are to learn before the teacher teaches, students are more apt to be interested and involved.

Stage 3: Initial Instruction

Teach using a variety of teaching–learning modes. One teaching style does not reach all students. A variety of strategies is essential to appeal to the many different ways students learn. Also be sure students are actively engaged in the learning process. Whoever does the most work gets the most learning.

Stage 4: Guided Practices and Adjustments

Most correctives and adjustments are made in this stage. It is at this time that students practice what they were just taught. This is a very personal stage where teachers walk around and make sure each student has learned the expected. This stage can also be implemented with student learning teams in which discussions and clarifications are conducted with peers. This stage must be managed carefully. It is generally of very short duration but can be repeated many times during a lesson. This is "check" time—a time to see how effective you were and how effectively students were learning.

Stage 5: Summary and Closure

You reviewed, taught, and corrected, and now it is time to summarize and bring closure to each lesson. This can be done in many ways and times during the lesson as well as in the conclusion. Obviously teachers can take the initiative and provide the summary. But students should be involved in summarizing what they learned that day. This can be done verbally or in writing. If done verbally you should write the summary on the board. It will also give you an opportunity to correct any misunderstandings or to emphasize a point.

Stage 6: Assessment and Testing

Align all assessment and testing to what you expect each student to learn. Assessment must not be a surprise. Align outcomes, teaching, and testing to get maximum learning. All assessment and testing should be used to correct learning errors and to help students learn. Reduce the use of tests to get a grade.

Managing Curriculum Planning

Without proper curriculum planning, which must include all the expected standards of the course and what students must know and be able to do, teaching may not be aligned, standards may not be achieved, and learning will be random. The better the planning, the better the teaching. And the better the teaching, the better the learning.

Proper curriculum planning helps to ensure that what is required is taught and allows teachers to go well beyond mandates.

Chapter 11 included seven necessary planning tools: acquiring knowledge, course learning goals, course outlined by units, unit planning, acquiring skills, lesson learning goals, and lesson planning.

The planning process is a detailed systemic curriculum plan and can't be completed in one year. Be patient while teachers go through the process. If you or they become impatient and try to complete the process too quickly, many valuable and important ideas will be missed.

There is no doubt that proper planning encourages alignment of the lesson and unit plan and prevents teachers from going into class unprepared or "winging it." But teachers must have a private as well as a professional life. Work with teachers to devise a plan and organize their curriculum. Many teachers actually create their course learning goals at the conclusion of the course. They develop their unit and lesson goals first and then from these, they develop their course learning goals. While this approach is not the optimum approach, it is doable and prevents burnout.

When these teachers are developing their unit and lesson plans, they should estimate the amount of time necessary to teach all the units. At the conclusion of the course, they should adjust their planning to guarantee completion and they should also adjust the time allocated for each unit.

Most teachers should concentrate on the required standards during the first year or so. Then, as they gain experience, they will be able to include other activities and learning goals.

If we want to make meaningful changes in our nation's schools, it is essential that leaders rethink their staff development program and the time teachers need to plan. More will be said about this in chapter 15.

The principal's job is to be sure planning takes place and is sufficient for effective teaching. If you have a good understanding of the curriculum planning process, you can help teachers as they plan. You don't have to do the planning; you have to guide and monitor it.

Managing Classroom Practices

Chapter 12 outlines five critical classroom practices that influence student learning both positively and negatively. When these practices are used correctly, more students will choose to learn. Many schools, however, use these practices incorrectly and in a negative way. This is not done intentionally but in most cases these practices go unexplored and are not discussed. When these practices are used correctly, students' attitude toward learning will become more positive. They will understand that all testing and assessment will be used to help them learn. Corrections will be made to learning errors, and students, if they are responsible, will be allowed to retest. Grades will be adjusted to reflect new and better learning.

Naturally these processes must be carefully managed; otherwise, teachers will get frustrated and give up. These practices will not go smoothly at first since they may be new to everyone. When teachers do what is suggested and don't get discouraged, major improvements will take place.

The principal must monitor to ensure effective use of the process and to ensure teachers are living by the purposes of each practice and resisting the nonpurposes. Successfully using the classroom practices is vital to changing and improving the culture of your school for teachers and students. Most of us have been victims of the nonpurposes listed for each practice. We can't let students relive our bad experiences even though we managed to be successful in spite of them.

Manage all the activities presented in this chapter. You should arrive at a set of classroom practice procedures acceptable to all. Finally, ask if each procedure is consistent with the vision, mission, beliefs, psychology, and knowledge base of your school.

Making Decisions

Teachers do not want to be involved in every decision the principal must make. They don't have the time and school would be chaotic if they were. But teachers do want to be involved and consulted, if possible, in every major decision that affects their lives. Naturally, policy and state law prevents them from being involved in every decision.

In many schools, committees represent all teachers in the decision-making process. This does not mean they make the decisions. During the process it is the committee's responsibility to keep all teachers informed and involved so the final decision will not be a surprise. Committees must listen to staff's concerns, gather their suggestions, and use them in refining their recommendations. Although this process takes time, in the end, it yields beneficial results.

Voting on decisions has a tendency to polarize the staff, so it is usually not a great option for decision making. What does it mean for a decision to be approved by a 52% to 48% vote? Does it make the 48% feel alienated while those in the 52% can claim victory? Making decisions should not be a win/lose proposition but a consensus process.

When you get to the point in the process where teachers have had considerable input, their recommendations were considered, and most teachers feel comfortable with the process, the committee must make their best recommendation. When this process is followed, the probability that the decision is the correct one will be high.

Even though the entire staff may not agree with the final decision, most will agree to abide by it. They will understand that making a decision using this process is a judgment call, but as long as they were involved they will accept it.

There are six actions that contribute to the process of making meaningful decisions or solving complex problems.

1. Allow involvement of all in major decisions affecting them. This is done within established parameters such as school policy and state law. Not every decision or problem needs to involve everyone. Most teachers will choose not to get involved in many decisions. Most will choose to get involved in major decisions. School policy and state law can be influenced by teachers and principals but there is no guarantee they will be involved in its formation or change. Furthermore, not every teacher wants to be involved in every major decision and that desire should be honored. However, they must accept the decision or solutions of others.
2. Obtain agreement that the process of decision making will involve no blame, humiliation, sarcasm, or excuses. All ideas will be considered fairly, no matter how different they appear. No one will use "killer phrases" or "put-downs" of others. An individual's position or title in the school or district will not be used as power. All people are equal in the process. All decisions will be knowledge- and research-driven and not opinion-driven.
3. Align actions of the decision-making process with your vision, beliefs, and knowledge. The decision-making process should be based on the following questions for each decision or plan:
   A. The Want Questions (about the decision): What do we want? What do we really want?
   B. The Knowledge Questions (about the decision): What do we know? What do we need to know? What do we want to know? What data do we have? What data do we need?

   C. The Belief Questions (about the decision): What do we believe? What should we believe?
   D. The Psychology Questions (about the decision): Is what we are doing or going to do needs-satisfying for everyone? Is what we are doing or going to do psychologically safe and nurturing for everyone?
4. To reach consensus, strive for 100% agreement. Everyone's ideas will be considered. No idea will be rejected without a fair hearing. All ideas will be screened through the knowledge and compelling observations base. Is the idea based on knowledge or is it just an opinion? Always ask if the idea will contribute to achieving the vision. Is it consistent with the beliefs? Is it psychologically nurturing? If a committee is trying to make a decision for the entire faculty, they should use the above process. They should also keep the entire staff informed and involved in the process and the committee's thinking. They should listen to the ideas and concerns staff have. They should then return to their committee for discussions and refinement of the decisions. Repeat this process as often as necessary to get as close to 100% agreement as possible. Again, don't vote. Make the final decision when you believe most staff members are favorable and it feels right.
5. Once consensus is reached, everyone agrees to live with the decision or agreement until such time as the decision is changed through the established process. This does not mean the decision can't be changed. It can, but a process must be used. It is not acceptable to complain, undermine the decision, or even kill it before it is implemented. There must be no clandestine meetings to alter or change the decision. There can be many discussions, but the entire process must be an open one, with open discussion and conclusions. At a meeting with the teachers' union personnel in another district, the teachers were receptive to the process with one reservation: they agreed to use the process if their administration did the same. And it did. Any new process can produce some bumps and bruises. Everyone was warned and agreed to correct any problem. Both sides worked together and had a process to make meaningful decisions.
6. All intended decisions and existing ones should be screened using the following process:
   A. Is it based on the best knowledge, data, and compelling observations available?

B. Is it consistent with the stated beliefs and values?
C. Will it help achieve the vision for your students and staff?
D. Is it psychologically safe and nurturing for all staff and students?
E. Is it needs-satisfying?

Managing Change

Every school has some teachers who don't want to change or even examine the possibilities. Try to understand why these teachers and some principals resist anything presented to them. They are tired of the all-purpose quick-fixes that find their way onto the educational table each year. As stated earlier, many of these ideas are good, but not one of them is the answer to the complex challenge of getting all students to learn and all teachers and principals to perform well.

There are many other reasons why teachers may choose to resist change. Some of these are the mindless mandates and imposed policies they are expected to support each year, as well as coercion, fear of making mistakes, fear of failure, and anger about not being involved in the decision-making process. Some also feel their voice doesn't count and that some teachers are favored over others. All these are barriers and should be overcome.

When teachers are convinced that what they are being asked to do will be supported with the necessary training and support, most will not resist change. Most teachers and administrators don't mind changing; they don't want to be changed. Yet most questions regarding educational change involve how we can change them or why they won't change.

Other statements regarding change are those that find fault and blame. Some would argue that the problems in education are teacher tenure and teacher unions. These are not the problems. Even if they were removed, education would still face the challenge to improve.

Let us begin with the assumption that the job of the principal is not to change someone else but to provide knowledge and skills to help teachers do their jobs better. The real issues are how to get more students to learn better and how to provide teachers and principals with the support they need to do so. I don't know many teachers or principals who wouldn't gladly learn new skills to have all students learn well and be prepared for a bright future.

When teachers are convinced that what they are being asked to do is meaningful, systemic, and will lead to significantly better student achievement, most teachers will willingly change. Therefore, it is essential to establish the need for change by gathering information and knowledge about how to get students to learn better. Then show teachers how they will be supported. When these are present, resistance will be reduced.

It has been my experience that even when teachers make a commitment to change what they are doing, administrators and boards do not. They should and they must make meaningful commitments to teachers to illustrate their support of any proposed changes.

Following are some commitments that must be established in the process of change:

1. Involve all teachers in establishing the need for change.
2. Reach a consensus on the plan and design of change.
3. Assure teachers that it is OK to make mistakes and that that is how we learn. Also tell them no judgments will be made.
4. Ask teachers not to bury problems but to identify them. Then involve everyone including the principal and other leaders in the solution.
5. Assure teachers that help will be provided whenever needed. Whenever possible, use your existing staff to provide the help.
6. Assure that teachers and principals are colearners, coworkers, and codoers. Also assure them that position will never be used as power even though principals must make final decisions.
7. Assure teachers that continuing education for them will be provided.

More will be said about this in chapter 15.

No matter what principals may say or do, some teachers will still resist making any significant change. A school may do everything absolutely perfectly, but it may not be enough to convince some teachers to change what they are doing. It is my observation there is a 7% rule operating in schools and perhaps in every organization. It seems that approximately 7% of the teaching staff will decide that any kind of change is not for them or anyone else.

In many schools too much time is spent on trying to convince the seven-percenters to consider change or to fend off their degrading comments. As suggested earlier, place newsprint in strategic locations such as the faculty room, faculty lunchroom, and the principal's office and when anyone hears a "killer phrase," have him or her write it on the newsprint and then publish the list. Sensitivity to negative statements and how we respond to each other is a necessary first step to abolish this kind of behavior. If possible, get everyone to agree to abolish all negative or derogatory statements by everyone, to everyone, in your school.

You may want to make a list of validation phrases. For example, when someone says, "I have an idea," you might use validation phrases like "tell me more," "let's hear it," or "let's consider it." Write these on newsprint and publish them.

However, make no mistake about it, if a teacher is hurting students by embarrassing them, putting them down, or humiliating them, you as the principal should not tolerate this behavior. The teacher must be directed at first verbally and, if it continues, in writing to discontinue this behavior immediately. This is not a request to stop, but a directive. Mental abuse is every bit as destructive as physical abuse. If this teacher's behavior continues after receiving a directive to stop, legal action must be taken. Refusing to solve a problem after being directed to do so is insubordination.

Naturally, no one wants this to happen and the goal is to solve the problem. No one wants to hurt teachers, but students must be protected. None of us would tolerate a disruptive or insubordinate student who can't live by the agreed-upon rules. We can't tolerate the same behavior from any member of the staff who can't or won't live by the agreed-upon decisions.

Some teachers, however, try but still have difficulty performing well. If this is the case, then it will be necessary to compensate for them. First, provide education for these teachers, giving them the necessary skills to be effective. Do what you can, including mentoring, to improve their teaching skills. Second, do not allow students to be placed with these teachers for instruction for long periods of time. Students can adjust to a less than competent teacher for a short period of time but it is unfair to have students spend all day with a less-than-average teacher. It becomes the responsibility of the principal to provide training for these teachers so they can become competent.

Nurture those teachers who want to change and build a culture in which the seven-percenters, who are negative about everything, will no longer be valued or have a voice in the decision-making process until they agree to live by the decisions of the faculty without belittling them.

None of us is self-employed, and if teachers want a genuine voice in all major decisions that affect their lives, then everyone must agree to and live by the decisions until they are changed. However, asking good questions and seeking ways to get better is not being negative. This is a healthy, proper process and should be encouraged.

Spend most of your time on those teachers who want to get significantly better, who want to make a major difference in the lives of children, and who know that getting better should be a way of life. While working with those who want to make a change, do what it takes to involve everyone constructively.

From experience, I have observed that staff, teachers, and principals can be viewed in three ways. There are those who want to remain unaware of any change and are unwilling to examine even the best of the practices. There are those who are aware of changes and are willing to move ahead, to learn and even adopt them. Then there are those who are aware of those changes, but because of many and mostly valid reasons want to wait until they are sure that the school and its leaders are willing to sustain and support the desired change.

Following is a discussion of the three groups, their attitude, and possible action steps to be taken with each:

Unaware and Unwilling Staff

Attitude:

- feel that ignorance is bliss
- have the Alfred E. Neuman mentality of "What, me worry?"
- don't know and don't care
- think that this too shall pass
- will be here long after they are gone
- prefer to wait this one out

Action plan—ask good questions like:

1. If your students did exactly what you wanted, what would they do that would be good for them and you?
2. Are you getting what you want now?

3. What do you think you can do to get more of what you want?
4. What do you think you can stop doing because it may be getting in the way of what you want?
5. Do you know of some teachers who are getting much of what they want?
6. Would you be willing to examine their practices and discuss with them what they are doing?

If you are making progress with the above questions, you may wish to ask some of the following:

1. What is your dream or vision for this school?
2. What are your beliefs about students and learning? How did you arrive at these beliefs? Are these beliefs getting you what you want?
3. What is your psychology for managing your students? How did you arrive at this psychology? Is this psychology getting you what you want?
4. Do you want to be involved in the important decisions made in this school? Would you be willing to live by them even if you don't agree? If you disagree with the decisions, how will you challenge them in ways that are effective and socially acceptable?

Aware and Willing Staff

Attitude:

- willing to act if they see the need
- willing to give change a try
- willing to use a process and be knowledge-driven
- realize there is much to learn and are eager to do it

Action plan:

1. Protect and encourage them.
2. Support them so they can succeed.
3. Form a mutual support group.
4. Provide much training and time to learn and plan.
5. Have them reach out to their peers.

6. Caution them not to be zealous.
7. Have them explain to everyone what is working and what is not working. Be open and honest.
8. Never call too much attention to this group and don't treat them as specials. Treat them as professionals, which they are.

Aware and Waiting Staff

This group is the largest and usually consists of 60% to 80% of the staff.
Attitude:

- generally willing to listen but not yet ready to commit, at least not at this time
- have seen and been involved in the fix of the year each year
- want to wait to see if there is support for the willing group
- generally cautious at this time but will be the important swing group

Action plan:

1. Keep them informed about what is working and what is not.
2. Nurture this group.
3. Involve them in decision making.
4. Ask them to support the willing group.
5. Establish the need for change.
6. Build their capacity so they will get ready.
7. Do not give mandates.
8. Never try to coerce.
9. Provide training when they choose to be involved.
10. Get the next willing group from here.
11. Have them involved with the willing group.
12. Ask for their advice and ideas.
13. Show you understand their position.
14. Show your encouragement.

A long time ago, I vowed to take the word "no" out of my vocabulary. Instead, whenever I got a request that would set a precedent or change the terms and conditions of the existing contract, I would say, "Help me find a way." In my head, "no" is an ugly word. It implies that I have the power and you do not. Interestingly enough, the more you give of yourself and the more power you give away, within certain parameters, the more it comes back to you. By asking for meaningful employee involvement, we can say yes to possibilities that we have never thought about. We can share the power.

If we could only understand that all of us are better than any one of us, we'd be much better off. My greatest fear as a leader was that people were overextending themselves. I knew the extent of their dedication and that concerned me. I used to tell the staff they were trying to give too much back to the school and to the district but their response would be "it's good for kids."

When people know they are valued and trusted, they are eager to demonstrate commitment. When we as school leaders act on what we say, when we actually live by the words we speak, people know our sincerity. When that trust is reciprocated, the school can go faster and farther than we ever thought possible.

We do not always know, though, who can make a contribution. We think we know because of what we have seen and heard in the past. But, we simply do not know how much people can contribute. Until we start to tap into the talents of all, we can't reach our potential, for that talent can be used to drive any organization toward excellence. My philosophy has always been, "Every person has a wonderful brain, and if you think they don't, just pretend they do."

Even when employees' viewpoints do not match ours, we have to trust them and show we care about them. They have to see, hear, feel, and taste the school's respect for what they have to say. The very fact that they are saying it indicates some level of concern on their part. Once the trust has been built, then a systems approach comes next. The quick-fix approaches may give us the illusion of a fast solution, but not a long-lasting one. While rarely are hot solutions bad, they alone will not change the school district over the long haul.

Sometimes I ask people, "What is the first thing you do when you are putting a puzzle together?" Some say they concentrate on the corners, others say they find the unusual shapes, but the best answer is to look at the big picture first. The same is true of schools. We cannot fit the pieces together if we do not have a sense of the big picture.

The big picture must include a clearly stated vision for students and staff. It must include a well-defined meaningful set of beliefs, values, and convictions. It must include an internal-motivated psychology that satisfies the basic human needs of everyone. But all of these must be based on the best educational knowledge, data, research, and compelling observations available.

The big picture must also include a well-defined instructional process, curriculum planning, and classroom practices. Everyone must be encouraged to take risks and succeed. Success in schools is for everyone. All students must learn and succeed, all teachers must do the job well and get satisfaction, and each principal must lead as the professional he or she is.

For any school to maintain progress and continually develop, that organization must view its employees as their most valuable resource. When employees feel valued, they will view change as necessary and the obtained results will be long lasting. When conditions permit them to be meaningfully involved, they will assume responsibility for their own behavior, productivity, and renewal. Most people want to be responsible and do a quality job, but without the conditions of trust, caring, and respect, school and personal renewal and improvement are almost impossible to achieve.

Renewal and self-assessment are the thrusts to sustaining momentum. We cannot keep asking vague questions like "What can we do to get better?" or "How can I improve?" Most will work hard when they know what the answers look like. We need to have leaders and those they lead working together to determine the attributes and performance indicators that spell excellence. Once this is done, each person can continually self-assess against the agreed-upon performance indicators and continually adjust for improvement. Renewal through self- and co-assessment is the only way to excellence. This will be discussed in the next chapter.

Chapter Fourteen

Continuous Assessment, Renewal, and Improvement

In highly successful schools there is a nurturing, collaborative, self-informing culture.

Focus Questions

1. What is the role and purpose of assessment in improving teaching, managing, and learning?
2. How are state and national tests used to improve teaching, managing, and learning?
3. How well is your school performing and how can you share information with your community in a clear and meaningful manner? Consider (a) evidence, (b) test data, and (c) nontest data.
4. How can you measure your effectiveness in terms of achieving your vision, your beliefs, your mission, and your desired culture and climate?
5. How can you measure your effectiveness as teachers and administrators?
6. How do you know if your school is getting better through continuous assessment, reflection, and renewal?

One of the real challenges facing any school is how to continually get better and avoid stagnation. Even those schools that make great efforts to improve and those that show significant improvement will always face the real challenge of continual renewal. With an effective continuous assessment and renewal process based on self- and co-assessment and reflection, teachers and administrators will find that getting better and improvement is a way of life.

Renewal can not happen when teachers are not encouraged or allowed to be fully responsible and professional. Renewal can not happen when administrators assume the responsibility for assessing and making suggestions to improve. When principals are the sole evaluators of teacher performance, rather than coevaluators, improvement will not happen. Furthermore, when principals or any leaders use assessment as a vehicle for controlling or intimidating staff, improvement will not take place.

Directing teachers to improve, or evaluating their performance hoping they will improve, are the very activities that interfere with real productivity, growth, and student achievement. Any controlling and manipulating action generally dooms schools or any organization to mediocrity. This kind of behavior results in staff distrust, frustration, anger, and diminished personal effectiveness. When teachers feel invited, supported, and empowered, they will act individually and collectively making unlimited effort for responsible change and improvement.

While principals must create the condition of trust for self-renewal to occur, it is everyone's responsibility to take care of his or her own improvement. It is everyone's responsibility to ensure the success of each student and the school. While principals must create the needs-satisfying conditions to nurture individual responsibility, it is still their job to handle problems and to lead.

Most teachers will be responsible when given the opportunity and trust but some will still choose not to be. When this happens, principals must exercise leadership and do what it takes to correct the situation. If a child is acting irresponsibly, parents will or should exercise control and correct the situation, hopefully in a caring, learning way. Principals must do the same. They must do it without using harsh and threatening language, fear, coercion, or humiliation. Dignity must be maintained at all times.

A word of caution: Don't treat all teachers like the seven-percenters discussed earlier, who are negative about everything and resistant to any change. Most teachers will be open and responsible and must be treated this way. When the conditions are such for teachers to be meaningfully involved, they will assume responsibility for their own behavior, personal growth, and continuous renewal. When most teachers feel valued, they will view change as necessary and the obtained results will be long-lasting.

Teaching and leading are complex, and improving teacher performance is equally complex. Teaching is more than transmitting knowledge: it is knowing how children learn and how they develop differently, and how one should manage individual learning rates.

Teaching is also knowing how to get students to construct knowledge, communicate effectively, study and learn their subjects, acquire the skills necessary for living a productive life, and develop social skills necessary for getting along. Teachers must also understand a variety of subjects, know how to teach them so students can learn, and simultaneously demonstrate enthusiasm for teaching and their subject matter. To do all of this, teachers spend many hours each day organizing and planning their curriculum in order to be prepared to teach in a manner that facilitates student learning.

Many students come to school with agendas other than learning, however. Many come to school to socialize and are content just getting by. Still others come to school with little sleep, a lack of a healthy diet, and an abusive home. Many have little parent concern or involvement. Some students even challenge their teachers to motivate them and then pass the blame on when they don't. Teachers must know how to compensate for these ills and set the conditions, culture, and climate for students to want to learn. Teachers must demonstrate a positive, inviting attitude even when all those around do not.

The principal's job, as previously stated, is very complex and at times may seem impossible. A principal, as the leader of the school, must create a positive atmosphere and culture as well as the needs-satisfying conditions that are necessary for productivity and growth.

With all the complexities of teaching and leading, it is still expected, and crucial, that teachers and principals learn new skills, renew, and continually strive to get better. Most educators really want to do this; however, not every school or educational setting promotes this practice.

Improving teacher performance is as complex and as important as teaching, and yet we rely on an outdated system. One of the most common methods used to improve performance is to have a supervisor or principal observe a teacher with a checklist in hand and make suggestions on how to improve in a follow-up conference. This superimposed approach rarely improves a teacher's performance and the process itself can actually be quite demeaning.

TRADITIONAL TEACHER ASSESSMENT

The traditional form of assessment doesn't work. Worse than not providing meaningful opportunities for teachers to learn, the system is often quite destructive. While the purpose of this system is to improve performance, it rarely does. In most cases it is nothing more than a ritual. Teachers openly admit that this outdated process does not help them to improve. Principals and supervisors confess that they employ this method because it is required, not because they believe it will be meaningful. They also admit that they do it to get it done. It's akin to the statement "We haven't had 100 years of experience but we had one year's experience 100 times." When will we learn?

Any time something is done to someone, there is rarely a benefit, and there is often damage. Trust is violated; individual responsibility is minimized and even discouraged. The traditional form of teacher assessment is often degrading and uninspiring. It also destroys motivation. In addition, teachers learn their way around the system and often play games with it. When Mr. Graham, my math supervisor, came to observe me when I was a high-school math teacher, I played the game that had been invented by many teachers before me. I warned my class ahead of time that my supervisor was coming to observe my performance:

> He wants to see my teaching and observe whether you are involved in the lesson. When he is present I will ask many questions. To be sure that I call on those who know the answer, raise your right hand if you do. If you don't know the answer, raise your left hand. Remember every hand must be raised. This way we both get a chance to perform.

I got the best evaluations and a few years later I was made chairman of the math department! However, I can truly say that this process did not, in any way, improve my teaching in any way.

Since the traditional system of teacher assessment rarely contributes to better teacher and student performance, the process must be altered. There is a pressing need both to alter the current system for assessing teacher performance and to create a system to assess total school performance. Until this point, this book has provided a comprehensive guide for improving our nation's schools. But to ensure that your school continues to get better, a process of continual assessment, adjustment, and reflection must be employed. Renewal through self- and co-assessment and adjustment is the key to long-term achievement and success.

A NEW SYSTEM

It is difficult to change old habits, but it is absolutely necessary if student achievement and morale are to improve. A new system of assessment is necessary that emphasizes self and joint responsibility. The new system must be one that emphasizes teachers' being responsible for assessing themselves. When one person assesses the performance of another, individual responsibility and self-motivation will be reduced. We learned this from quality corporations. We never got quality products until self- and co-assessment replaced "boss" assessment. When the workers were given responsibility to be part of a team and to participate in self- and co-assessment, their morale skyrocketed and they assumed more responsibility for producing quality.

Most successful teachers and students always look at their own performance to determine how they can get better. Successful people don't wait for someone else to assess how well they are doing; they assess their own performance. Being self-responsible is necessary for long-term success and renewal.

Improving teacher performance must be a continuous process and not just an hour's observation with a follow-up conference. Improving teacher performance and subsequently student achievement will come about only when a process of self- and co-assessment and renewal is in place.

In declining schools and organizations, there is little or no growth or positive change. Trust, caring, and individual responsibility are nonexistent. The values in these schools and organizations are coercion, blame, sarcasm, and humiliation. People are not valued and rarely do they assume self-responsibility. Slogans and not people are most important.

In contrast, people in highly successful schools and organizations are always responsible and seek ways to do even better. They know what to do and find ways to do it. They can't wait to go to work and work until the job is done. They are not driven by clocks but want to perform well because it is the right thing to do. They are self-motivated, and the only concern the principal or leader has is to be sure employees don't spend all their time on the job and ignore their families and personal needs.

In highly successful schools and organizations, there is a nurturing collaborative culture where people are trusted, valued, and encouraged to be responsible. You will always see people caring about and nurturing each other. These are the prerequisites for transforming the process to self- and co-assessment. Unless these values are present or at least there is a willingness to adopt them, changing the current system will be impossible. You can succeed only when they are present. Self- and co-assessment, self-responsibility, self-renewal, and self-discipline will be accomplished only in an atmosphere where everyone feels psychologically safe and nurtured. These values must always be present and never violated. If they are violated, they will cease to be part of the culture and the new system will be in danger of collapse.

The new system of assessment is based on mutual trust and respect. It is also based on having clear and measurable competencies, attributes, and performance indicators. Without these, assessment simply doesn't work because there is no clear picture of what is being assessed. Vague references and ill-defined performance indicators must be replaced by criterion-referenced and well-defined performance indicators.

Self- and co-assessment and reflection are necessary ingredients for any organization or person to continually renew and achieve. However, encouraging self- and co-assessment is not enough in and of itself. Sufficient guidelines and direction must be provided to ensure success. Individuals may want to self-assess and renew but frequently don't know where to begin. It is not good enough to ask simple questions like "How can I get better?" "Where can I improve?" or "What needs improvement?" While these are important and necessary questions, they are not enough to achieve significant results or change. Self-assessment and renewal go awry when individuals are not guided to real growth and improvement.

For self-assessment and renewal to be effective, a self-renewal guide including a process is needed. The guide will assist each person to assess, reflect, and renew using predetermined competencies and performance indicators. The guide will provide a systematic and systemic process for continuous and personal renewal. This process will eliminate fear, coercion, and intimidation. This process will help achieve the real purpose of assessment: to improve teacher performance and get significant improvement, thereby improving overall school performance.

To get a clear picture of what is being assessed, it is necessary to determine all the major competencies that would be expected of any successful teacher, principal, or school. This chapter will define the performance indicators for each section and chapter of this book. As always, you should feel free to add, delete, or modify any of the indicators to better suit your school's needs. It is your school, your assessment, and your renewal.

It is advised that the entire staff be involved in creating an assessment and renewal guide. There is much to be learned by doing so. Owen was a fifth-grade teacher who was mediocre at best. He was involved in creating the assessment and renewal guide for his school district. At the completion of the document, with acceptance by the staff, Owen reported that principals kept saying that he had to improve. They even offered some advice. He also said that the new renewal document provided many ideas and suggestions for improvement and that he was now able to write a five-year growth plan. His principal agreed with the plan and helped him to develop it. Owen did improve.

With the performance indicators that follow, you will be ready to self- and co-assess. This process is not a once-a-year affair; it should be done several times each year to chart progress. Not every chapter or parts of chapters must be assessed every time. Decide what is important at each assessment and assess and change as necessary. When working with a school district in North Carolina with a committee of approximately 25 teachers and administrators, I was getting mixed signals. The teachers said they weren't involved in important decisions that affected their lives, while the administrators said they were. I decided to do a perceptual check, which is another term for the assessment that is presented in this chapter. I wrote the following statement on some newsprint: "We the teachers are involved in all major decisions that affect our lives within the established parameters." I used the following rating scale:

1. Almost Never
2. Rarely
3. Sometimes
4. Usually
5. Almost Always

Each person received an identical piece of paper and recorded a number from the rating scale corresponding to their perception. I then collected all the slips of paper and proceeded to read the numbers aloud while a teacher recorded them. The average turned out to be 1.6, which meant almost never to rarely.

This exercise was not used to fault the administrators but to check perceptions and to design a plan to change. With this data the group was able to develop a plan to get staff involved. The plan was implemented and this exercise was repeated two months later. The new average was 3.1. Everyone was excited that they were making progress in this important area. By the end of the year the average was 3.8. This was significant progress and there was a noticeable improvement in the climate and culture of the school.

Using an instrument similar to the one presented in this chapter, with a similar rating scale, allowed this district to check perceptions and make significant progress. With personal and school perceptual checks, assessments, and adjustments, not only did the overall climate improve but student achievement got significantly better.

The performance indicators that follow correspond directly to chapters in this book. Keep in mind that the process of self- and co-assessment, both personally, and for total school continual adjustment, can be repeated as often as needed. The scale used, 1–5, was shown previously.

However, you can create your own scale with your own descriptors. What is important is checking perceptions and writing a plan of adjustments. Some schools have actually purchased hand-held devices and use a computer to get immediate anonymous feedback. Continuous adjustment sheets are provided here to facilitate the process of writing an improvement plan when areas of concern are identified.

CONTINUOUS ASSESSMENT: CHAPTERS 1 TO 3

Chapter 1: Here We Go Again
Chapter 2: Characteristics of an Ideal School
Chapter 3: It's All in the Perception

The questions below, which relate to the first three chapters of this book, should be answered by teachers and administrators. If you desire, you can also get parents' perceptions of these areas. Answer the questions in this section using the previously shown 1–5 scale.

Chapter 1: Here We Go Again

1. I know I have a profound influence on the life of each child that I teach and try to ensure it is a positive one.

Rating:	1 2 3 4 5	1 2 3 4 5	1 2 3 4 5
Date:	__/__/__	__/__/__	__/__/__

2. Our school avoids quick-fix solutions in trying to improve.

Rating:	1 2 3 4 5	1 2 3 4 5	1 2 3 4 5
Date:	__/__/__	__/__/__	__/__/__

3. I try to keep the excitement of opening day alive all year.

Rating:	1 2 3 4 5	1 2 3 4 5	1 2 3 4 5
Date:	__/__/__	__/__/__	__/__/__

4. Our school uses a comprehensive, systemic process for ensuring improvement.

Rating:	1 2 3 4 5	1 2 3 4 5	1 2 3 4 5
Date:	__/__/__	__/__/__	__/__/__

Chapter 2: Characteristics of an Ideal School

Develop the Unique Talents of Each Student

1. In our school, students want to learn and are learning well.

Rating:	1 2 3 4 5	1 2 3 4 5	1 2 3 4 5
Date:	__/__/__	__/__/__	__/__/__

2. The unique talents within each student are nurtured, developed, and unleashed.

Rating:	1 2 3 4 5	1 2 3 4 5	1 2 3 4 5
Date:	__/__/__	__/__/__	__/__/__

Expect All Students to Learn

1. In our school, students work hard and achieve.

Rating:	1 2 3 4 5	1 2 3 4 5	1 2 3 4 5
Date:	__/__/__	__/__/__	__/__/__

2. Students are expected to learn.

Rating:	1 2 3 4 5	1 2 3 4 5	1 2 3 4 5
Date:	__/__/__	__/__/__	__/__/__

3. Students feel that what they are asked to learn is relevant, interesting, and personally meaningful.

Rating:	1 2 3 4 5	1 2 3 4 5	1 2 3 4 5
Date:	__/__/__	__/__/__	__/__/__

Have High and Clear Expectations

1. Teachers are very clear on what learning is expected.

Rating:	1 2 3 4 5	1 2 3 4 5	1 2 3 4 5
Date:	__/__/__	__/__/__	__/__/__

2. Students know what learning is expected.

Rating:	1 2 3 4 5	1 2 3 4 5	1 2 3 4 5
Date:	__/__/__	__/__/__	__/__/__

3. Students and teachers strive to attain expectations.

Rating:	1 2 3 4 5	1 2 3 4 5	1 2 3 4 5
Date:	__/__/__	__/__/__	__/__/__

Create a No-Excuse School

1. Teachers are demanding and teach well.

Rating:	1 2 3 4 5	1 2 3 4 5	1 2 3 4 5
Date:	__/__/__	__/__/__	__/__/__

2. There are no excuses when students don't learn.

Rating:	1 2 3 4 5	1 2 3 4 5	1 2 3 4 5
Date:	__/__/__	__/__/__	__/__/__

3. No one accepts excuses.

Rating:	1 2 3 4 5	1 2 3 4 5	1 2 3 4 5
Date:	__/__/__	__/__/__	__/__/__

Be Caring and Compassionate as well as Demanding

1. Teachers are caring, compassionate, and demanding.

Rating:	1 2 3 4 5	1 2 3 4 5	1 2 3 4 5
Date:	__/__/__	__/__/__	__/__/__

2. Teachers encourage students to take risks.

Rating:	1 2 3 4 5	1 2 3 4 5	1 2 3 4 5
Date:	__/__/__	__/__/__	__/__/__

3. Teachers correct learning errors until students learn well and succeed.

Rating:	1 2 3 4 5	1 2 3 4 5	1 2 3 4 5
Date:	__/__/__	__/__/__	__/__/__

Invite All Students to Be Creative Thinkers

1. Teachers invite and encourage thinking.

Rating:	1 2 3 4 5	1 2 3 4 5	1 2 3 4 5
Date:	__/__/__	__/__/__	__/__/__

2. Students are thinking and demonstrate this.

Rating:	1 2 3 4 5	1 2 3 4 5	1 2 3 4 5
Date:	__/__/__	__/__/__	__/__/__

Be Excited about Teaching and about the Subject

1. Teachers know their subject well.

Rating:	1 2 3 4 5	1 2 3 4 5	1 2 3 4 5
Date:	__/__/__	__/__/__	__/__/__

2. Teachers are excited about teaching and about what they are teaching and students know it.

Rating:	1 2 3 4 5	1 2 3 4 5	1 2 3 4 5
Date:	__/__/__	__/__/__	__/__/__

Create a Psychologically Safe and Nurturing School

1. Everyone is accepted unconditionally.

Rating:	1 2 3 4 5	1 2 3 4 5	1 2 3 4 5
Date:	__ / __ / __	__ / __ / __	__ / __ / __

2. Everyone is valued and included.

Rating:	1 2 3 4 5	1 2 3 4 5	1 2 3 4 5
Date:	__ / __ / __	__ / __ / __	__ / __ / __

3. Teachers create a psychologically safe and nurturing environment.

Rating:	1 2 3 4 5	1 2 3 4 5	1 2 3 4 5
Date:	__ / __ / __	__ / __ / __	__ / __ / __

Remove All Sarcasm, Humiliation, and Blame

1. Everyone cares for each other.

Rating:	1 2 3 4 5	1 2 3 4 5	1 2 3 4 5
Date:	__ / __ / __	__ / __ / __	__ / __ / __

2. There is no sarcasm, humiliation, and blame.

Rating:	1 2 3 4 5	1 2 3 4 5	1 2 3 4 5
Date:	__ / __ / __	__ / __ / __	__ / __ / __

3. Everyone is validated for honest effort.

Rating:	1 2 3 4 5	1 2 3 4 5	1 2 3 4 5
Date:	__ / __ / __	__ / __ / __	__ / __ / __

Find Pleasure and Joy in Teaching and Learning

1. Everyone finds time to laugh.

Rating:	1 2 3 4 5	1 2 3 4 5	1 2 3 4 5
Date:	__ / __ / __	__ / __ / __	__ / __ / __

2. Teaching and learning are satisfying and enjoyable.

Rating:	1 2 3 4 5	1 2 3 4 5	1 2 3 4 5
Date:	__ / __ / __	__ / __ / __	__ / __ / __

3. Pleasure and fun occur on and off the job.

Rating:	1 2 3 4 5	1 2 3 4 5	1 2 3 4 5
Date:	__/__/__	__/__/__	__/__/__

Have a Few Positive Rules, Including Respect and Responsibility

1. There are very few rules.

Rating:	1 2 3 4 5	1 2 3 4 5	1 2 3 4 5
Date:	__/__/__	__/__/__	__/__/__

2. Rules are created cooperatively by students, teachers, and the principal.

Rating:	1 2 3 4 5	1 2 3 4 5	1 2 3 4 5
Date:	__/__/__	__/__/__	__/__/__

3. Respect and responsibility foster peace and harmony.

Rating:	1 2 3 4 5	1 2 3 4 5	1 2 3 4 5
Date:	__/__/__	__/__/__	__/__/__

Develop a Well-Defined, Clear Vision

1. Everyone creates and knows the vision of the school.

Rating:	1 2 3 4 5	1 2 3 4 5	1 2 3 4 5
Date:	__/__/__	__/__/__	__/__/__

2. All agree to the vision.

Rating:	1 2 3 4 5	1 2 3 4 5	1 2 3 4 5
Date:	__/__/__	__/__/__	__/__/__

3. Everyone is committed to attaining the vision.

Rating:	1 2 3 4 5	1 2 3 4 5	1 2 3 4 5
Date:	__/__/__	__/__/__	__/__/__

Strive to Make Your Ideal School Better

1. Everyone contributes to making their school an ideal school.

Rating:	1 2 3 4 5	1 2 3 4 5	1 2 3 4 5
Date:	__/__/__	__/__/__	__/__/__

2. Everyone feels a sense of pride and responsibility.

Rating:	1 2 3 4 5	1 2 3 4 5	1 2 3 4 5
Date:	__/__/__	__/__/__	__/__/__

3. All strive to make their ideal school even better.

Rating:	1 2 3 4 5	1 2 3 4 5	1 2 3 4 5
Date:	__/__/__	__/__/__	__/__/__

Chapter 3: It's All in the Perception

1. I perceive that all students can demonstrate and accomplish well in my class.

Rating:	1 2 3 4 5	1 2 3 4 5	1 2 3 4 5
Date:	__/__/__	__/__/__	__/__/__

2. I expect all students to learn well.

Rating:	1 2 3 4 5	1 2 3 4 5	1 2 3 4 5
Date:	__/__/__	__/__/__	__/__/__

3. I will always be willing to think, talk, and model positively with and about my students.

Rating:	1 2 3 4 5	1 2 3 4 5	1 2 3 4 5
Date:	__/__/__	__/__/__	__/__/__

4. I will always be open to new ideas and knowledge and to change what I am doing when new compelling observations and knowledge are available.

Rating:	1 2 3 4 5	1 2 3 4 5	1 2 3 4 5
Date:	__/__/__	__/__/__	__/__/__

5. I believe and perceive that all students, given the opportunity, will be responsible for their own behavior.

Rating:	1 2 3 4 5	1 2 3 4 5	1 2 3 4 5
Date:	__/__/__	__/__/__	__/__/__

6. I learn about and connect with each student on personal levels and let each know how I care.

Rating:	1 2 3 4 5	1 2 3 4 5	1 2 3 4 5
Date:	__/__/__	__/__/__	__/__/__

7. I connect with each student.

Rating:	1 2 3 4 5	1 2 3 4 5	1 2 3 4 5
Date:	__/__/__	__/__/__	__/__/__

8. I model appropriate dress and behaviors for my students.

Rating:	1 2 3 4 5	1 2 3 4 5	1 2 3 4 5
Date:	__/__/__	__/__/__	__/__/__

9. I emphasize the strengths, potential, and positive characteristics of each student.

Rating:	1 2 3 4 5	1 2 3 4 5	1 2 3 4 5
Date:	__/__/__	__/__/__	__/__/__

10. I help each student feel more connected to others and me.

Rating:	1 2 3 4 5	1 2 3 4 5	1 2 3 4 5
Date:	__/__/__	__/__/__	__/__/__

CONTINUOUS ADJUSTMENT: CHAPTERS 1 TO 3

Chapter 1: Here We Go Again
Chapter 2: Characteristics of an Ideal School
Chapter 3: It's All in the Perception

Write a plan to get better. Determine which of the statements of your continuous assessments were ranked low. Then write a plan to improve each of these areas:

1. Develop the unique talents of each student.
2. Expect all students to learn.
3. Have high and clear expectations.
4. Create a no-excuse school.
5. Be caring and compassionate as well as demanding.
6. Invite all students to be creative thinkers.

7. Be excited about teaching and about the subject taught.
8. Create a psychologically safe and nurturing school.
9. Remove all sarcasm, humiliation, and blame.
10. Find pleasure and joy in teaching and learning.
11. Have a few positive rules like respect and responsibility.
12. Develop a well-defined, clear vision.
13. Strive to make your ideal school better.

CONTINUOUS ASSESSMENT: CHAPTERS 4 TO 8

Chapter 4: The School
Chapter 5: Vision and Mission
Chapter 6: Best Knowledge, Research Literature, and Data
Chapter 7: Beliefs, Values, and Dominant Philosophy
Chapter 8: Relationships, Culture, and Dominant Psychology

Answer the questions in this section using the 1–5 scale listed earlier in the chapter.

Chapter 4: The School

The questions below, which relate to chapter 4, should be answered by parents.

1. I feel welcome to visit my school.

Rating: 1 2 3 4 5 1 2 3 4 5 1 2 3 4 5
Date: __ / __ / __ __ / __ / __ __ / __ / __

2. I am encouraged to participate in the activities of my school.

Rating: 1 2 3 4 5 1 2 3 4 5 1 2 3 4 5
Date: __ / __ / __ __ / __ / __ __ / __ / __

3. I feel the school's educational program is moving in the right direction.

Rating: 1 2 3 4 5 1 2 3 4 5 1 2 3 4 5
Date: __ / __ / __ __ / __ / __ __ / __ / __

4. I have a good understanding of how the teachers are working with my child/children.

Rating: 1 2 3 4 5 1 2 3 4 5 1 2 3 4 5
Date: __/__/__ __/__/__ __/__/__

5. I feel the instruction and pace of learning is just right for my child/children.

Rating: 1 2 3 4 5 1 2 3 4 5 1 2 3 4 5
Date: __/__/__ __/__/__ __/__/__

6. The teacher's tests are appropriate and fair.

Rating: 1 2 3 4 5 1 2 3 4 5 1 2 3 4 5
Date: __/__/__ __/__/__ __/__/__

7. My child/children are encouraged to work hard, take reasonable risks, and try new ideas.

Rating: 1 2 3 4 5 1 2 3 4 5 1 2 3 4 5
Date: __/__/__ __/__/__ __/__/__

8. My child/children's teachers believe all students can learn well.

Rating: 1 2 3 4 5 1 2 3 4 5 1 2 3 4 5
Date: __/__/__ __/__/__ __/__/__

9. I feel the amount and kind of homework is appropriate.

Rating: 1 2 3 4 5 1 2 3 4 5 1 2 3 4 5
Date: __/__/__ __/__/__ __/__/__

10. My child/children attend school with enthusiasm.

Rating: 1 2 3 4 5 1 2 3 4 5 1 2 3 4 5
Date: __/__/__ __/__/__ __/__/__

11. The teacher appears to be excited about teaching and about what he or she is teaching.

Rating: 1 2 3 4 5 1 2 3 4 5 1 2 3 4 5
Date: __/__/__ __/__/__ __/__/__

12. My child/children are achieving well in school.

Rating: 1 2 3 4 5 1 2 3 4 5 1 2 3 4 5

Date: __ / __ / __ __ / __ / __ __ / __ / __

Chapter 5: Vision and Mission

1. The vision of the school was created by teachers, administrators, parents, and others involved in the community.

Rating: 1 2 3 4 5 1 2 3 4 5 1 2 3 4 5

Date: __ / __ / __ __ / __ / __ __ / __ / __

2. The vision is compelling, measurable, and gives the school clear direction.

Rating: 1 2 3 4 5 1 2 3 4 5 1 2 3 4 5

Date: __ / __ / __ __ / __ / __ __ / __ / __

3. The vision is used to plan, make decisions, and solve problems.

Rating: 1 2 3 4 5 1 2 3 4 5 1 2 3 4 5

Date: __ / __ / __ __ / __ / __ __ / __ / __

4. Long- and short-term goals are derived from the stated vision.

Rating: 1 2 3 4 5 1 2 3 4 5 1 2 3 4 5

Date: __ / __ / __ __ / __ / __ __ / __ / __

5. The vision is composed of what all students should know and be able to do.

Rating: 1 2 3 4 5 1 2 3 4 5 1 2 3 4 5

Date: __ / __ / __ __ / __ / __ __ / __ / __

6. The mission of our school is more than a slogan. It is understood by everyone and guides our actions.

Rating: 1 2 3 4 5 1 2 3 4 5 1 2 3 4 5

Date: __ / __ / __ __ / __ / __ __ / __ / __

Chapter 6: Best Knowledge, Research Literature, and Data

1. Teachers are kept informed of the educational literature.

Rating:	1 2 3 4 5	1 2 3 4 5	1 2 3 4 5
Date:	__/__/__	__/__/__	__/__/__

2. Educational literature is obtained from a variety of sources such as research reviews, summaries, books, articles, and journals.

Rating:	1 2 3 4 5	1 2 3 4 5	1 2 3 4 5
Date:	__/__/__	__/__/__	__/__/__

3. Teachers agree to knowledge-driven educational observations and determine how to use them.

Rating:	1 2 3 4 5	1 2 3 4 5	1 2 3 4 5
Date:	__/__/__	__/__/__	__/__/__

4. All practices are screened through agreed-upon educational literature.

Rating:	1 2 3 4 5	1 2 3 4 5	1 2 3 4 5
Date:	__/__/__	__/__/__	__/__/__

5. All decisions are made and screened through the most compelling educational observations available.

Rating:	1 2 3 4 5	1 2 3 4 5	1 2 3 4 5
Date:	__/__/__	__/__/__	__/__/__

Chapter 7: Beliefs, Values, and Dominant Philosophy

1. Teachers believe all students are capable of achieving at high levels.

Rating:	1 2 3 4 5	1 2 3 4 5	1 2 3 4 5
Date:	__/__/__	__/__/__	__/__/__

2. Teachers believe that trust, caring, and nurturing should pervade the entire school.

Rating:	1 2 3 4 5	1 2 3 4 5	1 2 3 4 5
Date:	__/__/__	__/__/__	__/__/__

3. Teachers believe that change, renewal, and continual improvement are absolutely necessary.

Rating:	1 2 3 4 5	1 2 3 4 5	1 2 3 4 5
Date:	__/__/__	__/__/__	__/__/__

4. Teachers believe that students should cooperate so all can learn and minimize competition.

Rating: 1 2 3 4 5 1 2 3 4 5 1 2 3 4 5
Date: __/__/__ __/__/__ __/__/__

5. Teachers believe they should search continuously for ways to include all students.

Rating: 1 2 3 4 5 1 2 3 4 5 1 2 3 4 5
Date: __/__/__ __/__/__ __/__/__

6. Teachers believe all students have talent to be developed.

Rating: 1 2 3 4 5 1 2 3 4 5 1 2 3 4 5
Date: __/__/__ __/__/__ __/__/__

7. Teachers believe in the alignment of learning outcomes, testing, and teaching.

Rating: 1 2 3 4 5 1 2 3 4 5 1 2 3 4 5
Date: __/__/__ __/__/__ __/__/__

8. Teachers have an optimistic "can do" attitude.

Rating: 1 2 3 4 5 1 2 3 4 5 1 2 3 4 5
Date: __/__/__ __/__/__ __/__/__

Chapter 8: Relationships, Culture, and Dominant Psychology

1. I reject external motivation psychology and the use of punishment and rewards to motivate students.

Rating: 1 2 3 4 5 1 2 3 4 5 1 2 3 4 5
Date: __/__/__ __/__/__ __/__/__

2. I believe that getting students to choose to be responsible for their own behavior is achievable.

Rating: 1 2 3 4 5 1 2 3 4 5 1 2 3 4 5
Date: __/__/__ __/__/__ __/__/__

3. I create the conditions and practices so that all students belong, connect, and fit into the class.

Rating: 1 2 3 4 5 1 2 3 4 5 1 2 3 4 5
Date: __ / __ / __ __ / __ / __ __ / __ / __

4. I create the conditions and practices so that all students feel self-worth, have voices in the classroom, and feel they are in control of their lives.

Rating: 1 2 3 4 5 1 2 3 4 5 1 2 3 4 5
Date: __ / __ / __ __ / __ / __ __ / __ / __

5. I create the conditions and practices so that all students are free to take risks, create, think, and try new ideas.

Rating: 1 2 3 4 5 1 2 3 4 5 1 2 3 4 5
Date: __ / __ / __ __ / __ / __ __ / __ / __

6. I create the conditions and practices so that all students will find joy, fun, and contentment in learning.

Rating: 1 2 3 4 5 1 2 3 4 5 1 2 3 4 5
Date: __ / __ / __ __ / __ / __ __ / __ / __

7. The school creates the conditions so that all staff has the four basic needs satisfied effectively.

Rating: 1 2 3 4 5 1 2 3 4 5 1 2 3 4 5
Date: __ / __ / __ __ / __ / __ __ / __ / __

CONTINUOUS ADJUSTMENT: CHAPTERS 4 TO 8

Chapter 4: The School (Parents' Assessment of the School)
Chapter 5: Vision and Mission
Chapter 6: Best Knowledge, Research Literature, and Data
Chapter 7: Beliefs, Values, and Dominant Philosophy
Chapter 8: Relationships, Culture, and Dominant Psychology

Write a plan to get better. Determine which of the statements of your continuous assessments were ranked low. Then write a plan to improve each of the areas discussed in chapters 4 to 8.

CONTINUOUS ASSESSMENT: CHAPTERS 9 AND 10

Chapter 9: Children as Students
Chapter 10: Teaching, Learning, and the Teacher

These questions should be answered by teachers and administrators. If you desire, you can also get parents' perceptions of these areas. Answer the questions in this section using the previous 1–5 scale.

CHAPTER 9: CHILDREN AS STUDENTS

1. I encourage students to learn in a very natural way using their imaginations and creativity, and to explore, express themselves, and discover.

Rating:	1 2 3 4 5	1 2 3 4 5	1 2 3 4 5
Date:	__/__/__	__/__/__	__/__/__

2. I make each child feel very special.

Rating:	1 2 3 4 5	1 2 3 4 5	1 2 3 4 5
Date:	__/__/__	__/__/__	__/__/__

3. I am caring and welcoming of all students and show each one respect.

Rating:	1 2 3 4 5	1 2 3 4 5	1 2 3 4 5
Date:	__/__/__	__/__/__	__/__/__

4. I make sure my classroom and what students are studying is not mindless and tedious but meaningful and personally interesting.

Rating:	1 2 3 4 5	1 2 3 4 5	1 2 3 4 5
Date:	__/__/__	__/__/__	__/__/__

5. I make sure my classroom is free of fear, humiliation, rejection, or criticism.

Rating:	1 2 3 4 5	1 2 3 4 5	1 2 3 4 5
Date:	__/__/__	__/__/__	__/__/__

6. I don't moralize, preach, yell, blame, or create a coercive classroom.

Rating:	1 2 3 4 5	1 2 3 4 5	1 2 3 4 5
Date:	__ / __ / __	__ / __ / __	__ / __ / __

7. I help each student become a responsible self-directed learner.

Rating:	1 2 3 4 5	1 2 3 4 5	1 2 3 4 5
Date:	__ / __ / __	__ / __ / __	__ / __ / __

8. I am always prepared, organized, and make learning interesting and fun.

Rating:	1 2 3 4 5	1 2 3 4 5	1 2 3 4 5
Date:	__ / __ / __	__ / __ / __	__ / __ / __

9. I model and expect each student to show concern for each other.

Rating:	1 2 3 4 5	1 2 3 4 5	1 2 3 4 5
Date:	__ / __ / __	__ / __ / __	__ / __ / __

10. I follow the guidelines for maximum inclusion of all children.

Rating:	1 2 3 4 5	1 2 3 4 5	1 2 3 4 5
Date:	__ / __ / __	__ / __ / __	__ / __ / __

Chapter 10: Teaching, Learning, and the Teacher

Respect

1. In our school everyone is respected equally.

Rating:	1 2 3 4 5	1 2 3 4 5	1 2 3 4 5
Date:	__ / __ / __	__ / __ / __	__ / __ / __

2. In our school, all teachers are treated as thinking, caring people.

Rating:	1 2 3 4 5	1 2 3 4 5	1 2 3 4 5
Date:	__ / __ / __	__ / __ / __	__ / __ / __

3. In our school, all teachers are considered to be important contributors.

Rating:	1 2 3 4 5	1 2 3 4 5	1 2 3 4 5
Date:	__ / __ / __	__ / __ / __	__ / __ / __

4. In our school, teachers are proud to be teachers and students are proud of their school.

Rating: 1 2 3 4 5 1 2 3 4 5 1 2 3 4 5
Date: __/__/__ __/__/__ __/__/__

5. In our school, the administration respects the teachers and teachers respect the administration.

Rating: 1 2 3 4 5 1 2 3 4 5 1 2 3 4 5
Date: __/__/__ __/__/__ __/__/__

6. Administration and other teachers respect me.

Rating: 1 2 3 4 5 1 2 3 4 5 1 2 3 4 5
Date: __/__/__ __/__/__ __/__/__

7. I respect each and every one of my students and treat them as people.

Rating: 1 2 3 4 5 1 2 3 4 5 1 2 3 4 5
Date: __/__/__ __/__/__ __/__/__

Caring

1. In our school, teachers and administrators demonstrate mutual caring.

Rating: 1 2 3 4 5 1 2 3 4 5 1 2 3 4 5
Date: __/__/__ __/__/__ __/__/__

2. In our school, teachers feel they are cared for by each other and me.

Rating: 1 2 3 4 5 1 2 3 4 5 1 2 3 4 5
Date: __/__/__ __/__/__ __/__/__

3. This school is a nice place to be because most of us feel wanted and needed.

Rating: 1 2 3 4 5 1 2 3 4 5 1 2 3 4 5
Date: __/__/__ __/__/__ __/__/__

4. I care about each of my students and they know it.

Rating: 1 2 3 4 5 1 2 3 4 5 1 2 3 4 5
Date: __/__/__ __/__/__ __/__/__

5. All children feel wanted and needed in my classroom.

Rating: 1 2 3 4 5 1 2 3 4 5 1 2 3 4 5
Date: __/__/__ __/__/__ __/__/__

Involvement

1. All teachers are involved in important decisions.

Rating:	1 2 3 4 5	1 2 3 4 5	1 2 3 4 5
Date:	__/__/__	__/__/__	__/__/__

2. Teachers are involved in the selection of new teachers.

Rating:	1 2 3 4 5	1 2 3 4 5	1 2 3 4 5
Date:	__/__/__	__/__/__	__/__/__

3. I feel that I personally have a voice in the direction our school is taking.

Rating:	1 2 3 4 5	1 2 3 4 5	1 2 3 4 5
Date:	__/__/__	__/__/__	__/__/__

4. I involve students in formulating the rules of my classroom and being responsible for their own behavior.

Rating:	1 2 3 4 5	1 2 3 4 5	1 2 3 4 5
Date:	__/__/__	__/__/__	__/__/__

Trust

1. In our school, teachers feel that the administration is on their side.

Rating:	1 2 3 4 5	1 2 3 4 5	1 2 3 4 5
Date:	__/__/__	__/__/__	__/__/__

2. In our school, teachers can share their concerns openly with each other and with the administration even if they don't agree.

Rating:	1 2 3 4 5	1 2 3 4 5	1 2 3 4 5
Date:	__/__/__	__/__/__	__/__/__

3. In our school, teachers and administrators can count on me and each other to listen and support them.

Rating:	1 2 3 4 5	1 2 3 4 5	1 2 3 4 5
Date:	__/__/__	__/__/__	__/__/__

4. In my classroom, children can trust me to help them learn, never compare them to other students, and never embarrass them.

Rating: 1 2 3 4 5 1 2 3 4 5 1 2 3 4 5
Date: __/__/__ __/__/__ __/__/__

5. In my classroom, students can count on me to be fair, listen to them, and be on their side.

Rating: 1 2 3 4 5 1 2 3 4 5 1 2 3 4 5
Date: __/__/__ __/__/__ __/__/__

Communication

1. An honest and open communication system is present in our school.

Rating: 1 2 3 4 5 1 2 3 4 5 1 2 3 4 5
Date: __/__/__ __/__/__ __/__/__

2. I feel that teachers and administrators are friendly and I can talk with them.

Rating: 1 2 3 4 5 1 2 3 4 5 1 2 3 4 5
Date: __/__/__ __/__/__ __/__/__

3. I feel that I am easy to communicate with and I listen well.

Rating: 1 2 3 4 5 1 2 3 4 5 1 2 3 4 5
Date: __/__/__ __/__/__ __/__/__

4. In my classroom, all students feel free to talk with me openly and frankly.

Rating: 1 2 3 4 5 1 2 3 4 5 1 2 3 4 5
Date: __/__/__ __/__/__ __/__/__

5. In my classroom, students are taught effective communication skills and I model them all the time.

Rating: 1 2 3 4 5 1 2 3 4 5 1 2 3 4 5
Date: __/__/__ __/__/__ __/__/__

Morale

1. In our school, teachers and administrators feel enthusiastic about their job.

Rating: 1 2 3 4 5 1 2 3 4 5 1 2 3 4 5
Date: __ / __ / __ __ / __ / __ __ / __ / __

2. In our school, everyone feels pride in its accomplishments and defends the school if it is challenged.

Rating: 1 2 3 4 5 1 2 3 4 5 1 2 3 4 5
Date: __ / __ / __ __ / __ / __ __ / __ / __

3. In our school, attendance is high and teachers and students stay away for urgent and good reasons.

Rating: 1 2 3 4 5 1 2 3 4 5 1 2 3 4 5
Date: __ / __ / __ __ / __ / __ __ / __ / __

4. I like working in this school and am proud to be a teacher.

Rating: 1 2 3 4 5 1 2 3 4 5 1 2 3 4 5
Date: __ / __ / __ __ / __ / __ __ / __ / __

5. In my classroom, students are enthusiastic about being there and about learning.

Rating: 1 2 3 4 5 1 2 3 4 5 1 2 3 4 5
Date: __ / __ / __ __ / __ / __ __ / __ / __

6. In my classroom, students demonstrate pride in their learning and achievements.

Rating: 1 2 3 4 5 1 2 3 4 5 1 2 3 4 5
Date: __ / __ / __ __ / __ / __ __ / __ / __

Chapter 10: Teaching, Learning, and the Teacher

Stage 1: Preparation for Success

Attitudinal Readiness

1. I assess and observe each student's attitude toward learning what I am going to teach.

Rating: 1 2 3 4 5 1 2 3 4 5 1 2 3 4 5
Date: __ / __ / __ __ / __ / __ __ / __ / __

2. I assure all students that I am on their side and if they put forth the effort they will succeed.

Rating: 1 2 3 4 5 1 2 3 4 5 1 2 3 4 5
Date: __/__/__ __/__/__ __/__/__

3. I assure all students they are accepted unconditionally and their self-worth is never in question.

Rating: 1 2 3 4 5 1 2 3 4 5 1 2 3 4 5
Date: __/__/__ __/__/__ __/__/__

4. I assure all students that it is possible for everyone to do well and get high grades.

Rating: 1 2 3 4 5 1 2 3 4 5 1 2 3 4 5
Date: __/__/__ __/__/__ __/__/__

Academic Readiness

1. I prepare all students for academic success each day by reviewing what is necessary for success.

Rating: 1 2 3 4 5 1 2 3 4 5 1 2 3 4 5
Date: __/__/__ __/__/__ __/__/__

2. I try to turn all remedial programs into prevention programs.

Rating: 1 2 3 4 5 1 2 3 4 5 1 2 3 4 5
Date: __/__/__ __/__/__ __/__/__

3. When other teachers such as special-needs teachers or remedial teachers are providing help for my students, I make sure they know what will be taught so they can prepare students for success in my class.

Rating: 1 2 3 4 5 1 2 3 4 5 1 2 3 4 5
Date: __/__/__ __/__/__ __/__/__

4. For those students who need correctives regularly, I often preteach the next day's lesson ahead of time.

Rating: 1 2 3 4 5 1 2 3 4 5 1 2 3 4 5
Date: __/__/__ __/__/__ __/__/__

5. For those students who have difficulty reading, I make sure I compensate for them. I never make reading the prerequisite for success while still trying to teach the student to read.

Rating:	1 2 3 4 5	1 2 3 4 5	1 2 3 4 5
Date:	__/__/__	__/__/__	__/__/__

Stage 2: Getting and Focusing Student Attention

1. I ensure that students know what they are to learn, why they are to learn it, and how they will learn it.

Rating:	1 2 3 4 5	1 2 3 4 5	1 2 3 4 5
Date:	__/__/__	__/__/__	__/__/__

2. I create conditions and experiences that optimize the possibilities that students will be motivated to want to achieve the learning goals I set.

Rating:	1 2 3 4 5	1 2 3 4 5	1 2 3 4 5
Date:	__/__/__	__/__/__	__/__/__

3. I try to capture and focus students' attention on what is to be learned.

Rating:	1 2 3 4 5	1 2 3 4 5	1 2 3 4 5
Date:	__/__/__	__/__/__	__/__/__

Stage 3: Initial Instruction

1. I maximize student understanding of new ideas and concepts by using at least two different modes of instruction to appeal to the many and varied ways students learn.

Rating:	1 2 3 4 5	1 2 3 4 5	1 2 3 4 5
Date:	__/__/__	__/__/__	__/__/__

2. I provide many opportunities for students to be actively involved in the teaching–learning process.

Rating:	1 2 3 4 5	1 2 3 4 5	1 2 3 4 5
Date:	__/__/__	__/__/__	__/__/__

3. I accommodate different learning rates when providing initial instruction.

Rating: 1 2 3 4 5 1 2 3 4 5 1 2 3 4 5
Date: __ / __ / __ __ / __ / __ __ / __ / __

4. I understand that when initial instruction is done well, the need for correctives is minimized.

Rating: 1 2 3 4 5 1 2 3 4 5 1 2 3 4 5
Date: __ / __ / __ __ / __ / __ __ / __ / __

Stage 4: Guided Practice and Adjustments

1. I provide many opportunities for students to practice what they have learned during the lesson.

Rating: 1 2 3 4 5 1 2 3 4 5 1 2 3 4 5
Date: __ / __ / __ __ / __ / __ __ / __ / __

2. Many of my correctives and adjustments are done during the guided practice part of instruction.

Rating: 1 2 3 4 5 1 2 3 4 5 1 2 3 4 5
Date: __ / __ / __ __ / __ / __ __ / __ / __

3. I make sure guided practice is short, intense, and frequent and prepares students for independent practice.

Rating: 1 2 3 4 5 1 2 3 4 5 1 2 3 4 5
Date: __ / __ / __ __ / __ / __ __ / __ / __

4. I use guided practice to determine how effective my initial instruction has been. I use it to make adjustments to my teaching.

Rating: 1 2 3 4 5 1 2 3 4 5 1 2 3 4 5
Date: __ / __ / __ __ / __ / __ __ / __ / __

Stage 5: Summary and Closure

1. I provide opportunities for students to experience daily review and closure in a variety of ways.

Rating: 1 2 3 4 5 1 2 3 4 5 1 2 3 4 5
Date: __/__/__ __/__/__ __/__/__

2. I involve students either as a class or in small learning teams to provide the summary of the lesson.

Rating: 1 2 3 4 5 1 2 3 4 5 1 2 3 4 5
Date: __/__/__ __/__/__ __/__/__

Stage 6: Assessment and Testing

1. I align all assessment and testing with what I expect students to know and do.

Rating: 1 2 3 4 5 1 2 3 4 5 1 2 3 4 5
Date: __/__/__ __/__/__ __/__/__

2. I use all assessments to help students learn by making the necessary correctives or by reteaching.

Rating: 1 2 3 4 5 1 2 3 4 5 1 2 3 4 5
Date: __/__/__ __/__/__ __/__/__

3. I am reasonably sure that when I give a test, students will do well and succeed.

Rating: 1 2 3 4 5 1 2 3 4 5 1 2 3 4 5
Date: __/__/__ __/__/__ __/__/__

Experiences throughout Teaching and Learning

1. I align all teaching and learning experiences, including assessments, to the learning goals.

Rating: 1 2 3 4 5 1 2 3 4 5 1 2 3 4 5
Date: __/__/__ __/__/__ __/__/__

2. I implement meaningful learning experiences that actively engage students throughout the teaching and learning process.

Rating: 1 2 3 4 5 1 2 3 4 5 1 2 3 4 5
Date: __/__/__ __/__/__ __/__/__

3. I ensure that, when appropriate, students assess and track their own progress.

Rating: 1 2 3 4 5 1 2 3 4 5 1 2 3 4 5
Date: __ / __ / __ __ / __ / __ __ / __ / __

4. I continually assess student learning and provide timely and regular feedback.

Rating: 1 2 3 4 5 1 2 3 4 5 1 2 3 4 5
Date: __ / __ / __ __ / __ / __ __ / __ / __

5. I provide opportunities for students to explore learning in more depth and to connect learning to new situations.

Rating: 1 2 3 4 5 1 2 3 4 5 1 2 3 4 5
Date: __ / __ / __ __ / __ / __ __ / __ / __

6. I identify students who need reteaching and make instructional adjustments to accommodate them.

Rating: 1 2 3 4 5 1 2 3 4 5 1 2 3 4 5
Date: __ / __ / __ __ / __ / __ __ / __ / __

7. I identify students who need to be challenged and make instructional adjustments to accommodate them.

Rating: 1 2 3 4 5 1 2 3 4 5 1 2 3 4 5
Date: __ / __ / __ __ / __ / __ __ / __ / __

CONTINUOUS ADJUSTMENT: CHAPTERS 9 AND 10

Chapter 9: Children as Students
Chapter 10: Teaching, Learning, and the Teacher

Write a plan to get better. Determine which of the statements of your continuous assessments were ranked low. Then write a plan to improve each of these areas:

1. Respect
2. Caring

3. Involvement
4. Trust
5. Communications
6. Morale

Stage 1: Preparation for Success (Attitudinal Readiness and Academic Readiness)
Stage 2: Getting and Focusing Student Attention
Stage 3: Initial Instruction
Stage 4: Guided Practice and Adjustments
Stage 5: Summary and Closure
Stage 6: Assessment and Testing
Experiences Throughout Teaching and Learning

CONTINUOUS ASSESSMENT: CHAPTERS 11 AND 12

Chapter 11: Curriculum Planning
Chapter 12: Classroom Practices

Answer the questions in this section using the 1–5 scale. The questions below should be answered by teachers and administrators. If you desire, you can also get parents' perceptions of these areas.

Chapter 11: Curriculum Planning

Acquiring Knowledge (Know)

1. I teach all concepts for understanding as well as having students memorize information and facts.

Rating:	1 2 3 4 5	1 2 3 4 5	1 2 3 4 5
Date:	__ / __ / __	__ / __ / __	__ / __ / __

2. I help all students understand the structure of my discipline.

Rating:	1 2 3 4 5	1 2 3 4 5	1 2 3 4 5
Date:	__ / __ / __	__ / __ / __	__ / __ / __

Acquiring Skills (Do)

1. I help all students use the connecting skills to think critically, create, develop, apply, construct new ideas, and determine patterns.

Rating: 1 2 3 4 5 1 2 3 4 5 1 2 3 4 5
Date: __/__/__ __/__/__ __/__/__

2. I help all students to develop their communication skills in my discipline.

Rating: 1 2 3 4 5 1 2 3 4 5 1 2 3 4 5
Date: __/__/__ __/__/__ __/__/__

3. I provide many opportunities for all students to develop the life skills of using technology, creating and testing hypotheses, and solving problems.

Rating: 1 2 3 4 5 1 2 3 4 5 1 2 3 4 5
Date: __/__/__ __/__/__ __/__/__

4. I teach students to carry on investigations, use the tools of my discipline, make learning connections, and develop their learning skills.

Rating: 1 2 3 4 5 1 2 3 4 5 1 2 3 4 5
Date: __/__/__ __/__/__ __/__/__

5. I help all students understand the importance of social skills and what it means to interact in a positive way with others.

Rating: 1 2 3 4 5 1 2 3 4 5 1 2 3 4 5
Date: __/__/__ __/__/__ __/__/__

Course Learning Goals

1. I use national, state, and local standards to develop my course learning goals.

Rating: 1 2 3 4 5 1 2 3 4 5 1 2 3 4 5
Date: __/__/__ __/__/__ __/__/__

2. I include the three parts of Acquiring Knowledge and the five parts of Acquiring Skills in my course learning goals.

Rating: 1 2 3 4 5 1 2 3 4 5 1 2 3 4 5
Date: __/__/__ __/__/__ __/__/__

Course Outlined By Units

1. Accounting for all goals, I have placed the course learning goals into appropriate units, chapters, themes, or events.

Rating:	1 2 3 4 5	1 2 3 4 5	1 2 3 4 5
Date:	__/__/__	__/__/__	__/__/__

2. I have determined the approximate amount of time needed to teach and have students learn each unit.

Rating:	1 2 3 4 5	1 2 3 4 5	1 2 3 4 5
Date:	__/__/__	__/__/__	__/__/__

3. I will adjust the time for each unit at the completion of the unit and course.

Rating:	1 2 3 4 5	1 2 3 4 5	1 2 3 4 5
Date:	__/__/__	__/__/__	__/__/__

Unit Planning

1. I will ensure that the content of each unit is aligned to the national, state, and local standards.

Rating:	1 2 3 4 5	1 2 3 4 5	1 2 3 4 5
Date:	__/__/__	__/__/__	__/__/__

2. I will estimate the amount of time needed to teach and have students learn the unit.

Rating:	1 2 3 4 5	1 2 3 4 5	1 2 3 4 5
Date:	__/__/__	__/__/__	__/__/__

3. I will determine both formal and informal assessments to determine what students know and are able to do.

Rating:	1 2 3 4 5	1 2 3 4 5	1 2 3 4 5
Date:	__/__/__	__/__/__	__/__/__

Acquiring Skills Model

1. I use the acquiring skills planning tool to ensure that the five skills are taught and learned and included in my planning.

Rating: 1 2 3 4 5 1 2 3 4 5 1 2 3 4 5
Date: __/__/__ __/__/__ __/__/__

2. As I plan each unit I look at past planning and determine which skills have not yet been included.

Rating: 1 2 3 4 5 1 2 3 4 5 1 2 3 4 5
Date: __/__/__ __/__/__ __/__/__

Lesson Learning Goals

1. I determine for each lesson what students should know and do.

Rating: 1 2 3 4 5 1 2 3 4 5 1 2 3 4 5
Date: __/__/__ __/__/__ __/__/__

2. I align my lesson learning goals to the unit and course learning goals.

Rating: 1 2 3 4 5 1 2 3 4 5 1 2 3 4 5
Date: __/__/__ __/__/__ __/__/__

Planning for the Instructional Process

Preparation for Success

1. I identify all the essential prerequisites that students need to know and be able to do to prepare them for successful learning.

Rating: 1 2 3 4 5 1 2 3 4 5 1 2 3 4 5
Date: __/__/__ __/__/__ __/__/__

Focusing Student Attention

1. I plan for a variety of ways to focus students on what they are to learn, why they are to learn it, and how they will learn it. I plan to create conditions and experiences that optimize the possibilities for students to be motivated enough to want to achieve the learning goals.

Rating: 1 2 3 4 5 1 2 3 4 5 1 2 3 4 5
Date: __/__/__ __/__/__ __/__/__

Initial Instruction

1. I identify and plan to use a wide range of materials and strategies that address the learning styles, rates, and needs of all students.

Rating:	1 2 3 4 5	1 2 3 4 5	1 2 3 4 5
Date:	__ / __ / __	__ / __ / __	__ / __ / __

2. I plan to align all standards, teaching, learning, and assessments.

Rating:	1 2 3 4 5	1 2 3 4 5	1 2 3 4 5
Date:	__ / __ / __	__ / __ / __	__ / __ / __

Guided Practice and Adjustments

1. I design guided practice activities that are short and intense and help each student make the necessary adjustments.

Rating:	1 2 3 4 5	1 2 3 4 5	1 2 3 4 5
Date:	__ / __ / __	__ / __ / __	__ / __ / __

Summary and Closure

1. I design opportunities for students to experience daily review, summary, and closure in a variety of ways.

Rating:	1 2 3 4 5	1 2 3 4 5	1 2 3 4 5
Date:	__ / __ / __	__ / __ / __	__ / __ / __

Assessments and Testing

1. I plan ways to continually assess student learning and provide timely and regular feedback.

Rating:	1 2 3 4 5	1 2 3 4 5	1 2 3 4 5
Date:	__ / __ / __	__ / __ / __	__ / __ / __

2. When appropriate, I plan for ways that students can assess and track their own progress.

Rating:	1 2 3 4 5	1 2 3 4 5	1 2 3 4 5
Date:	__ / __ / __	__ / __ / __	__ / __ / __

3. I plan for alignment of all assessment and testing to the expected course, unit, and lesson learning goals.

Rating: 1 2 3 4 5 1 2 3 4 5 1 2 3 4 5
Date: __ / __ / __ __ / __ / __ __ / __ / __

Other Planning

1. I plan opportunities for students to explore learning in more depth and to make corrections with new situations.

Rating: 1 2 3 4 5 1 2 3 4 5 1 2 3 4 5
Date: __ / __ / __ __ / __ / __ __ / __ / __

2. I plan for challenges and consider instructional adjustments for those students who need them.

Rating: 1 2 3 4 5 1 2 3 4 5 1 2 3 4 5
Date: __ / __ / __ __ / __ / __ __ / __ / __

Chapter 12: Classroom Practices

Testing and Assessment

1. I will align all assessment and testing to the course, unit, and lesson learning goals.

Rating: 1 2 3 4 5 1 2 3 4 5 1 2 3 4 5
Date: __ / __ / __ __ / __ / __ __ / __ / __

2. I will communicate to students what is to be learned and how they will demonstrate that learning.

Rating: 1 2 3 4 5 1 2 3 4 5 1 2 3 4 5
Date: __ / __ / __ __ / __ / __ __ / __ / __

3. I will use my assessments to measure both knowledge and skills.

Rating: 1 2 3 4 5 1 2 3 4 5 1 2 3 4 5
Date: __ / __ / __ __ / __ / __ __ / __ / __

4. I will give a test only when I am reasonably sure all students will do well.

Rating: 1 2 3 4 5 1 2 3 4 5 1 2 3 4 5
Date: __/__/__ __/__/__ __/__/__

5. I will use both traditional and alternative assessments to measure what students know and are able to do.

Rating: 1 2 3 4 5 1 2 3 4 5 1 2 3 4 5
Date: __/__/__ __/__/__ __/__/__

Grading

1. I will use a grade to reflect achievement against predetermined standards or competence, never how fast it took a student to learn and never for comparing students with one another.

Rating: 1 2 3 4 5 1 2 3 4 5 1 2 3 4 5
Date: __/__/__ __/__/__ __/__/__

2. I will not give a grade until a student has achieved the standard of competence.

Rating: 1 2 3 4 5 1 2 3 4 5 1 2 3 4 5
Date: __/__/__ __/__/__ __/__/__

3. I will alter (not average) a grade when a student can demonstrate new and improved learning.

Rating: 1 2 3 4 5 1 2 3 4 5 1 2 3 4 5
Date: __/__/__ __/__/__ __/__/__

4. I will not give a grade for effort but for demonstrated performance.

Rating: 1 2 3 4 5 1 2 3 4 5 1 2 3 4 5
Date: __/__/__ __/__/__ __/__/__

Retesting and Managing Time

1. I will give a retest when a student prepares and demonstrates an attitude and readiness to take it. I will make it clear that a retest is an earned privilege and opportunity and not a right.

Rating: 1 2 3 4 5 1 2 3 4 5 1 2 3 4 5
Date: __/__/__ __/__/__ __/__/__

2. I will give a retest to encourage responsibility by having students earn excellent achievement at the competent or highly competent levels.

Rating: 1 2 3 4 5 1 2 3 4 5 1 2 3 4 5
Date: __ / __ / __ __ / __ / __ __ / __ / __

3. I encourage all students to achieve well on the first test and avoid taking a retest.

Rating: 1 2 3 4 5 1 2 3 4 5 1 2 3 4 5
Date: __ / __ / __ __ / __ / __ __ / __ / __

4. I will manage my time by trying to stay within the allocated time to teach and learn each unit.

Rating: 1 2 3 4 5 1 2 3 4 5 1 2 3 4 5
Date: __ / __ / __ __ / __ / __ __ / __ / __

Homework

1. I will give homework (depending on my grade level) to provide independent practice, promote retention, reinforce understanding and skills, encourage responsible learning, promote self-directed learning, and encourage creativity.

Rating: 1 2 3 4 5 1 2 3 4 5 1 2 3 4 5
Date: __ / __ / __ __ / __ / __ __ / __ / __

2. I will give homework that is relevant, meaningful, and aligned to the course, unit, and lesson learning goals.

Rating: 1 2 3 4 5 1 2 3 4 5 1 2 3 4 5
Date: __ / __ / __ __ / __ / __ __ / __ / __

3. When I give homework, I will be reasonably sure students will be able to do it.

Rating: 1 2 3 4 5 1 2 3 4 5 1 2 3 4 5
Date: __ / __ / __ __ / __ / __ __ / __ / __

Classroom Discipline

1. I will create conditions and procedures so that all students are physically and psychologically safe.

Rating: 1 2 3 4 5 1 2 3 4 5 1 2 3 4 5
Date: __ / __ / __ __ / __ / __ __ / __ / __

2. I will create, with the students, rules and consequences to produce a positive climate and culture in the classroom.

Rating: 1 2 3 4 5 1 2 3 4 5 1 2 3 4 5
Date: __ / __ / __ __ / __ / __ __ / __ / __

3. I will create needs-satisfying conditions in my classroom that will be positive and prevent discipline problems.

Rating: 1 2 3 4 5 1 2 3 4 5 1 2 3 4 5
Date: __ / __ / __ __ / __ / __ __ / __ / __

CONTINUOUS ADJUSTMENT: CHAPTERS 11 AND 12

Chapter 11: Curriculum Planning
Chapter 12: Classroom Practices

Write a plan to get better. Determine which of the statements of your continuous assessments were ranked low. Then write a plan to improve each of these areas.

Chapter 11: Curriculum Planning

- Acquiring Knowledge
- Acquiring Skills
- Course Learning Goals
- Course Outlined by Units
- Unit Planning
- Acquiring Skills Model
- Lesson Learning Goals
- Planning for the Instructional Process
- Focusing Student Attention
- Initial Instruction
- Guided Practice and Adjustments
- Summary and Closure

- Assessments and Testing
- Other Planning

Chapter 12: Classroom Practices

- Testing and Assessment
- Grading
- Retesting and Managing Time
- Homework
- Classroom Discipline

CONTINUOUS ASSESSMENT: CHAPTER 13

Chapter 13: The Principal

Answer the questions in this section using the 1–5 scale. These questions should be answered by teachers and administrators. If you desire, you can also get parents' perceptions of these areas.

Personal Skills

1. Our principal has many personal skills such as (a) values every child and teacher, (b) understands teaching and learning, (c) inspires everyone through personal example to have high expectations and intellectual pursuits and to achieve, (d) knows that schools are in a people business and that people are the most important resource, (e) takes the long-term view and avoids fads, and (f) is optimistic and positive through the routine ups and downs.

Rating:	1 2 3 4 5	1 2 3 4 5	1 2 3 4 5
Date:	__/__/__	__/__/__	__/__/__

2. Our principal takes a systems approach, sees the complete picture of managing a school, and provides clear direction.

Rating:	1 2 3 4 5	1 2 3 4 5	1 2 3 4 5
Date:	__/__/__	__/__/__	__/__/__

3. Our principal creates a positive school culture by creating the needs-satisfying conditions for everyone.

Rating:	1 2 3 4 5	1 2 3 4 5	1 2 3 4 5
Date:	__/__/__	__/__/__	__/__/__

4. Our principal creates a positive school culture by creating needs-satisfying conditions for everyone in the school.

Rating:	1 2 3 4 5	1 2 3 4 5	1 2 3 4 5
Date:	__/__/__	__/__/__	__/__/__

Communicating Skills

1. Our principal listens intentionally and attentively to others, shows he or she understands what others are saying, and is not judgmental of their ideas.

Rating:	1 2 3 4 5	1 2 3 4 5	1 2 3 4 5
Date:	__/__/__	__/__/__	__/__/__

2. Our principal shows he or she is sensitive to new ideas, positive and encouraging, and a good listener.

Rating:	1 2 3 4 5	1 2 3 4 5	1 2 3 4 5
Date:	__/__/__	__/__/__	__/__/__

Using Knowledge

1. Our principal uses the most compelling research and educational observations along with data to plan and make decisions.

Rating:	1 2 3 4 5	1 2 3 4 5	1 2 3 4 5
Date:	__/__/__	__/__/__	__/__/__

2. Our principal uses a well-defined process to introduce and bring knowledge to the teaching staff.

Rating:	1 2 3 4 5	1 2 3 4 5	1 2 3 4 5
Date:	__/__/__	__/__/__	__/__/__

3. Our principal values the use of educational research and models using it for the staff.

Rating: 1 2 3 4 5 1 2 3 4 5 1 2 3 4 5
Date: __/__/__ __/__/__ __/__/__

Creating a Vision and Mission

1. Our principal involved all teachers in creating the vision and mission for the students in our school.

Rating: 1 2 3 4 5 1 2 3 4 5 1 2 3 4 5
Date: __/__/__ __/__/__ __/__/__

2. Our principal involved all teachers in creating the vision and mission for the staff in our school.

Rating: 1 2 3 4 5 1 2 3 4 5 1 2 3 4 5
Date: __/__/__ __/__/__ __/__/__

3. Our principal assesses, models, and defends the mission and vision of our school.

Rating: 1 2 3 4 5 1 2 3 4 5 1 2 3 4 5
Date: __/__/__ __/__/__ __/__/__

Generating Beliefs

1. Our principal involved all teachers in creating the beliefs for students in our school.

Rating: 1 2 3 4 5 1 2 3 4 5 1 2 3 4 5
Date: __/__/__ __/__/__ __/__/__

2. Our principal assesses, models, and defends the beliefs of our school.

Rating: 1 2 3 4 5 1 2 3 4 5 1 2 3 4 5
Date: __/__/__ __/__/__ __/__/__

Managing the Instructional Process, Curriculum Planning

1. Our principal ensures that the Instructional Classroom Practices process is followed and the teacher is effective in its delivery.

Rating: 1 2 3 4 5 1 2 3 4 5 1 2 3 4 5
Date: __/__/__ __/__/__ __/__/__

2. Our principal understands the complex planning process and ensures that all teachers plan effectively.

Rating:	1 2 3 4 5	1 2 3 4 5	1 2 3 4 5
Date:	__ / __ / __	__ / __ / __	__ / __ / __

3. Our principal ensures that all teachers follow the classroom practices as intended.

Rating:	1 2 3 4 5	1 2 3 4 5	1 2 3 4 5
Date:	__ / __ / __	__ / __ / __	__ / __ / __

Making Decisions

1. Our principal involves everyone, if they choose, in major decisions affecting them.

Rating:	1 2 3 4 5	1 2 3 4 5	1 2 3 4 5
Date:	__ / __ / __	__ / __ / __	__ / __ / __

2. Our principal creates a positive climate for everyone participating in the decision-making process.

Rating:	1 2 3 4 5	1 2 3 4 5	1 2 3 4 5
Date:	__ / __ / __	__ / __ / __	__ / __ / __

3. Our principal follows the decision-making process when making decisions.

Rating:	1 2 3 4 5	1 2 3 4 5	1 2 3 4 5
Date:	__ / __ / __	__ / __ / __	__ / __ / __

Managing Change

1. Our principal establishes the need for change and helps everyone to understand it.

Rating:	1 2 3 4 5	1 2 3 4 5	1 2 3 4 5
Date:	__ / __ / __	__ / __ / __	__ / __ / __

2. Our principal creates a positive-change atmosphere and assures staff that we must learn from our mistakes and that it is not acceptable to bury problems.

Rating:	1 2 3 4 5	1 2 3 4 5	1 2 3 4 5
Date:	__ / __ / __	__ / __ / __	__ / __ / __

3. Our principal does what he or she can to provide whatever help teachers need and continuing education for the entire staff.

Rating:	1 2 3 4 5	1 2 3 4 5	1 2 3 4 5
Date:	__ / __ / __	__ / __ / __	__ / __ / __

4. Our principal never belittles any staff member even if he or she doesn't want to open his or her mind to new possibilities. He uses a positive process with these teachers.

Rating:	1 2 3 4 5	1 2 3 4 5	1 2 3 4 5
Date:	__ / __ / __	__ / __ / __	__ / __ / __

5. Our principal is quite patient with those teachers who want to wait and observe the teachers who are leading the change.

Rating:	1 2 3 4 5	1 2 3 4 5	1 2 3 4 5
Date:	__ / __ / __	__ / __ / __	__ / __ / __

6. Staff can trust the principal to support them during the change process.

Rating:	1 2 3 4 5	1 2 3 4 5	1 2 3 4 5
Date:	__ / __ / __	__ / __ / __	__ / __ / __

CONTINUOUS ADJUSTMENT: CHAPTER 13

Chapter 13: The Principal

Write a plan to get better. Determine which of the statements of your continuous assessments were ranked low. Then write a plan to improve each of these areas:

- Personal Skills
- Process Skills
- Communication Skills
- Using Knowledge
- Creating a Vision and Mission

- Generating Beliefs
- Managing the Instructional Process, Curriculum Planning, and Classroom Practices
- Making Decisions
- Managing Change

Chapter Fifteen

Continuing Professional Education for Staff

The only way to produce significant student achievement is to provide continuing education for all staff.

Focus Questions

1. Is there a clear, systematic, continuous, and well-defined education model that all staff understand and can rely on to help them continue with their professional education?
2. Is there a clear, systematic, continuous, and well-defined education model that ensures that all staff will be provided support and assistance as they use new teaching techniques?
3. Is there a clear, systematic, continuous, and well-defined education model that helps all staff implement national, state, and local standards so that all children will achieve well?
4. Is there a clear, systematic, continuous, and well-defined education model that helps all staff to fully implement the vision, beliefs, mission, culture, and climate of the school and classroom?
5. Is there a clear, systematic, continuous, and well-defined education model that describes the different roles of teachers and principals?

To significantly improve our schools, guarantee that teachers and principals perform well, all children learn well, and our educational system becomes respected throughout the world, it is absolutely necessary to alter the current process of continuing education (staff development) for our teachers and principals.

As stated earlier, teaching may be the most complex of all the professions. It is difficult to teach those who want to learn, but trying to teach those who don't seems impossible. Try teaching students who come to school only because it is mandated. Now include students with disabilities in the regular classroom without support and teacher training, and teaching can be overwhelming. Try teaching students who spend most of their time in front of a television or playing video games.

With all these challenges there is little time during the school day for teachers to meet, plan, or learn. And when the school day is over, teachers must go home and plan for the next day, complete reports, correct papers, and make suggestions for students to improve. This often leaves little time for family.

A teacher's day can be so consuming that, at times, teachers even find it difficult to get a bathroom break during the school day. After a day like this, there is very little chance that a teacher will be motivated or receptive to new ideas. Staff development sessions that take place at the end of the school day are rarely productive. Most teachers will tell you this and the existing research on staff development confirms this fact.

Some schools provide one-day seminars with an outside "motivational speaker" presenting some good thoughts. Do you think those seminars are effective and can make a lasting impact? Again, read the research. These types of seminars are meant to increase awareness of new ideas and possibilities—nothing more.

Some schools set aside several continuing education days each year when teachers are not required to teach. These days are usually spread out over the entire school year. While these may be valuable, they are not sufficient to improve teaching and learning. It is like teaching long division on five separate days spread out over the entire year. Not good. Meaningful learning opportunities must be provided when teachers are not tired and when large blocks of time can be provided. Block scheduling is necessary for effective continuing education for teachers.

Virtually every politician has an educational agenda to gather votes. They frequently state how poorly schools are performing and then offer a slogan as a solution. Most of the time, these politicians appeal to the public with accountability hype. Some state education departments fall into the same trap and offer quick-fix solutions to deep problems. More student testing is often proposed as the answer. These external solutions rarely produce lasting results, yet the beat goes on. And when it comes time to provide financial support to keep with the mandate, little is forthcoming.

Meaningful and long-lasting results will be obtained only when teachers and principals are committed to changing and improving the status quo. Most teachers and principals do the best they can. They do not purposely hold back on teaching students or managing the school. They are educators and want to help all students learn well. They came into the profession full of optimism and hope, but they soon get mired in the difficulties of teaching and leading.

Except for the seven-percenters mentioned earlier, most teachers and principals would gladly give more of themselves given the opportunities and skills to do so. All teachers enter the profession with basic skills, but those skills are not enough to ensure year after year of effective teaching and learning. Once they start teaching, new-to-the-profession teachers find that their previous training is beginning to make sense. However, it is at this time that teachers realize how much they need to learn. It is essential to expand on the basic skills and to be sure that teachers are constantly gaining new knowledge.

Some states have mandated further education and even a master's degree for teachers to get permanent certification. But this type of education does not usually address the real challenges teachers actually encounter on a daily basis. There are many reasons for this. The professors providing this training often lack the practical experiences to accompany the theory. Furthermore, there are very few professors who have broad knowledge or a comprehensive approach to improve the total school. This is not their job. As is the case with most educators in higher education, they are experts in a very narrow field. This academic work and the writing and research it produces is quite important. It is not, however, practical and general enough to make a difference in the daily lives of most teachers.

A change must occur in how teachers and principals continue their education. When the Russians launched the first satellite, Sputnik, into orbit in the 1950s, our nation decided that it was time to make a massive investment to improve the knowledge and skills of our math and science teachers. The universities responded and provided academic math and science courses and year-long academic institutes. This led to a huge improvement of the quality of math and science instruction as well as an improvement of knowledge for teachers in all subjects.

There were some problems, however. Some children and some teachers were having trouble with the new math and science ideas and understandings. A call for Back to Basics was heard. There were problems with the new approaches and content and students didn't understand what they were learning. But rather than adjust the system and ensure basics were learned, the new ideas were tossed out.

The new, new system was called Competency Based Education. While basic competencies are necessary, they alone will never make our schools and students competitive. Our most talented students can compete with students from other countries. But this is not good enough. If we are ever to be the world's leader in education we must make all our schools ideal schools. We must do what is necessary to have all teachers and principals involved in all decisions that affect their lives. They are the ones who must do the planning and implementation. Change cannot be imposed. It must come from within.

Although not perfect, the 1960s were the "golden years" in intellectual stimulation and excitement in our nation's schools. What is now needed is another event or commitment that will rally our nation into action and get the same intellectual stimulation that occurred when the National Science Foundation sprung into action and positively influenced our math and science teachers and in turn raised the math and science standards for students. An investment in our teachers and principals will improve student achievement. Demanding more testing will not.

It is now time for another massive effort to improve the education and knowledge of all our teachers in all our schools—suburban, urban, and rural. Many teachers in our intermediate and middle schools are teaching subjects like math and science and do not have sufficient subject knowledge to teach them for understanding. They can teach basic skills but not in-depth comprehension. How can you teach something when you don't have a competent understanding and the skills to do so?

Universities and colleges can do much to improve subject competence for teachers. Professors have an abundance of subject knowledge and can provide continuing education for teachers to become subject-competent. The better a teacher's knowledge, the greater the enthusiasm for their subject and the better student achievement. It is a teacher's responsibility to improve their understanding of the subjects they are teaching.

When it comes to implementing a comprehensive guide for creating your own ideal school, it must be done with the cooperation of all teachers. You can use outside consultants who have experience with implementing a comprehensive plan, but it is the responsibility of everyone in the school to commit to the plan and to develop each of the components. This process takes much time but with summer employment, much can be accomplished.

All continuing education for staff must have a common focus and a comprehensive plan. Without this there would be no unifying effort to make your school an ideal school. Training would be random and although there may be some benefit, it would not be lasting or significant. It is important to be sure that everyone knows that all continuing education must fit into the comprehensive plan or it will not be approved. Fragmented education will produce fragmented results.

If summer employment is to be provided, each school and the staff who want to be included must make a commitment that the time will not be wasted and that while individual planning time will be provided, they are committing themselves to the larger purpose of making their school an ideal school. They are committing themselves to be a team member without losing their individual identity.

A Comprehensive Plan. We are committed to developing and using a comprehensive plan to improve student learning. We are committed to preparing each student, every student, for a productive life in an uncertain world. We will avoid any attempts at adopting quick-fix approaches to improve student achievement. There are none. Teaching and learning are much too complex for that.

Characteristics of an Ideal School. We will develop and publish our list of ideal school characteristics. We will then make every effort to implement all of them, knowing that it will take much time and new skills.

Perceptions and Expectations. We will perceive that all students are excellent learners and we will expect each to learn. Some will need more time to learn and some less. We also recognize there are many and varied learners and learning styles. We, as a staff, will examine our own expectations and be sure they are positive ones.

Vision and Mission. We will develop our vision of what we want all of our students to know and be able to do. We will involve the community and parents in the process. We will also ensure that our stated and published vision will guide all of our actions and decisions.

Compelling Research and Observations. We are committed to reject baseless opinions. We are committed to ideas that are backed with compelling research and observations. We will make all decisions, do all planning, and design our ideal school based on the most compelling research and observations.

Beliefs, Values, and Dominant Philosophy. We will develop and share our beliefs about students and learning with our community. All faculty will be involved in the formulation of the beliefs. We will make every effort to live by the stated beliefs and screen all decisions through them.

Relationships and Dominant Psychology. We will develop a positive relationship and culture in our school. We will encourage everyone to become personally responsible for his or her behavior. We will establish the conditions so that everyone in the school will have his or her basic psychological needs satisfied effectively.

Children as Students. We will stay focused on helping each child learn well with much knowledge, understandings, and skills. We will make every effort to include each student, as much as possible, in every classroom and every activity in our school.

The Climate and Culture of a School. We will make every effort to ensure that we have a positive influence on every single child in our school. We will create the conditions so that the culture and climate of our school are psychologically safe and nurturing for each child and staff.

Teaching and Learning. We will use a well-defined teaching and learning process. As we learn more about new and proven teaching–learning strategies, we will include them in the process. We are committed to continually get better. While we will do all we can to get each student to learn well, we recognize that parents play a major role in the learning process. We will ask all parents to prepare their children for attending school. They should ensure that their children have adequate nutrition and clothing. They should be involved in the functions of the school, showing interest in all that is happening. They should prepare a place for their children to study and do their homework.

Curriculum Planning. We will, given time, develop a complete curriculum guide for each course. These guides will be made available for anyone interested. We will ensure that these guides include the mandated national, state, and local standards. We will also ensure that these guides include what all students should know and be able to do for a productive future. The required mandates aren't enough. We understand that the better the planning, the better the teaching and learning. We also understand that planning is an ongoing process and is best done in collaboration with our colleagues.

Classroom Practices. We will develop our classroom practices as a total faculty so that all students get the same messages. These practices will be based on the most compelling educational knowledge and observations available. We will share these practices with our parents so they understand what our teachers are trying to accomplish. These practices play a major role in influencing student achievement.

Continuous Assessment, Renewal, and Improvement. We will assess each component of the comprehensive guide to determine what has been achieved and what must be changed, modified, or improved. This process can be influenced by the parents and community. Our principals will monitor the process to be sure that all staff are using the stated components. They will also co-assess performance with teachers.

Continuing Education for Staff. The Johnson City Board of Education, while I was superintendent of schools, made the bold move to offer paid continuing education for all its teachers during the summer break. The following is the process used for those teachers (approximately 90% of the entire staff) who decided to take advantage of the board's offer to continue their education. The same process has been used by many school districts.

Understanding that the most acceptable and perhaps the best trainers of our teachers are our own teachers, we embarked on a process to train teacher trainers. Small groups of teachers were immersed in an agreed-upon knowledge base that contributed to our instructional process. Teachers volunteered, after some awareness sessions, to receive initial instruction. They understood that they would use the knowledge base, after they felt comfortable, in their classroom. They also agreed to demonstrate their new skills for other teachers who wanted to observe them.

The initial groups were either sent away to receive their training or outside consultants were brought to the district. Consultants were identified for their work in improving instruction.

An example of this occurred when some teachers attended a conference and heard a presentation by one of Dr. William Glasser's associates. The teachers were excited by this conference and believed it was very important for our district to explore adopting and adapting this knowledge base. After further awareness and discussions, we were convinced that control theory, now choice theory, was very important and our teachers and administrators should get training in this theory.

While all teachers were being made aware of choice theory, every administrator, including myself, the counselors, and a group of volunteer teachers received in-depth training by associates of the Glasser Institute. This training continued for years. This resulted in a well-trained cadre of teachers and administrators who received certification from the institute. This group, as agreed, presented these new skills and theory to the entire staff. More teachers became trained and certified. Eventually every teacher received this education. The institute continued to consult with the district for many years and their psychological base became our standard.

During the training of any initial group, the entire staff was informed about their progress and what was being learned. When teachers see their colleagues excited about new knowledge, most opt for the training. When a knowledge base does not generate a positive response with an initial group, it is also shared with all teachers and is soon dropped.

Another example occurred when some teachers attended a presentation by professional educator Bernice McCarthy on learning styles. They learned how to design instruction for the many and varied learning styles of children. The initial group continued their training with Bernice, and were soon using this new knowledge base in their classrooms. They kept other teachers informed about what they were learning and how it was working.

Following the same format, teachers were invited to observe the new knowledge base in operation. After learning more about the theory and seeing it in practice, more teachers wanted the training. No training was imposed by the school district. It was allowed to grow naturally from theory to practice to observation, and to self-selection by staff.

As the number of knowledge bases increased, more and more teachers were asking for training and to be involved in the initial groups. The school district continued to send teachers away for training and to bring consultants to the district to train initial groups and eventually other teachers.

It is important to note that since the entire staff already had a well-defined instructional process using many of the ideas of Madeline Hunter (Hunter, 2004), one of my heroes in education, they would view each knowledge base as fitting into the process. They did not think the district was switching direction but adding to their existing knowledge.

There were times when consultants wanted us to drop what we were doing and adopt their knowledge base as the answer. They were convinced that what they had to offer was the solution to all problems. However, our staff knew that each knowledge base was part of the solution but not the whole solution. Furthermore, it was not expected that every teacher would use every knowledge base. It was their choice based on their subject and their own creativity. This was sometimes influenced by the teacher's supervisor or principal. As a matter fact, it was not unusual for teachers to integrate knowledge bases and create something unique and quite wonderful. This creativity was always encouraged. It is precisely what professionals are trained to do. Academic freedom is the freedom to create within the process. And this academic freedom was expected from everyone, including students.

Teachers who were not only using knowledge bases as part of the instructional process but were doing so in a creative manner were identified as trainers in that knowledge base. These teachers became the teachers of teachers. This was a natural process for selecting trainers. Other teachers observed, admired what they saw, and then asked to learn the knowledge base.

These well-trained teachers were not simply trainers. They often became mentors and coaches for their peers and were given release time to help their colleagues learn and grow professionally. These mentors and coaches were available during all the implementation stages. When teachers had difficulty with a new knowledge base, they were coached to success. This prevented teachers from giving up and going back to what they had always done. When it was time to plan for summer continuing education, teachers and principals were involved in the planning process, and together they decided what knowledge bases would be emphasized during the summer. It was expected, however, that the district's vision, mission, beliefs, psychology, and compelling knowledge were always reviewed for the veteran teachers and presented to the new teachers.

Each knowledge base had two levels of instruction. If teachers were not yet applying the knowledge base on a regular basis, they would enroll in Level 1. Teachers who were using the knowledge base on a regular basis but were not yet comfortable with it were encouraged to enroll in Level 2. Each teacher would meet with his or her principal to discuss which knowledge bases and which levels to study.

Teachers, like students, go through five stages of learning when they are studying a knowledge base. None of these stages can be eliminated and neither are they mutually exclusive. They often overlap.

Stage 1: Awareness

Stage 1 is where ideas and information are presented and introduced. It is in this stage where the need to change or improve is established and the hearts and minds of staff are engaged. Often, when hearing a presentation, teachers begin to make up their mind about the suitability of the idea. Theory, successful practices, and results are presented and discussed during this stage.

Stage 2: Knowledge and Information

Stage 2 is when teachers acquire relevant facts, knowledge, and information. Teachers should acquire a basic understanding of the new practice or knowledge base and how it will contribute to more effective teaching and learning. Teachers gain new vocabulary and continue to make judgments concerning the efficacy of this new knowledge.

Stage 3: Personal Understanding and Comprehension

Stage 3 furthers connections of this knowledge base and teachers gain a more in-depth understanding. Key concepts, theories, and many examples are presented and teachers are provided many opportunities to process and discuss these new ideas. It is in this stage that teachers ask many questions in an attempt to make the practices and knowledge base personally meaningful.

Stage 4: Application

During Stage 4, teachers actually use the new skill or practice in a classroom. When teachers are in this stage, they may feel lonely and even frightened, especially when no experienced teacher is available to guide and coach them.

Change often stops when teachers feel uncomfortable, lack the necessary understanding to make decisions to continue, or don't have the necessary time. When this happens, teachers revert to their comfort zone and that may include giving up on the new knowledge base.

In this stage, teachers need encouragement, understanding, and help in implementing and applying new ideas.

Stage 5: Creation

In Stage 5, teachers should have many and varied opportunities to integrate different knowledge bases and to create new and extended practices. Teachers' creativity emerges as they begin to tinker, make connections, and develop new ideas. Not all teachers will feel comfortable in this creative stage and that is OK.

In-House Training

In-house trainers and coaches emerge from teachers in the creative stage. These trainers use the instructional process and guide other teachers through the five learning stages. They start by providing an overview of the knowledge base, modeling it in their classrooms, and inviting other teachers to observe.

The trainers provide the theory of the knowledge base and even demonstrate with other teacher's students. After presenting an awareness, theory, basic knowledge, and modeling, the next step for the trainer is to help the adopting teacher to plan and implement.

Time and assistance are provided so teachers can plan units of instruction to incorporate this new practice. The Curriculum Planning Model, presented earlier, is used to help the teacher plan. Planning must be done in a safe environment with the assistance of a trainer. Planning time must not be rushed, for the planning is crucial to the success of the implementation. Most ideas never get to the implementation stage since most teachers are not provided enough time or help for implementation. Education in general cannot get significantly better unless much time is provided. This should be clear to anyone who understands schools. It is essential for teachers and principals to continue their education during summers.

Finally, teachers must have mentoring and coaching by trainers who know how to apply the knowledge base and how to solve problems when they arise. Some schools have hired permanent substitutes so that trainers can have released time to manage the implementation process.

The learning–training process described is a vibrant one. It is alive and always developing as it is monitored, adapted, and adopted by each school district. Getting better must be a way of life. Furthermore, trainers change according to their creativity with a knowledge base. A teacher may be a trainer with one knowledge base but a learner may have another one.

Funding for staff training and trainers can be made in agreement with the teachers association. Teachers who are trainers might receive their prorated salary. Teachers who are involved as learners may receive an agreed-upon stipend.

Summers include time for teachers to receive training and planning time to implement new knowledge bases, write the curriculum plans, and develop instructional plans for the next year. Teachers should also have personal time, interactive time, and even leisure time for fun. Skills will be developed and teachers from all grade levels will gain respect for each other. Secondary teachers learn what elementary teachers do and they in turn learn about secondary education. Teachers learn that the instructional process is the same for every grade although the implementation may be different. All teachers are encouraged to be creative with the process.

This kind of training often results in teachers' using the same instructional and planning vocabulary and language. They develop a common nonjargon, yet professional language that allows them to communicate effectively with every teacher in the district. This process, with summer time provided, seems ideal, but remember we are trying to create an ideal school.

Funding

To create an ideal school, it is necessary that summer continuing education be available. This will almost always require an increase in the school budget. Before we examine cost, consider the following activity.

Activity: Regaining Market Share

Assume you are a CEO of a major corporation in this country. You produce some good products, some better than others, but you are losing market share to foreign competitors. You have been advised that if you increase your budget by approximately 4% you can retool your corporation, recapture your market share, and increase your profit. Would you do so? If yes, why? If not, why? What assurances would you need before you make your decisions?

Let us recognize one simple fact about any organization. Throwing money at a problem is not necessarily the solution to a problem. It depends on how the money will be used. To spend money and hope something good will happen will only result in a waste of that money.

When someone calls for increased spending to solve a problem, he or she should be able to say how that money will solve the problem and explain the expected results. These expected results should drive all spending and decisions. Hoping and wishing that results will happen is not the way to go. Expected results should drive all actions.

To increase funding for continuing education without a detailed comprehensive plan for how time will be managed would probably produce few results. Much time will be wasted if a plan is not in place. Having an abundance of courses or workshops without a plan may produce some results, but it will not improve the teaching–learning process significantly. New ideas may emerge from these workshops but disconnected ideas will not make a difference.

This book provides a comprehensive guide to create your own ideal school but this isn't necessarily your comprehensive plan. It may be, but as suggested many times, you may want to create your own. You may want to use the guidelines presented in a modified manner to develop a plan that suits your particular needs.

It is time that we as educators tell our communities what we value and what we are all about. It is time that we state our vision, our beliefs, and the compelling educational knowledge we possess. It is time that we share our instructional process, curriculum planning, and our classroom practices. It is time that we form true partners with our community within the established framework. When our parents are involved and we share our comprehensive guide, they will not only support our efforts but provide the funding. Parents understand test results and they often use these scores to measure success. If you follow the guide, test results will be positive. Success brings more success and also brings community support. What follows is a typical budget for a four-week continuing education program for teachers. All of the following figures are approximate. Use your school budget to determine your actual cost.

Total school budget	$30,000,000.00
Number of students	2,650
Cost per student	$11,320.75
Number of teachers	225
Average salary per teacher	$45,000.00
Teachers' salary if teachers accept the continuing education for 4 weeks	$843,750.00
Percent budget increase	2.81%
Approximate $300,000 for awareness conferences, substitutes to free trainers for mentoring and coaching, and teachers interacting during the year	1%
Total percent increase	3.81%

You may want to limit training for the first year to two weeks. This will give you time to increase awareness and for an understanding of the process to develop. You can then increase the training to three weeks in the second year, and to four weeks in the third. This model will also increase the budget gradually and make it easier to manage. Some other considerations:

1. Provide day care for faculty children during the training.
2. Provide summer camp for faculty children using the facilities of the school.
3. Provide continuing education for some students who need to have their skills updated, reviewed, enhanced, and extended.

While a plan and a process has been suggested, each school district must adapt it to meet its own needs. Following are the comments of teachers and administrators on the subject of continuing education.

Larry. The process described allows for new ideas and knowledge bases to come into the schools and to be acted upon by all teachers and principals. The process also provides opportunities for teachers and principals to plan together, work together, and to implement new knowledge bases and ideas. The important idea is that new knowledge is constantly brought into the district by everybody. This keeps the district vibrant. Of all the places where learning should automatically happen, it should be in the schools. In most schools the amount of time that staff interacts about new knowledge is very small. With continuing education as described, the amount of time for interacting of teachers and principals is very high.

Jane. I think a poorly planned staff development program is a major factor in teacher burnout. A well and thoroughly planned staff development program is the best energizer you can have as a professional. My self-concept as a teacher got much better when I was learning the educational research. Learning new knowledge bases, understanding the underpinning theory, working and planning with my peers, sharing ideas, and seeing the results of staff development and student learning further improved my self-concept as a teacher.

Joe. Many times I have talked to other principals about staff development in their building. Their major concern is having enough knowledge in a variety of areas to lead staff development programs in their school. However, with a process of continuing education as just described there is a building full of teachers who can become trainers of other teachers. This is within the capacity of every teacher if they choose and is quite empowering. My job is to establish the conditions for teachers to get the proper training so everyone, if they wish, can become a trainer. I also encourage teachers to attend conferences and workshops and help in whatever ways I can to make this happen. Teachers need to learn together and then process these new skills. I find time for teachers to meet to determine what the research and educational literature is saying. I often lead the discussions that lead to conclusions and actions. I also help get coaches and mentors into the classroom when teachers are trying new ideas and practices. I monitor the process to ensure success. I spend a great deal of time trying to keep up with everything that is going on but I know I have a building of teachers who can provide assistance. They are willing to do this. To me the greatest benefit of continuing education as described is that teachers help teachers. My job has changed to set the conditions for this to happen.

Frank. Before we adapted this continuing education process, I would hear teachers say, "Well it doesn't work," and tell the principal that. The problem was given to the principal. I don't see this happening anymore.

Nancy. As a first grade teacher I was told that the knowledge base cooperative grouping wasn't for kindergarten and first grade. I went to my in-house trainer and asked why first grade couldn't be involved to lay the groundwork for second grade. We worked together and came up with a creative way to do this. My principal arranged for the time and assistance but it was the trainer who was using this practice that had the skill. Teachers like other teachers to help them.

Cindy. In a system like this nothing is forced on teachers. When other teachers are using a practice and are willing to model it, teachers will see the need and get involved in a natural way. I was a trainer for cooperative grouping but a learner with the knowledge base program for more effective teaching. It is nice to be a learner and a trainer at the same time.

Jane. As an example of a knowledge base being introduced, I was asked to attend a week-long seminar on cooperative grouping. I went away very reluctantly and returned with much knowledge. The first question my principal asked me was, "How does this fit into our philosophy and our instructional process?" "Is it an add-on or an enhancer?" We decided it fit into what we were doing except for the final assessment and grading phase. We modified what we learned and soon it became acceptable to all of us. We knew a grade reflected what an individual learned and was not the grade of the group. Our principal provided time for a voluntary group of eight teachers from third to eighth grade to work together for a week in the summer to develop a plan and activities. The ideas were implemented with the eight of us and they soon began to spread throughout the district.

Larry. With any new knowledge base principals receive intense training to gain a basic understanding. They are not expected to teach the new skills but they are expected to understand it and be able to provide feedback to teachers. The principal can't become the instructional leader with a knowledge base but rather sets the conditions. There are times, however, that a principal becomes a trainer. This happened when we implemented choice theory.

Jane. It is exciting to see everyone become a trainer, and this includes our superintendent as well as principals. When this happens, a school becomes a real learning school.

Larry. Everybody is asking the question, "What does a principal do as an instructional leader?" I have had principals ask me that all the time.

Probably the most important job a principal can do is champion his or her teachers. If teachers think a knowledge base is good and they get the help they need, excitement is going to spread. Principals need to be supportive in spreading ideas. They can facilitate meetings and bring teachers together. A principal can be an idea giver. A principal can't do what teachers do. The role of the principal changes in this continuing education process.

Tim. I am currently president of the teachers association and want to say that our staff development process is so different than what is going on in other districts. Our teachers are part of the process and take a strong role in their continuing education. They feel comfortable in the process because they know it enhances their role as professionals. Teachers are able to learn new ideas, model them, use them, teach others, and have others observe them. The process that we use gives teachers a strong voice and ownership. They feel good about what they are doing and this naturally carries over into their classroom. Our creative staff development program gets all teachers actively involved in learning, gives them time not encumbered with students, to plan, to create, and to try new ideas. Teachers are supported throughout the process. This is a valuable experience and prevents teacher burnout. Also, our staff development program gives every teacher a clearer picture of what is happening at all grade levels. We then understand everyone's role in helping each child develop from kindergarten through graduation. Teachers don't work in an isolated vacuum anymore and there is always another teacher or principal there to help. Teachers particularly like the opportunity to be both a learner and a trainer. This keeps us all growing as professionals. The process is non-threatening, stimulating, and enjoyable. This is the essence of a learning organization.

Cheryl. In our district, the power is not just in the administration. Principals have a great respect for the practitioners. Teachers are not just in the classroom teaching students, they have a different role. A principal would make available educational experiences and opportunities. They manage the time, encourage staff, and guide teachers into appropriate training. But they also give teachers a chance to become leaders. Principals support teachers, look at what teachers are doing objectively; have a good, solid knowledge base; and give us good, positive feedback. Principals find time for teachers to meet and ensure that a competent substitute is available. By using a substitute that was well trained in our process, I was able to train other teachers and still be available to teach my students. This is the best of both worlds. I was able to experience a feeling of power, professional growth, while still staying in touch with my classroom.

Tim. I also like, as most teachers do, that any new idea must fit into our instructional process. We don't just take an idea, use it for a while and then discard it. We rework it and fit it into our process. My growth as a teacher has been an evolutionary process. I have grown, thrived, and prospered because I have learned many new ideas and techniques. Teachers are given a database, are given a chance to use the databases, and then are able to align them with district goals. Teachers are then given freedom to exercise professionalism and to use what they have learned.

Al. Nancy may be involved with one knowledge base while Tim is more interested in another. Tim, Nancy and all teachers have a choice of where they want to grow. Naturally this is negotiable with their principal. It is not a choice whether a teacher wants to continue to learn; it is a degree of choice where they want to learn.

Nancy. We as teachers are modeling what we want for our children. We model that we are learners and that we have concern for each other. They see us as learners and this is what we want them to be.

CONCLUSION

A good continuing education program builds on the expertise of teachers. It is an empowering process where teachers are teaching teachers, principals are teaching teachers, teachers are teaching principals, and principals are setting the conditions for this to happen.

While some continuing education can occur during the school year, it is recommended that an eleventh month be added to the teachers' contract so that teachers will have a continuing education program that allows teachers and principals to continue to learn new skills, plan to use them, and interact and share them with peers.

Epilogue

It Is Our Choice

It is our choice whether to create an ideal school or simply continue doing what we have always done. Are we bold enough to choose a different path—one that will prepare all students for the competitive futures they face?

When they enter the profession, most teachers see every possibility. They see everything as good, see all children as wanting to learn and as the beautiful people that they are. However, these new teachers are soon instructed in the way things are done in their new school and are discouraged from doing it any other way. They are told that while some children can learn well, some can't, and that that's just the way it is. In other words, we have enough to do, and we don't need to do any more than what we are already doing.

But in spite of all this, many of these new teachers are still excited and want to do what they feel is right. They see every child as wanting to learn, wanting to be included, wanting to be accepted, and wanting to feel loved and cared for.

After some time though, some of these idealistic teachers begin to conform to the schools' implied values. They too want to "fit in" and be included. They soon begin to say and do what is expected. This is not what should happen to idealistic professionals and, as a result, to students. They deserve better. They are just kids who want their teachers to like them and help them learn.

It is essential to realize that this pattern of doing only what is expected can and must be broken. When teachers are recognized and treated like professionals, when they are involved in the decision-making process of the school and have a comprehensive plan and direction, and when they are provided with continuing education to update their skills, they will do what is necessary to create an ideal school.

To create your own ideal school, consider the following thoughts inspired by the book *One* written by Richard Bach (2001). "We are each given a block of marble when we begin a lifetime" and especially when we enter the noblest of professions, teaching. We are also given "the tools to shape it into sculpture." We can shape our sculpture into a wonderful ideal school even though it may seem impossible. And it isn't impossible. It just takes time, cooperation, a willingness, a desire, and a choice to do so. Bach gives us three choices concerning our marble block:

> We can drag it behind us, untouched,
> We can pound it to gravel,
> We can shape it into glory.

We have the same choices in education. Some teachers and principals drag the education block of marble behind them, untouched. They have always been too busy. They leave the profession the way they found it when they entered. Their contributions are minimal even though some of their students might have learned well.

Some teachers pound their educational block of marble into gravel. These teachers are pessimistic about education and maybe even their own lives and end up dragging everyone into the muck with them. These teachers do a great disservice to the teaching profession and are responsible for many imposed mandates.

Most teachers shape the educational block of marble into something magnificent and wonderful. They leave their classroom, their school, and their profession much better than they found them. Their students are lucky to have been taught by them, parents are grateful for having such teachers for their children, and principals would love to have a school filled with them.

Given a choice, almost all teachers would want to remain in their profession. And most teachers, with the help of good leadership, involved parents, and the support of the community along with a comprehensive plan and continuing education, will succeed in creating schools that would make us all proud.

Near the end of their careers when these teachers' education sculpture is nearly finished, they can spend time smoothing and polishing what they started as young novices. New teachers often look to veteran teachers for advice and direction at this stage, and veterans must leave a legacy for all new teachers to admire and emulate.

We can get exactly what we want and even what we desire. We can create a wonderful life for all our students. We can create a beautiful sculpture, and this will be our legacy.

It is our choice, not someone else's, what we want to leave behind. We can choose to live a life of service to our children and create, shape, and polish our education block of marble—a block that will get better with age.

References

Bach, R. (2001). *One*. London: PanMacmillan.

Ballard, E. S. (1976). Three letters from Teddy. *Home Life*. Sunday School Board of the Southern Baptist Convention.

Bloom, B. (1983). *Human characteristics and school learning*. New York: McGraw-Hill.

Cohen, A. (1987). Instructional alignment: Searching for a magic bullet. *Educational Researcher*, 16(8), 16–20.

Glasser, W. (1999). *Choice theory. A new psychology of personal freedom*. New York: Harper Paperbacks.

Glasser, W. (1986). *Control theory in the classroom*. New York: HarperCollins.

Hunter, M. (2004). *Mastery teaching: Increasing instructional effectiveness in elementary and secondary schools*. Thousand Oaks, CA: Corwin Press.

Kohn, A. (1999). *Punished by rewards. The trouble with gold stars, incentive plans, As, praise, and other bribes*. Boston: Houghton Mifflin.

Popik, B. (2005). You gotta believe. Retrieved April 25, 2007 from http://www.barrypopik.com.

Silverstein, S. (2004). *Where the sidewalk ends*, 30th anniversary edition. New York: HarperCollins.

U.S. Department of Labor. (1992). *Secretary's commission on achieving necessary skills: What work requires of schools*. Washington, DC: U.S. Government Printing Office.

About the Author

Dr. Albert Mamary has made his career in the field of education. He has been a high-school mathematics teacher, a department chairperson, a supervisor of mathematics, a university professor, an assistant superintendent, and a superintendent of schools. He has coauthored more than twenty textbooks in secondary mathematics, published by Holt, Rinehart and Winston, and Harcourt. These books achieved the distinction of gaining 25% to 35% of the national market. He has been a frequent speaker and lecturer, as well as keynote speaker at virtually every major educational conference. He has been a consultant for more than two hundred school districts as well as several state education departments. His articles have appeared in national and international publications. The amazing transformation of the Johnson City school district during Dr. Mamary's tenure as superintendent has been nationally recognized and lauded.